Sri Sri Swami Satchidananda,
Founder/Spiritual Head of Satchidananda Ashram; Founder, Light of Truth Universal Shrine (LOTUS); renowned yoga master and visionary; Yogaville, Virginia

Lemurian Scrolls is a fascinating work. I am sure the readers will find many new ideas concerning ancient mysteries revealed in this text, along with a deeper understanding of their importance for the coming millenium.

Patricia-Rochelle Diegel, Ph.D,
well known teacher, intuitive healer and consultant on past lives, the human aura and numerology; Las Vegas, Nevada

I have just read the *Lemurian Scrolls* and I am amazed and pleased and totally in tune with the material. I've spent thirty plus years doing past life consultation (approximately 50,000 to date). Plus I've taught classes, seminars and retreats. But I've never found as complete a book on many important pieces of information as *Lemurian Scrolls*. The *Lemurian Scrolls* will enlighten all who read it and it will become a "Source" that will constantly be referred to by serious students, teachers, leaders and metaphysical and spiritual groups. I've told many clients and students about their origin from the Pleiades, and it's exciting to know that we've discovered the Eighth Sister (only one more to find in the next century). It's now time for the people on Earth to remember who they were and what their original purpose is about. There are a few who are remembering their origin and what their purpose is on Planet Terra (Earth). As they awaken they will start to awaken others and they in turn will awaken others, etc. When humankind gave up their "spiritual bodies" and took on earthling bodies, they forgot who they really were. Now is the time for them to reawaken, so they can help the rest of the people on the planet. The time is now! Thank you so much for the wonderful information in your book! It has also opened up many new doorways for me.

K.L. Seshagiri Rao, Ph.D.,
Professor Emeritus, University of Virginia; Editor of the quarterly journal *World Faiths Encounter*; Chief Editor of the forthcoming *Encyclopedia of Hinduism;* Columbia, South Carolina

Sivaya Subramuniyaswami, a widely recognized spiritual preceptor of our times, unveils in his *Lemurian Scrolls* esoteric wisdom concerning the divine origin and goal of life for the benefit of spiritual aspirants around the globe. Having transformed the lives of many of his disciples, it can now serve as a source of moral and spiritual guidance for the improvement and fulfillment of the individual and community life on a wider scale.

Ram Swarup,
intellectual architect of Hindu spirituality and culture in India; founder of Voice of India; author: *The Word as Revelation, Understanding Islam Through Hadis;* New Delhi, India

Lemurian Scrolls is a very unusual kind of book both in content and even more so in methodology. Lately we have gotten used to the idea of man's journey to the moon and to his possible journey to other more distant planets in the future, but *Lemurian Scrolls* tells you about man's actual journey to the Earth from the Pleiades millions of years ago. The idea goes against our present scientific wisdom, but on that account alone we need not reject its possibility altogether. ¶Though man is apparently terrestrial, there is no difficulty in admitting that he derives energies, impulsions and influences from the farthest corners of the world. Some scientists believe that life

Continued on page 334

THE BEAUTIFUL GOUACHE PAINTING ON THE COVER IS THE 1995 WORK OF NEW YORK ARTIST VERA ROSENBERRY, commissioned by Himalayan Academy, based on one of 27 ink drawings done for this book by Bruce Andre in the early '70s. It illustrates man's arrival on Earth some four million years ago during a golden era, as described in this collection of ancient *ākāśic* records read clairvoyantly in 1973 by Satguru Sivaya Subramuniyaswami, chronicling the origin of man on this planet and his early life and experiences. According to these mystical revelations, this generation of souls migrated here in their subtle, soul bodies, many traveling first through the Sun. Shown in the foreground are two beings who arrived earlier and have fully manifested physical bodies. They are offering fruits and flowers (which were much larger then than now) to assist a new arrival in developing an Earth body. The arriving soul has taken his place on a sacred pedestal established for this purpose. A physical body will coalesce around his soul body and become more and more dense as he absorbs the subtle *prāṇas* of the fruits, flowers and other substances. As Hindus believe, the ultimate attainment, *nirvikalpa samādhi,* realization of the Self, God, is possible only in a physical body. This requires living on a fire planet such as our spinning blue-green globe called Earth.

Lemurian Scrolls

लिमुरियन् पत्राणि

First Edition, Second Printing, 3,000 Copies

Lemurian Scrolls, Angelic Prophecies Revealing Human Origins is published by Himalayan Academy. First edition 1973. Lovingly designed and typeset by the *āchāryas* and swāmīs of the Śaiva Siddhānta Yoga Order, 107 Kaholalele Road, Kapaa, Hawaii 96746-9304 USA.

Published by
Himalayan Academy
India • USA

PRINTED IN USA

Library of Congress Catalog Card Number 98-70384
ISBN 0-945497-70-9

Lemurian Scrolls

Angelic Prophecies Revealing Human Origins

लिमुरियन् पत्राणि

मानुषमूलप्रकाशकं दैविकभविष्यकथनम्

Satguru Sivaya
Subramuniyaswami

PORTRAIT OF SATGURU YOGASWAMI,
BY SRI INDRA SHARMA

ൎ

Dedication

समर्पणम्

THESE PAGES ARE TRULY MYSTIC IN MORE WAYS THAN ONE. THE SIDDHI THAT WAS USED TO READ THESE REVEALING MANUSCRIPTS IN TWO ANCIENT LANGUAGES WAS IMPREGNATED IN ME BY MY SATGURU DURING SANNYĀSA INITIATION. It is a very special *siddhi* that is only activated by the great ones on "the other side"—not unlike a real vision, which one does not attain at will but which comes as a grace—an opening allowed by the inner plane masters when they want to be seen or have their message heard by mankind. *Lemurian Scrolls* is sincerely dedicated, with full *prapatti,* a total surrender, to my *satguru,* Siva Yogaswami, born 126 years ago, on May 29, 1872. It is his darshan's *śakti* that is doing it all, it truly is, then as now. It was a wonderfully rewarding experience to have this momentary window open in the *ākāśa,* enabling me to read these epistles as easily as one would read the credits on television after the performance. The writing was clear, the language, though foreign to my external mind, was immediately translated through the superconscious intelligence. There are no words to convey the feelings of appreciation for these revelations being made available by the kind souls within the inner worlds wanting to make our history known to Earthlings. ¶ Satguru Yogaswami had developed the powers of clairvoyance and clairaudience while seated under an olive tree night and day for four years. His was an incomparable life as *satguru,* spiritual leader of over a million in the island country of Sri Lanka. He saw into the future with extreme, even uncanny, accuracy. He knew of happenings in his devotees' lives, though they may have been hundreds or thousands of miles away. He appeared to them in his subtle body in times of danger to give warning, in times of temptation to give strength, in times of uncertainty to give faith's gifts. His visions anticipated the present-day ethnic war in Sri Lanka, which he described to devotees decades before it happened, of his painful sight into their future, of their future anguish and suffering, of their dispersal and their despairing fate. Such was the profound insight of this Great One whose ability to see in subtle ways is still legendary. ¶ Appreciate *Lemurian Scrolls* as a treasure upon which your life and perceptions of life are reformed. They were for twenty-five years entrusted only to the resident monks of my monasteries, the *maṭhavāsis.* Now, from me to you, dear one. Read them, absorb them, honor them as we have all these many, many years. Jai! Satguru Siva Yogaswami. Jai!

Contents

विषयसूची

Chapter 6: Diet and Destiny आहारः प्रयोजनं च 53

Milk, seeds and nuts, honey, pollen and fruit mixed in right proportion provide our nourishment. Our main task now is preparing this planet for human life during the coming millennia. When a monastery is closed down, we form a lake to preserve the sacred vortex as a site of worship and austerity a million years hence.

Chapter 7: Monastic Training मठप्रशिक्षणम् 63

Training for our Lemurian priesthood is detailed and exacting, carefully outlined in *ākāśic* books. During years one and two, stories and games are the medium, as for a child. In the third year, a close interest is taken, marked by initiation, personal discipline and tests of will. During the fourth year, a pattern of duties is given.

Chapter 8: Lemurian Sādhakas लिमुरियन् साधकाः 71

Most of our monastics are still in original bodies. Our Lemurian *sādhakas*, seeking deeper admittance, are of animal lineage, and they are given duties according to the animal lineage they emerged from. Training given during the first four years prepares the young one for the rest of his life in serving as a channel for cosmic rays.

Chapter 9: Emulating Our Original State स्वस्वरूप स्पर्दन 79

It is the discipline of the Lemurians to continually strive to be like us who still live in the original body. It is our task, our mission, to set patterns so they can hold the cosmic force after we are gone. Our monasteries are laboratories for this purpose, establishing formulas for living and recording them securely in the ether for future use.

Chapter 10: Areas of Service सेवाक्षेत्राणि 87

All of the Lemurian monastics are of the male gender, and those who never mated are chosen. Through the artisan-apprentice system, each is taught to serve our guru and the Mahādevas in one of the four divisions of our culture. Deep reverence is held for artisans, who can train others and thus expand our monastery population.

Chapter 11: Mystic Skills गुह्यकौशलानि 95

As in all things, the accent is on refinement, be our skill that of weaving a fabric, carving a divine image, or writing a book. Our artisans sit with our guru for instructions, and our gurus conclave to discuss the future of the race. Those of the surrounding community listen to philosophical dissertation through holes in the wall.

Chapter 12: The Great God, Śiva महादेवः शिवः.......................... 103
We have reached the era of preservation. As we come to the end of the Tretā Yuga, our inner sight is dimming, as is our ability to fly. With every loss of an inner faculty, solutions are sought within our laboratories for knowledge of how to compensate. Predictions are now heard of the impending darker era called the Dvāpara Yuga.

Chapter 13: Continuity of Wisdom ज्ञानप्रवाहः 111
Great knowledge is being developed in our Dravidian monasteries on the five great winds of the physical body to aid in its refinement, so that Self can be realized. Our gurus, with secret orders from within, are our firm guides. Many monks are sent out on a daily basis to carry of the Śiva darshan and teach our ancient culture.

Chapter 14: Egoless Service निरङ्कारसेवा.................................. 119
We have many subtle sciences, including that of sound, the psychic perception by which we remain closely attuned to our guru, great souls who work closely with the Mahādevas. Serving our gurus is our reason for being here, and their mission is always the same, to establish many positive channels to stabilize existing communities.

Chapter 15: The Secret Order of Masters गूढनाथसंघः..................... 127
Apart from the gurus who own monasteries, there exists a secret group of masters, each extreme in his actions, either loved or feared, each possessing psychic powers and all meeting in an area of the Devaloka owned by them. Each *ṛishi* of this order of the *kuṇḍalinī* is an agent of Lord Subramaniam in setting old patterns anew.

Chapter 16: The Yoga of Celibacy ब्रह्मचर्य तपस्यः........................ 135
As the Kali Yuga looms closer, the *kuṇḍalinī* expresses itself through sexual desire. In our monasteries, those who previously mated perform *brahmacharya tapas* to dissolve psychic bonds and cease the mating instinct. Various forms of yoga are practiced to quiet the animal nerve system, mature the inner bodies and seek the Self.

Chapter 17: The Monastery Wall मठप्राकारः............................. 145
Sitting and living outside our wall are aspirants begging admittance, monks in transit and those from other monasteries adjusting to our forcefield. Devonic guards observe each one's activities during sleep. Our host speaks with them and sees to their needs. They all gather to listen when a discourse is given from the other side.

Chapter 18: Guru and Disciple गुरुः शिष्यश्च 153

Each of us works to follow our guru's instructions implicitly, to capture his power invested in the assignment and manifest his vision without putting our mental structure in the way of it. This is the main method of teaching to fulfill the mission. Our gurus travel constantly, and some remain incognito except to their senior disciples.

Chapter 19: The Senior Minority Group वरिष्ठाल्प संख्यकवर्गः............. 159

The guru inwardly looks at each monastery as one person, and at the groups within it like the winds of the body. Each of the monastery's four winds is special in its responsibilities—temple, education, business, crafts. The senior group, our guru's anonymous helpers, oversees the darshan flow, monastery cleanliness and training.

Chapter 20: Monastery Procedures मठचरितः 169

The senior minority group is made up of the senior third of the monastery population determined according to a special formula. They conclave in secret to channel the Śiva darshan, to receive the Guru's instructions via the Umāgaṇeśa and convey those instructions to the groups and individuals via the Hanumān and Umādeva.

Chapter 21: Training and Discipline प्रशिक्षणानु शासने 179

New monasteries, formed either by *sādhakas* gathering together with the guru's blessings or by the guru himself, are vital to us to preserve our message and culture as the Kali Yuga approaches. Great care is always taken to see that each monastic is well trained, for we know that a disciplined intellect does not inhibit the darshan flow.

Chapter 22: Wall Protocol प्राकार शिष्टाचारः 189

Ours is a time of transition, and as the instinctive forces within the population grow stronger, our monastery walls are becoming great way-stations for pilgrims, sites of austerity, training, testing and philosophical discussion. Newcomers not allowed admittance after many moons are sent to beg entrance at a monastery elsewhere.

Chapter 23: Purity of Purpose उद्देश्य पवित्रता 199

Within our monasteries there are those dressed in orange, yellow and white, among them realized beings and those yet to realize. But all seek for sameness as we serve our guru, perform our *sādhana* and surrender to the darshan of our Lord. We work joyfully under our artisans who are, in turn, apprentices to our guru and the Deity.

Chapter 24: Divine Qualities of Foods आहाराणां दिव्यगुणाः 209

The energies within milk from our cows and goats strengthens our bodies and allows us to soar within ourselves. Certain herbs and the oil from seeds have a deep healing effect. Caring for animals clears instinctive patterns of the past. Our nourishment is carefully regulated so that our nature is sublime and our nerve system strong.

Chapter 25: Kuṇḍalinī, the Primal Force कुण्डलिनी प्रधानशक्ति 219

Looking ahead, we see a time, after the clash of forces that marks the Kali Yuga, a new awakening and understanding as the *kuṇḍalinī* force rises in all beings on Earth in an even way. But the Kali Yuga will be a time of competition, fear and conflict. Yoga will be practiced by advanced souls for right alignment with the *kuṇḍalinī* ray.

Chapter 26: Kuṇḍalinī Tapas कुण्डलिनीतपः 229

Tapas, austerity, controls the fire as the *kuṇḍalinī,* the life force, makes adjustments within us. *Tapas* is given by our guru to throw our forces back within us, to make swift corrections and nullify our tendency to pull on his forces. On *guru tapas,* we work with the guru to fulfill a mission. *Mauna tapas,* silence, reverses externalization.

Chapter 27: Family Ties कटुम्ब क्बन्धनानि.............................. 239

Devout Śaivite families conceive a son for the monastery, being careful to show no emotion before, during or after conception so that attachments are minimal, then train him for monastic life. Traditionally, at age 14, he enters the monastery, never looking back. In all cases it is important that the mother surrender him to his destiny.

Timeline 245
Conclusion 255
Glossary.. 263
Index 297
Colophon 321
About Gurudeva
Come to Lemuria!
A Few Unusual Young Men
Hindu Heritage Endowment
Mini-Mela Giftshop

Preface

प्रस्तावनं

How Did Man Arrive on Earth?

EVERY CULTURE ON EARTH HAS PONDERED THE QUESTION, "HOW DID WE GET HERE?" PROFOUND, DIVINE ANSWERS HAVE BEEN FORMULATED THROUGH THE AGES. SEVERAL, DRAWN FROM THE WORLD'S OLDEST AND newest cultures and religions, are summarized or retold in this resource section. Today we seem to be on the verge of completely losing our sense of divine origin and purpose as more and more people accept the verdict of Darwinian science—that we are the chance result of billions of years of evolution from single-celled creatures, to seaborn creatures, to reptiles, birds, mammals, to apes and finally to man. We need not accept at face value this Godless judgment about our origins. Hinduism and other religions hold that there is more to existence than mere physical reality, and that a transcendent intelligence inheres and instructs the development of this universe, including the observed processes of evolution. Here we introduce their poignant citations from legends and ancient texts. Then we present the likelihood of intelligent life elsewhere in our galaxy, exploring the intriguing fact that man did not originate on Earth at all, but came here from other planets. So, before we begin what may be the greatest creation myth of all, let's view some of the accounts that our international monthly magazine, HINDUISM TODAY, researched in June of 1996. All this serves to lend a complementary view to that found in *Lemurian Scrolls, Angelic Prophecies Revealing Human Origins.*

What the World's Religions Teach

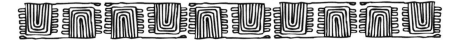

The **Australian Aborigines** are likely the oldest tribe on our planet, with a known continuity of cultural history dating back 50,000 years. They speak of the "Dreamtime" of the distant past when the Gods walked on the Earth and created people, sacred places, animals and the ways of human society. They believe a *jiva* or *guruwari,* a "seed power," is deposited in the Earth, "a symbolic footprint of the metaphysical beings whose actions created our world," states Australian author Robert Lawlor. "We have been here since the time before time began," explains an Aboriginal elder. "We have come directly out of the Dreamtime of the great Creative Ancestors. We have lived and kept the Earth as it was on the First Day. All other peoples of the world came from us."

Hinduism has several creation accounts, of which the central is found in the *Ṛig Veda,* telling of the Cosmic Man, Purusha, who was sacrificed, as in a *yajña,* by the Gods to create man. The Purusha is a divine emanation of God, understood in at least one sense as the individuation of consciousness, the personal aspect of Divinity. It is this individuated consciousness that is offered and divided by the Gods to create all of the physical universe, humans, animals and plants. Three-fourths of the Purusha remains "ascended high" and "one fourth took birth again down here," the hymn explains, meaning that what we see is only one quarter of reality, the remaining being in divine form. Further elaborations of the creation are told in the *Purāṇas, Dharma Śāstras* and other scriptures. *Manu Dharma Śāstra* I.11–119, for example, describes the creation of heaven and Earth, of the soul and of individual creatures. Manu, son of the first being, performed *tapas,* very difficult austerities, to create ten great sages who then created seven other Manus, the progenitors of the human race in each age.

Man, according to the *Vedas,* is the result of the Gods' sacrifice of the divine, primordial form of man. In a concept also found among many other peoples, the parts of this first being became the various living creatures, including man. The *Ṛig Veda* states, "Thousand-headed is the Man [Purusha] with a thousand eyes, a thousand feet; encompassing the Earth on all sides, he exceeded it by ten fingers' breadth. That Man, indeed, is this All, what has been and what is to be, the Lord of the immortal spheres which he surpasses by consuming food. Such is the measure of his might, and greater still than this is Man. All beings are a fourth of him, three-fourths are the immortal in heaven. Using the Man as their oblation, the Gods performed the sacrifice. This evolved Man, then first born, they besprinkled on the sacred grass. With him the Gods performed the sacrifice, as did also the heavenly beings and seers. From this sacrifice, fully accomplished, were born the hymns and the melodies; from this were born the sacrificial formulas. When they divided up the Man, his mouth became the *brāhmin;* his arms became the warrior-prince, his legs the common man who plies his trade. The lowly serf was born from his feet. The Moon was born from his mind; the Sun came into being from his eye; from his mouth came Indra and Agni, while from his breath the Wind was born."

The *Purāṇas* speak of Manu, progenitor of our race. In the *Śiva Purāṇa,* Brahmā said, "Dharma, the means for achievement of everything, born of me, assumed the form of Manu at my bidding. I created from the different parts of my body innumerable sons. I was then prompted by Śiva present within me and hence I split myself into two; one had the form of a woman and the other half that of a man. That man was Svayambhuva Manu, the greatest of the means of creation. The woman was Satarupa, a *yoginī,* an ascetic woman. Together they created beings. Their sons and progeny are spread over the world both mobile and immobile."

Sikhism follows Hindu traditions of origins. **Buddha** taught that this world will come to an end, but that in time a new world will evolve again. Certain *karmas* will cause souls to again seek life in the body. Others will follow and become more and more attached to the body, developing passion, selfishness and other evils. The Buddhist scripture *Saddharma Pundarika* mentions that there are so many worlds beyond this one that no one "should be able to imagine, weigh, count or determine their number." The **Jains** hold that the world, souls and time are uncreated, unbeginning and unending. The world exists through its own being and is divided into heaven, earth and hell.

Abrahamic Religions: The **Hebrews, Christians** and **Muslims** all hold more or less to the creation story given in the Bible's first chapter. "In the beginning God created the heaven and the Earth. And the Earth was without form, and void; and darkness was upon the face of the deep. And the Spirit of God moved upon the face of the waters. And God said, Let there be light: and there was light. And God saw the light, that it was good: and God divided the light from the darkness. And God said, Let there be a firmament in the midst of the waters, and let it divide the waters from the waters.... And God said, Let the Earth bring forth the living creature after his kind, cattle, and creeping thing, and beast of the Earth after his kind: and it was so. And God said, Let us make man in our image, after our likeness: and let them have dominion over the fish of the sea, and over the fowl of the air, and over the cattle, and over all the Earth, and over every creeping thing that creepeth upon the Earth. So God created man in His own image, in the image of God created He him; male and female created He them. And God blessed them, and God said unto them, be fruitful, and multiply, and replenish the Earth, and subdue it: and have dominion over the fish of the sea, and over the fowl of the air, and over every living thing that moveth upon the Earth."

Christians and **Jews** believe in the making of man by God on the sixth day of creation (some 4,000 years ago) out of clay and in His own image, as told in the *Book of Genesis*. The **Muslims** believe, similarly, that Allah created Adam, the first man in Paradise, then the first woman, Hawa (Eve). There they lived a perfect life in a perfect universe, far vaster than ours. They were cast to Earth when they committed the first act of disobedience to God, after a jealous Satan tricked them. Their children are the ancestors of mankind. The **Zoroastrian** religion of Persia also holds to the creation story of Adam and Eve. There are mystical traditions within the Abrahamic religions—Christianity, Islam and Judaism—which go beyond *Genesis*. For example, **Sufi** master Shaykh Muhammad Nazim al-Haqqani taught, "Do you think there was only one Adam? No. There was not one Adam. In fact, there have been 124,000 Adams. Allah is not stingy; He is generous. His creation is endless." Sufi mystics also hold that there are many inhabited worlds in the universe. The **Jewish** *Kabbala* tradition teaches of man's descent from the highest spiritual world through a series of planes ending with his incarnation in a physical body.

The **Shinto** teaching is that the Japanese people are descendants of the Gods Izanagi and Izanami, who were ordered to "make, consolidate and give birth to this drifting land [of Japan]." This they did and then produced the many Gods, fire, water and men. Among the Gods, the most important was Amaterasu, the Sun God, whose descendent was Jimmu, the first emperor of Japan.

Theosophy believes in countless universes, each the home of numerous solar systems with planets where beings are evolving. Human history is recounted in terms of seven succeeding "root races." The first, descended from residents of the moon, dwelt on a continent named the imperishable Sacred Land. The second, known as the Hyperborean, inhabited a vast territory in the vicinity of the North Pole. Since neither of those races had physical bodies, they reproduced by spiritual means. The third root race lived and died in Lemuria; the fourth in Atlantis—both now at the ocean bottom. The fifth and present root race is the Aryan; the sixth and seventh have yet to appear. When they do, humanity will have run its course on Earth and will move to another planet to begin the cycle again.

American Indians: The Omaha tribe live in the American Midwest. Their stories emphasize the oneness of man and nature. "At the beginning all things were in the mind of Wakonda. All creatures, including man, were spirits. They moved about in space between the Earth and the stars (the heavens). They were seeking a place where they could come into bodily existence. They ascended to the sun, but the sun was not fitted for their abode. They moved on to the moon and found that it also was not good for their home. Then they descended to the Earth. They saw it was covered with water. They floated through the air to the North, the East, the South and the West and found no dry land. They were sorely grieved. Suddenly from the midst of the water uprose a great rock. It burst into flames and the waters floated into the air in clouds. Dry land appeared; the grasses and the trees grew. The hosts of the spirits descended and became flesh and blood. They fed on the seeds of the grasses and the fruits of the trees, and the land vibrated with their expressions of joy and gratitude to Wakonda, the maker of all things."

Mayan: *The Popol Vuh* is nearly the only surviving text of the Central American Mayans. It tells their story of creation. "Admirable is the account of the time in which it came to pass that all was formed in heaven and upon Earth as was spoken by the Creator and Maker, the Mother, the Father of life and of all existence, that One by whom all move and breathe, Father and Sustainer of the peace of peoples, by Whose wisdom was premeditated the excellence of all that doth exist in the heavens, upon the Earth, in lake and sea. Lo, all was in suspense, all was calm and silent; all was motionless, all was quiet, and wide was the immensity of the skies. Lo, the first word and the first discourse. There was not yet a man, not an animal; only the sky existed. The face of the Earth was not yet to be seen; only the peaceful sea and the expanse of the heavens. Alone was the Creator, the Maker, Tepeu, the Lord, and Gucumatz, the Plumed Serpent, those who engender, those who give being, alone upon the waters like a growing light. They spoke, 'Let it be thus done. Let the waters retire and cease to obstruct, to the end that Earth exist here, that it harden itself and show its surface, to the end that it be sown, and that the light of day shine in the heavens and upon the Earth; for we shall receive neither glory nor honor from all that we have created and formed until human beings exist, endowed with sentience.' "

The **Mayans** and the ancient **Babylonians** taught that the Gods created man to honor them. "I will create a savage; Man shall be his name," declared the victorious God Marduk in Enuma Elish. "Verily, a savage man I will create. He shall be charged with the service of the Gods, that they might be at ease! Let one of the [lesser] Gods be handed over. He alone shall perish that mankind may be fashioned."

Chinese: The Chinese story of the original man, Pangu, parallels that of Hindu creation. "In the beginning was a huge egg containing chaos, a mixture of yin-yang—female-male, passive-active, cold-heat, dark-light and wet-dry. Within this yin-yang was Pangu, that which was not yet anything but which broke forth from the egg as the giant who separated chaos into the many opposites, including Earth and sky. Each day for 18,000 years Pangu grew ten feet between the sky, which was raised ten feet and the Earth, which grew by ten feet. So it is that heaven and Earth are now separated by 30,000 miles. Pangu was covered with hair; horns sprang from his head and tusks from his mouth. With a great chisel and a huge mallet, he carved out the mountains, valleys, rivers and oceans. During his 18,000 years, he also made the sun, moon and stars. He created all knowledge. All was suffused by the great primal principles of the original chaos, yin and yang. When Pangu finally died, his skull became the top of the sky, his breath the wind, his voice thunder, his legs and arms the four directions, his flesh the soil, his blood the rivers and so forth. The people say that the fleas in his hair became human beings. Everything that is is Pangu, and everything that Pangu is is yin-yang. With Pangu's death a vacuum was created, and within this vacuum pain and sin were able to flourish."

Africa: The Bantu people live in Equatorial and Southern Africa. Their story includes the introduction of death. "In the beginning there was only one man on Earth, and he was called Kintu; the daughter of the sky saw him, fell in love with him and persuaded her father to make him her husband. Kintu was summoned to the sky, and such were the magic powers of the daughter of the sky that he emerged successful from the ordeals imposed on him by the great God. He then returned to Earth with his divine companion, who brought to him as her dowry domestic animals and useful plants. As he bade them farewell, the great God advised the newly weds not to return to the sky. He feared that they might have incurred the anger of one of his sons, Death, who had not been informed of the marriage, since he had been absent at the time. On his way to Earth, Kintu realized he had forgotten to bring grain. In spite of his wife's supplications, he went back up to the sky. By then the God of Death was there. He followed in the man's footsteps as he returned to Earth, hid near his home and killed all the children who were eventually born to Kintu and the daughter of the sky." The **African Dogon** tribe teaches that the primal Cosmic Egg was shaken by seven huge stirrings of the universe. It divided into two birth sacs, each containing a set of androgenous twins who were fathered by the Supreme Being, Amma. From one set of twins was born the Earth, from the other, mankind.

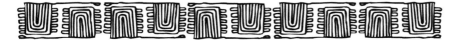

Ancient Egypt: This creation story is recorded in *The Book of Overthrowing Apophis,* an ancient text in hieroglyphics. "The Lord of All, after having come into being, says: I am he who came into being as Khepri, the Becoming One. When I came into being, the beings came into being, all the beings came into being after I became. Numerous are those who became, who came out of my mouth, before heaven ever existed, nor Earth came into being, nor the worms, nor snakes were created in this place. I, being in weariness, was bound to them in the Watery Abyss. I found no place to stand. I thought in my heart, I planned in myself, I made all forms being alone, before I ejected Shu, before I spat out Tefnut I before any other who was in me had become. Then I planned in my own heart, and many forms of beings came into being as forms of children, as forms of their children. I ejected Shu, I spat out Tefnut. After having become one God, there were now three Gods in me. When I came into being in this land, Shu and Tefnut jubilated in the Watery Abyss in which they were. I wept over them, and men came into being out of the tears which came out of my eyes. I created all that came into being with them. Shu and Tefnut produced Geb and Nut; Geb and Nut produced out of a single body Osiris, Horus the Eyeless one, Seth, Isis, and Nephthys, one after the other among them. Their children are numerous in this land."

Signs of a Common Heritage: In examining the creation stories of the world's faiths, one thing strikes a Hindu: nearly every account has some parallel within Hindu mythology. Anthropologists explain all these parallels in a psychological fashion—water symbolizes the womb, etc. But perhaps all cultures are harkening back to the experiences of a common ancestry. The American Indians of California, for example, tell of how God sent an animal down through the waters to bring up the Earth, in the same way that the Boar incarnation of Lord Vishnu rescued the Earth from beneath the waters. The Chinese Pangu is amazingly akin to the sacrificed original man in the *Purusha Śukta*. In many cultures, man was originally immortal, and only at a certain time did he start to die—just as Yama in Hinduism was the first man to die, and then became the Lord of death. Another common element is the breath of God being infused into man, bringing him to life.

Did We Come from the Sky? The authoritative *Larousse World Mythology* book states, "There is an almost universal belief in a visit by the first men to the sky, and consequently in the existence of a path between the Earth and the world above that was ultimately destroyed by human wrongdoing." There are common elements in the creation stories which indicate we had a different kind of existence before living in these physical bodies. One example is androgyny; the original people in the creation stories are often both male and female. Another is the absolute harmony of existence in an earlier time when people lived in peace and freely communicated with the animals and plants. A third is the initial absence of death, a fact of life which comes later, as previously described.

Hindu scriptures often speak of the many *lokas,* or planes of existence, and *dvipas,* or islands. They talk of beings coming from other *lokas* to this *loka,* possibly even of spaceships in which they could travel. These *lokas,* however, are more commonly interpreted as other dimensions of existence rather than physical planets.

His Divine Grace A.C. Bhaktivedanta Swami Prabhupada, founder of ISKCON, addressed this question in his commentary on *Śrīmād Bhāgavatam:* "According to Vedic understanding, the entire universe is regarded as an ocean of space. In that ocean there are innumerable planets, and each planet is called a *dvipa,* or island. The various planets are divided into fourteen *lokas.* As Priyavrata drove his chariot behind the sun, he created seven different types of oceans and planetary systems, known as Bhūloka." Srila Prabhupada also stated that according to the Vedic tradition there are 400,000 species in the universe with humanlike form, many of them advanced beyond us. Other parts of Hindu scripture refer to travel to other worlds. The *Ṛig Veda* hymns on death speak of man's soul traveling to the sun and the moon, then returning to Earth.

Certainly the most dramatic example of a people who believe they came from another planet is the Tana Toraja tribe in the Celebes Highlands of Java, Indonesia. They declare their ancestors came from the Pleiades in spaceships. In fact, they continue to build their homes to look like those ships today. This tribe had no contact with the outside world until this century, and had no way of knowing that space travel was even possible.

Creation According to Modern Science

The following descriptions are assembled from the statements of several eminent scientists. The universe was created *ex nihilo* [out of nothing]. At a particular instant roughly fifteen billion years ago, all the matter and energy we can observe, concentrated in a region smaller than a dime, began to expand and cool at an incredibly rapid rate. This knowledge comes from decades of innovative experiments and theories. This theory is known as the big bang cosmology. Yet many fundamental mysteries remain [such as] what was the universe like before it was expanding? Life developed spontaneously on Earth and slowly developed into more and more complex organisms through a process of natural selection. When the environment changes, individuals bearing traits that provide the best adaptation to the new environment meet with the greatest reproductive success. Science generally holds that without supernatural intervention, spontaneous interaction of the relatively simple molecules dissolved in the lakes or oceans of the prebiotic world yielded life's last common ancestor. Man has evolved by natural selection from earlier species. Our most recent ancestors are the primates. Evolution does not mean progress defined to render the appearance of something like human consciousness either virtually inevitable or at least predictable. As stated by noted astrophysicist Stephen Hawking, "We must come to entertain the strong possibility that *Homo sapiens* is but a tiny, late-arising twig on life's enormously arborescent bush—a small bud that would almost surely not appear a second time if we could replant the bush from seed and let it grow again."

The Greenbank Formula: The scientists who developed the Greenbank Equation on page xxiv make a convincing case for the existence of intelligent life elsewhere in our universe. Sentient life throughout the cosmos provokes the question, "Could man have originated elsewhere and migrated here, either physically or spiritually?" Most religions that address this question speak of the migration as purely spiritual, but at least one claims the journey was physical. Below are some of mankind's reflections about how we came to be here.

On a purely materialistic basis, scientists have made the case for at least the very first elementary life coming to Earth from outer space, probably arriving frozen solid inside a meteor. This hypothesis is called *panspermia,* meaning the migration of living spores from planet to planet throughout space. There is a class of meteors called carbonaceous chondrites with organic compounds in them and microscopic particles resembling, but not identical to, fossil algae of the kind that live in water.

There is another school among the scientists which includes Nobel Laureate Francis Crick, co-discoverer of the DNA molecule. Crick advocated a theory of "directed panspermia"—the possibility that an older civilization sent a mission to start life on our newly evolving planet. A single capsule of several elementary organisms would, he claimed, suffice to bring life to Earth. "This might suggest," Crick said, "that we have cousins on planets which are not too distant." In modern times the concept of coming from other planets is advocated by the Theosophists. The first two of their postulated seven root races had nonphysical bodies. They teach that when the last root race has appeared, humanity will have run its course of evolution on Earth and will move to another planet to begin the cycle again.

The Green Bank Formula is a way to statistically guess the possible number of intelligent civilizations in our galaxy, the Milky Way. It is not the result of a UFO conference, but rather sober calculations made when US scientists first set out to detect life elsewhere in the galaxy by listening for coded radio signals from them. The explanation of the equation on the next page is from the book *Cosmos* by my friend the late astrophysicist Dr. Carl Sagan. We were together in 1990 at the Moscow Global Forum and there spoke of ultimate matters from very different points of view.

Who could we talk to "out there" with our present level of technology? The answer, according to the *Encyclopedia Britannica,* is that with our present most powerful radio telescope we could send and receive intelligible signals "a rather astonishing 1,000 light years. Within that range are over ten million stars." The Green Bank formula's "bottom line" is that within our galaxy there are plausibly ten million advanced civilizations. That, of course, doesn't mean they are all close by. If equally distributed, the nearest might be several hundred light-years away—which is a really long way. Consider also that this formula only addresses one galaxy, ours. The total number of galaxies in the universe is estimated at 100 billion. Ten million civilizations per galaxy computes to a truly astronomical figure. We are very probably not alone in this vast universe.

Conclusion

We can now see that there is hope for a more secure future when we put together in our inner mind all the information that we have gathered on these pages. The wise look to the past to know the future. We do hope that by looking at our beginnings we have helped in some way the peoples of the world to forge a fulfilling future. Maybe, just maybe, all the answers are not to be found in our intellects. Some may exist in the old creation stories, or be projected to us from futurists within inner and outer space.

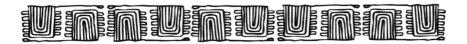

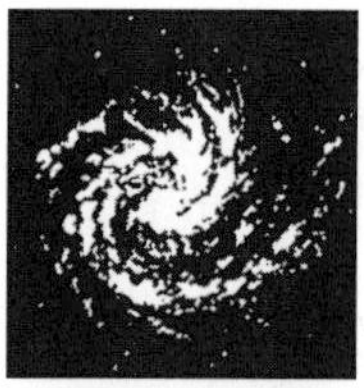

The Green Bank Formula: $N = n\, f_P\, n_E\, f_L\, f_I\, f_C\, L$
How Science concludes there is intelligent life elsewhere in our galaxy. **N** represents the number of stars in our Milky Way galaxy, estimated at 400 billion.

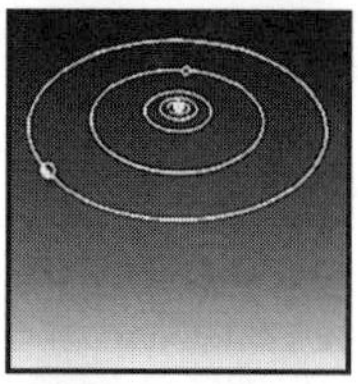

f_P is the number of planets. One in three stars may have a solar system, averaging perhaps 10 planets each, for a total of 1,300 billion planets. Since 1995, more than 6 nearby stars were confirmed to have planets around them.

n_E is the number of planets that can support life. Since life exists on Earth in a wide range of temperature and environment, this is guessed at two per system. That gives a total of 300 billion planets on which life might evolve.

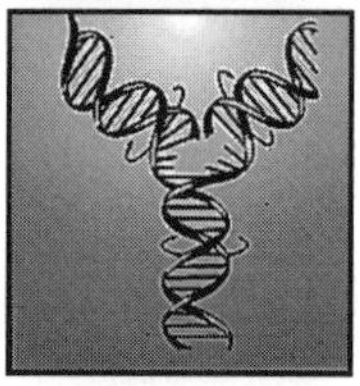

f_L is the number of such planets which might actually develop some form of life. It was estimated by Carl Sagan (based on the range of scientific opinion) at one in three. That means there might be 100 billion inhabited worlds.

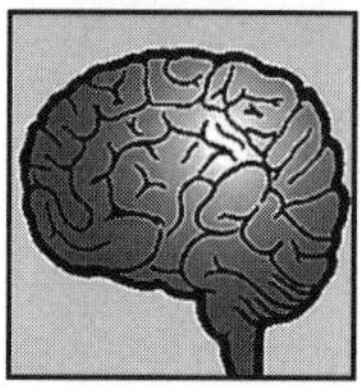

f_I is the likelihood of intelligent life developing. Such a development might be rare, or it might be inevitable. Sagan uses the conservative figure of one in ten. We could have in our galaxy an estimated ten billion worlds with intelligent life.

f_C is the number of those planets with intelligent life which develop a technological civilization capable of interstellar communication. This is estimated at one in ten, for a total of one billion technically advanced civilizations in the galaxy.

L is the final factor. Does an advanced civilization destroy itself, as we on Earth seem inclined to do, or does it endure for millions of years? If even one percent survive, states Sagan, "The number of such advanced living civilizations is in the millions."

Introduction

भूमिका

THE STORY OF THIS REVELATION BEGINS IN THE DISTANT AND STILL MAGICAL LAND OF INDIA. IT WAS A SPLENDID SEASON IN NEW DELHI, APPROACHING THE PASSAGE OF MAHĀŚIVARĀTRI, THE HOLIEST NIGHT OF THE YEAR. Having pilgrimaged with seventy-five monastics and devotees throughout India and Sri Lanka to saints and sages, ancient temples, *dharmaśālas, aadheenams* and modern *āśramas,* I happened late one morning, during a spontaneous walk, upon an extraordinary Lord Śiva Naṭarāja Deity at Nirmala's Copper Bazaar. I walked around the wondrous six-foot-tall bronze statue situated on the busy sidewalk and quietly said, "Hello!" It was the store's insignia and showpiece, too precious to sell, the owner declared, as no value could be attached. Bravely disregarding that fact, we bargained and traded through the morning hours and ultimately acquired it and as evening approached arranged for its shipment to our distant Garden Island of Kauai. At Mahāśivarātri time again a year later, in 1973, in the jungles of Kauai, our Kadavul Naṭarāja Deity, Lord of the Dance, arrived at Kauai Aadheenam and was placed in the gardens overlooking the sacred Wailua River, where it was spontaneously decorated, bathed and worshiped. That night the exact location of the Deity's installation was chosen by Lord Muruga Himself when He appeared to me in an early morning vision, upturned His glistening *vel,* His scepter of spiritual discernment, and powerfully pounded its point three times on the cement steps at the Aadheenam entrance, marking the precise spot to place the Deity. Soon after, a rotating 24-hour vigil was established, and it has been maintained without a single hour's lapse to this very day. Under this strict monastery discipline, monks take turns every three hours in the temple, night and day, 365 days a year. During this vigil they perform constant meditation, *pūjā,* yogas and chanting, quelling the mind and giving themselves in profound adoration, *prapatti,* to this remarkable icon. Thus the arrival of the Śiva Naṭarāja Deity transformed our life, and from that day onward life in and around the monastery has revolved around His divine presence. This establishment of Kadavul Hindu Temple on the same sacred grounds that had once harbored the area's fifth Hawaiian *heiau* (temple), established 1,500 years ago, eventually was recorded in the State archives by the Governor as the first Hindu temple in Hawaii. With the arrival of Lord Naṭarāja, thousands upon thousands of *devas* of the Second World and *devas* and Mahādevas of the Third World penetrated the inner atmosphere of the Lemurian mountaintop island of Kauai from several ancient temples—in Sri Lanka, the precious Kumbhalavalai Koyil, mystic Nallur and potent seaside Tiruketeeswaram, and in India, the mighty Chidambaram, Thanjavur's Brihadeesvara, which I am said to have built in a previous life as Rajaraja Chola, according to several *jyotisha nādīśāstrīs,* and the sin-dissolving Rameshvaram, overflowing in healing waters in twenty-two wells. The three worlds had at that moment become connected as one, and the Śaivite Hindu religion began to flourish on this side of the planet.

A Great Inner-Plane Library

Soon after we had placed the Deity, my inner eye, within the *ājñā* chakra, was opened upon an array of great manuscripts, and the inner library of Lord Subramaniam was seen. Upon each wish and fancy, the librarian, a tall, fine, elegantly robed, bearded man, would pull forth from one shelf or another great volumes and with firm hands open and turn the pages to the proper place to be read. I read these volumes one after another to the monastics at Kauai's Hindu monastery after this *siddhi* was obtained. They asked questions. The books were placed within the inner ether of my mind, the pages turned and read and enjoyed and understood. Thus, Śiva's great diamond-dust-like darshan flooding out opened the inner door of our Lord Subramaniam's private library, which contains the records accrued since His arrival on this planet. Lord Subramaniam, the South Indian God also known as Kārttikeya, Muruga, Skanda and Sanatkumāra, has always been near and dear to us.

In a Coconut Grove Near The Ocean

℄ The venue of this remarkable clairvoyant happening was the garden restaurant of Coco Palms Hotel. As the librarian presented each volume and turned page after page, I dictated slowly to a sincere monastic scribe, who pa-

The early morning vision in which Lord Muruga indicated the placement for the Śiva Deity after the icon's arrival from India in 1973

tiently and accurately wrote down each word. These were the days when cigarette smoke billowed forth from elite hotel guests at neighboring tables, clouding the atmosphere and creating an ambiance in which the *ākāśic* manuscripts could be clearly seen. The backdrop of Hawaiian music, the hubbub of people talking and the lower vibration of worldly feelings, too, helped screen out the conscious mind to make this clairvoyant *siddhi* a working reality. On some days reams of pages were turned and read; on other days nothing was seen. Vigilantly, morning after morning, week after week, month after month, we sat waiting, while enjoying fruit, yogurt and coffee, for my inner eye to open on the inner-plane library. The restaurant was not in an ordinary location. Our table overlooked tropical ponds amid the island's largest coconut grove near the ocean on the east side of Kauai, the oldest and northernmost of the Hawaiian archipelago. Not far away was the second of a series of seven ancient temples, or *heiaus,* each representing one of the seven chakras, or spiritual force centers. These seven rock-walled, open-air sanctuaries were built by the first Hawaiian priest, Kuamo'o Mo'okini, 1,500 years ago, along the Kuamo'o trail (now a highway), the spine of the dragon, that winds up a stony ridge toward Mount Waialeale, the island's central and tallest peak, site of the seventh *heiau,* representing the crown force center, *sahasrāra* chakra. Each day's writings, gleaned by my astral vision near the birthstone *heiau,* where royalty were birthed in olden times, were penned in letter-sized spiral notebooks. Before noon, we returned with them to my *āśrama,* Kauai Aadheenam, four miles inland at the site of the fifth ancient *heiau,* now the Kadavul Hindu Temple, on land revered in sacred Hawaiian chants as Pihanakalani, "where heaven touches Earth."

Monks Gobbled Up the Early Chapters

The early revelations were enjoyed by *maṭhavāsis* at Kauai Aadheenam and shared with others at our branch monasteries via an in-house teletype network, named *beneba* in Shum, our language of meditation. As the flow continued week after week, *maṭhavāsis* in San Francisco, California, and in Virginia City, Nevada, gathered 'round to read the spellbinding messages being clacked out on the piano-size communication devices. The monks were able to type questions to me and receive my responses in "real time" from Hawaii, thousands of miles away. We enjoyed many philosophical discussions in this way. As each volume finally drew to completion, it was typed up by the scribe on an electric IBM typewriter, from which a dozen or so copies were made and cased in plain, white soft-cover binding. These texts, restricted to monastics under vows, served us for twenty-four years. One chapter was read daily at the meditation sessions to mold a new standard of selfless living in the monasteries of Śaiva Siddhānta Church. Thus, the pages of this book you hold became a living message from one world to another, not merely an interesting encounter. It dramatically changed the life of many thousands of spiritual seekers on several continents. *Lemurian Scrolls* comprise twenty-seven chapters, one to be read each day of the lunar calendar, which is how they have been studied in our monasteries since 1973. Preceding each chapter is an intricate pen drawing by Bruce Andre, whom we commissioned in 1974–1975 to illustrate the prevailing concepts. Every two months *maṭhavāsis* took the 400-mile flight from Kauai to the Big Island of Hawaii, then drove to Captain Cook, near where Bruce lived alone in a simple coffee shack, to work out the imagery for one or two pieces at a time, drawing on his creative and imaginative understanding of the incredible story being told. Each pen-and-ink illustration took him over a month to produce, for which we paid an outrageous $35 (a lot of money for us in those days) on which he subsisted, augmented with mangos and avocados plucked from the local trees. I think you will agree he has brought to life these early eras through his envisioning interpretations. The large captions adjacent the art were written during the same period and edited in 1997 when we drew *Lemurian Scrolls* forward as a public book. The short introductions to the chapters, in my own hand, were composed in 1998.

The Ancient Lemurian Script

¶ After reading from these ancient scriptures, verification in the First World began to arrive as to the usefulness in the personal lives of the Śaivite monastics of much of this information. The language in which I read the first books was found to be similar to an old Lemurian language. It looks like this:

The books were large. This language was written in gold. Shimmering gold letters danced out at me, and I knew the meaning as the inner eye scanned each page. When questions were asked, the masterful librarian turned the page. Lord Subramaniam's librarian could read my thoughts. He read them well and presented the volumes systematically that were to create, when finished, The *Lord Subramaniam Śāstras* and change the course and direction of our Śaivite monasteries in the Western area of the world, then and into the future of futures.

Numerous Volumes Revealed

¶ The *Lord Subramaniam Śāstras* are divided thrice. The divisions are: *The Lemurian Śāstras, The Dravidian Śāstras* (which together constitute these *Lemurian Scrolls)* and *The Śaivite Śāstras* (now part of the *Maṭhavāsi Śāstras)* written for the guidance of and restricted to *āchāryas,* swāmīs, yogīs and *sādhakas* of our Śaiva Siddhānta Church. Along with these were unfolded two supplementary manuscripts, *The Book of Virtue* and

The Book of Attitudes, along with a larger work entitled *The Book of Remedies. The Lemurian Śāstras,* which make up the first half of these scrolls, unfold a remarkable story of how souls journeyed to Earth in their subtle bodies some four million years ago. The narrators of the ancient texts explain that civilization on their native planets had reached a point of such peacefulness that spiritual evolution had come to a standstill. They needed a "fire planet," such as Earth, to continue their unfoldment into the ultimate attainment—realization of the Self within. To persist in the lush atmosphere, genderless, organic bodies were formed through food-offering ceremonies. Later, through a slow process of mutation, the fleshy bodies we know today as human were established as vehicles for reincarnation. As the book progresses, a diminishing of the spiritual forces radiating from the Central Sun of the galaxy is described. As spiritual awareness wanes, the life force of man, *kuṇḍalinī,* sleeps and instinctive desire manifests in abundance. These amazing chronicles of early man's life on Earth are told from within great, walled monasteries where narrators look back and forward at the same time, often reading from ancient texts, describing the daily life of those within and outside these sacred citadels. The theme throughout is to continue channeling the pristine spiritual vibration from the Central Sun as long as possible and to preserve the Lemurian culture, its wisdom and knowledge for generations far into the future. This, under the guidance of powerful gurus working closely with great Gods, was the spiritual mission of the dedicated monastics of these eras. Largely it was done by implanting sacred writings in the *ākāśa* by mystical means.

From the "Dravidian" Manuscripts

The Dravidian Śāstras, which make up the second half of *Lemurian Scrolls,* will interest you from the point of view of how humans lived at the end of the Dvāpara Yuga, their society, internal and external government, the culture of those early years on the Earth and how some of it carried forth to this very day. Our narrators explain that it was in the far distant past that the people who formed societies realized they needed group spiritual guidance. This group guidance is, to this day, recognized as a viable form of community and leadership. Examples that come to mind are the Dalai Lama's Tibet, where something like one-third of the social order is a monastic group, serving the religious and political needs of the two-thirds family group. Thus their society was transparently stable for hundreds and hundreds of years. This and other societies, such as villages in Europe, where monks and nuns were valued, were settled with a certain percent of monastics who served the religious needs of the other residents. The division of lay community and monastic community results in a wealthy, highly productive, harmonious society. We learn in the *Dravidian Śāstras* just how this was accomplished in the long, long ago. It is prophesied that sustainable societies will once again emerge when mankind returns to the wise protocols of these earlier times, where spiritual men and women, spiritual principles and spiritual sharing guided both individual and society, where religious leaders were valued and sought after, for the populace knew that if they could be engaged in the social effort, they would lend it a light and wisdom that would not otherwise be available or important. These last sixteen chapters of *Lemurian Scrolls* explain the procedures of management, their gurus and their protocol. We can see its wisdom really worked, and our monastic order endeavored to emulate it as much as was possible in this modern, diverse age where divisions are normally accepted as signs of an advancing civilization and religion is considered an interference with scientific points of view.

Questions From Monks Answered

Now I shall ramble on a bit and explain some of the intricacies involved in completing this work, taken from my notes made along the way, as bringing through and recording these *śāstras* took over one year of retreat from outer activities for absolute one-pointed concentration each morning for many hours. Each *maṭhavāsi* was asked to send his questions about the *śāstras* through the top of his head, with an onrush of energy up through his spine following it. In this way his communication would penetrate into the Second World, the Antarloka, and even sometimes the Third, the Śivaloka, and be heard by the *devas* and Deities there. He was carefully taught an ancient method of writing his question or his prayer, a request for help from beings in the Second and Third World, neatly on a piece of paper which he signed. During the fire *pūjā* each evening, it would be burned, disappear as ash in the First World but reappear in the exact same way in the Second. This the librarian of Lord Subramaniam's valuable collection of ancient and modern manuscripts would read, and choose appropriate chapters and paragraphs for me to read and make notations of for the monastic's elucidation. One of my original notes from 1973 says, "On a great table in Lord Subramaniam's library I see many pieces of paper and am told by the librarian, hearing him through my inner ear, that these are the notes and questions that the Śaivite monastics in my monasteries have been burning during the fire ceremony and which have re-manifested there for answers and elucidations of their current needs and queries that will assist in the writing of the *Śaivite Śāstras.* These *Śāstras* will explain how the basic Lemurian laws and Dravidian culture can be made applicable at this time."

The Long Task Of Reading And Dictating

It was through the first nine months of inner research that the original writings of *The Lemurian and Dravidian Śāstras* were dictated to a young monastic who wrote patiently, word after word, what I read from the manuscripts shown to me in the inner *ākāśic* ether of the mind. Later in the year, many portions of the manuscripts were re-read in the *ākāśa* for verification and clarification and compiled together into a more comprehensive presentation, as the Lord Subramaniam's librarian and I had become accustomed to working together, and these two documents were brought into final form. My notes from that period explain, "Through the last several moons on my retreat, which incidentally ended yesterday, October 1, 1973, my third eye has developed to a great extent in precision and accuracy, the only catalyst being numerous cups of morning Kona coffee and a crowded room where the odic force is high, which acts as a mirror, especially if cigarette smoke is in the air, and enables me to see extremely clearly these *ākāśic* records. I want you to know that the *Lemurian Śāstras* are in two languages of which the meaning comes out to me and I interpolate it in English. When I began the *Lemurian Śāstras,* it came as a surprise. I had not been accustomed to reading the *ākāśa,* let alone books in the *ākāśa.* So when the books were presented by the librarian in the Lord Subramaniam Library, which I have verified actually is Lord Skanda's library, it came as a surprise. Truly, as Satguru Yogaswami said, 'It is an open book.' "

Reading of *The Dravidian Manuscripts*

The Dravidian Śāstras (chapters twelve through twenty-seven of *Lemurian Scrolls)* were read from a collection of manuscripts written in a language that looks like this:

The writing of the language was black upon yellow, gold-like paper, some of which appeared to look like ancient parchment, but of a kind which is not seen on Earth today. *The Śaivite Śāstras* were written for the Śaiva Siddhānta Yoga Order by a group of *devas* in the Second World, in English, clearly printed on white paper with black letters. They were easy to read, as a translation did not have to occur through the process of the universal language that happens within the *ākāśic* area of the mind when languages foreign to an individual are encountered. In the Antarloka, as well as the Śivaloka, each one hears another speak in the language he is accustomed to, due to the immediate process of translation that occurs. This is called the universal language. The Lemurian script and Dravidian script seemed to leave the page, travel toward me through the *ākāśic* ether, enlarging themselves as they did, and I would speak out the meaning. More than often, after speaking out the meaning, print would leave the page, and the actual scene, in vivid picture form, would appear in place of it, depicting what had been described. Some of these books stood three feet tall and when opened spanned about a four-or-five-foot area. These were the Lemurian collection, written during the Tretā Yuga. They all had heavy covers and were placed into the *ākāśic* library through certain prescribed methods used in that day. Some of the covers were decorated in gold, with a light-green, suede-leathery-type material covering them; others were brown and still others red and covered with jewels.

The Dravidian Volumes

The Dravidian collection were of different sizes. Some had large, floppy covers and loosely connected pages. Others were small, well bound. Still others were heavy, bulky, but were lifted and placed before me as if they weighed no more than a feather. At times, pages would crackle as they turned, and others would appear to be quite well preserved. Here is a note I made when encountering these *ākāśic* texts in 1974. "These *śāstras* were written at the end of the Dvāpara Yuga as a guideline for going into the Kali Yuga and are in a different language than the *śāstras* that were written at the end of the Tretā Yuga. They tell at great length about the time of night in the Kali Yuga when the *kuṇḍalinī* in the form of a snake would curl up and go to sleep, and since we know all the problems that this has caused through the nerve system of man in a state of sleep, we won't go into this particular section of the book, which is a thick section. The *śāstras* say that when the *kuṇḍalinī* is well balanced, the whole nature becomes very smooth, and that every effort should be made to surround oneself with people and circumstances that keep the *kuṇḍalinī* active in the deeper chakras. Another book is being presented now by the librarian which is a book of prophecy of the action of the *kuṇḍalinī* in the Sat Śiva Yuga. This book has big, floppy pages, and each page is about two by three feet, big and loose and floppy, with a soft cover. Occasionally, out of the center of a page comes a picture, and I see very clearly how these things look. So, between words and looking at the pictures in reading this book, unlike other books, you don't have to turn the page to get another picture; it just comes out of the place where the picture is. This book is the same as all the rest, sort of yellow-gold with golden writing on it, with a royal blue *ākāśic* background, and is sort of sitting there in space. Occasionally when we get into an area, the librarian will turn a few pages and a whole new area will come up. I just see now that the fibrous bodies are the same structure as a leaf on a tree and the sap running though the veins all equally, so they were kind of vegetable or tree constructed bodies. However, it shows clearly that they were not exactly a vegetation of this Earth because they were produced out of this *kuṇḍalinī* force and maintained by it."

First World Petitions

My original notes continue, "At one point I saw a table before my forehead with an array of paper and books and manuscripts on it. I had never seen this before, and here is how I described this experience: 'A large scroll tells me that this is the collection of petitions from all the esoteric groups

Artist's depiction of the vision of Lord Śiva, February 15, 1975, that was the inspiration for the San Mārga Sanctuary and its Iraivan Temple

and organizations in the world who are guided from this one library of our Lord Subramaniam in the *ākāśa*. The thoughts of the group leaders, it goes on to say, are listened to by the inner plane divine helpers and written down and given to the librarian here. Then these leaders of the various groups are brought to the library at night, and the librarian (the one who has been getting for me all the books I have been reading) gives them books to read, and specific helpful things are pointed out to them. In this way all the many groups heralding the Sat Śiva Yuga on Earth are guided in the same way, getting all their information and guidance from the same central source in the *ākāśa*. In this way, Lord Subramaniam, the God of the Pleiades, does His work through his international library, with records existing today that are over two million years old. These petitions on this table will be answered tonight when the particular person arrives, or the answer will be projected to him telepathically or clairaudiently. The organization leader may say in the morning, 'Oh, I had a good dream last night or in meditation and it was unfolded that we should do this or that,' and his people quite naturally would be inspired to make it manifest.' "

A Window On the Way of Wisdom

During the course of the months that followed, after the first entry into the library, we really came to love Lord Subramaniam's librarian, and he told us that on the Earth plane, the last time he was here, he was one of the Śaivite saints. He mentioned that Satguru Yogaswami of Columbuthurai (1872-1963) was also one of the Śaivite saints, Nayanars, and was sent by Lord Subramaniam back to a birth in the Bhūloka, the First World, to live in Jaffna to lay the foundation for and accrue the power to sustain Śaivism in the Western world. "There are more of us," he said, "and they will identify themselves on the physical plane from time to time." In reading this book, *Lemurian Scrolls,* use your inner eye to follow what is described. You will begin to see the intricacies to be found in the depth of the *ākāśa*. They outline "the way of wisdom" for the *āchāryas* and swāmīs of the Śaiva Siddhānta Yoga Order and offer a window into the origins of mankind and our purpose for being on planet Earth. We do hope that you gain some new insights and inspiration from *Lemurian Scrolls,* as have so many of my devotees during the past two decades. During the many months it took to bring through the entirety of the *Lord Subramaniam Śāstras* and their supplementary texts, I came to deeply appreciate the wonderful being whom I knew as Lord Subramaniam's librarian. To that very tall, efficient man, elegantly dressed in colorful robes, living and serving in the Antarloka, I now offer a profound "Mahalo," thank you, for granting us access to your master's extraordinary archive. I shall conclude with a quote from my dear friend, Lord Subramaniam's librarian, offered with a wise nod of approval: "An amazing work, well done." After that, the door gently closed. To this very day my inner eye has never opened again into Lord Subramaniam's *ākāśic* library, though other inner worlds continue to be revealed.

Another Vision And Direction For the Future

It was almost exactly two years after the arrival of the Lord Naṭarāja Deity, once the entirety of the *śāstric* reading had been completed, that another vision came that planted the seeds of our San Mārga Iraivan Temple, which

Artist's conception of the white granite Iraivan Temple being built on the banks of Kauai's sacred Wailua River, near the foot of Mount Waialeale, an extinct volcano—Hawaiian site of Gurudeva's Hindu monastery where this book was designed.

is being carved of white granite as a spiritual edifice to last a thousand years. For this decades-long project we built a village in Bangalore, India, in 1990. Today over 100 workers and their families daily carve by hand this magnificent edifice. Early on the morning of February 15, 1975, I experienced a three-fold vision of Lord Śiva. First, I saw Him walking in the meadow near the sacred Wailua River on our fifty-one acre Aadheenam land. Suddenly His face, composed of billions of tiny, hair-like quantums, was looking into mine. I remember this perfect face of all faces clearly today, and with each year the details of this vision become clearer and clearer. Then He was seated upon a great stone. Astonished, I was seated on His left side. Upon reentering earthly consciousness, I felt certain the great stone was somewhere on our land and set about to find it. Guided from within by my *satguru,* I hired a bulldozer and instructed the driver to follow me as I walked to the north edge of the property that was then a nearly impenetrable tangle of buffalo grass and wild guava. I hacked my way through the jungle southward as the dozer cut a path behind me. After almost half a mile, I sat down to rest near a small tree. Though there was no wind, suddenly the tree's leaves shimmered as if in the excitement of communication. I asked the tree, "What is your message?" In reply, my attention was directed to a spot just to the right of where I was sitting. When I pulled back the tall grass, there was a large rock, the self-created Liṅga on which Lord Śiva had sat. The bulldozer's trail now led exactly to the sacred stone, surrounded by five smaller boulders. San Mārga, the straight or pure path to God, had been created. All this happened on February 15, 1975.

San Mārga Iraivan Temple

Worship of the sacred stone with water and flowers was commenced immediately through daily *pūjā* rites, and a master plan was unfolded from the *devonic* worlds. Today, visitors to the sanctuary walk the path of the Tamil Nayanars around picturesque lotus ponds and visit the six shrines of the Kailāsa Paramparā on the banks of Saravaṇabhava Lake in Ṛishi Valley. Across rolling meadows, pilgrims will gaze upon the San Mārga Iraivan Temple, enshrining the world's largest single-pointed quartz crystal—a 700-pound, 39-inch-tall, six-sided natural gem, a *sphaṭika* Śivaliṅga, acquired in 1987. Iraivan, designed to stand a thousand years and more as a spiritual edifice for forty generations, is America's first traditional, all-stone temple. We now know that this vision and its blessings, as the seed for such a remarkable project for future generations, was a gift from the inner worlds following directly in the wake of *Lemurian Scrolls.* The foundation had been set long, long ago, and now it was time to bring forth Sanātana Dharma to the Western world in all its glory. And what better place to begin than Pihanakalani, "where heaven touches Earth," on an ancient mountaintop of Lemuria, the Garden Island of Kauai?

A Place Of Sacred Pilgrimage

Here is a quotation from the *Śaivite Śāstras* giving a vision of future fulfillment: "By the time 1995 arrived, the inner order and the outer Order of Śaivism worked in harmony with the band of Mahādevas in the Third World.

On August 16, 1987, the day of Harmonic Convergence, the world's largest, perfectly formed, single-pointed quartz crystal, 39 inches tall and weighing 700 pounds, was brought to Kauai from Arkansas to be the central icon of Iraivan Temple. As the focal point of worship and meditation, the crystal will be adored as a Śivaliṅga, or mark of God. In India, the crystal Śivaliṅga is considered to be the most sacred and unique of all Liṅgas, because of its integrated substance and natural self-manifestation, for it is not carved or crafted by human hands.

Lord Skanda and Umāgaṇeśa and Lord Śiva Himself were pleased at this band of great Lemurian souls working together in the Second World and the First World. Constant rays from cosmic galaxies began to penetrate these monasteries deep into the Earth, some so

strong they penetrated through the Earth. This permanent darshan that vibrated all the temple land resounded through the countryside, establishing a peace of mind and abundant consciousness for those who lived within the radiance of this darshan of the monasteries and temples. Looking into the future, we can see this vibration growing in the ground. Each pebble, each grain of sand became sacred. Each stone, like a *chakram*. The monastics were ecstatic and they spoke to all who came to visit with the radiance of their presence. There were constant streams of pilgrims flowing in and out of certain areas of these great monasteries, schools and temples." Now, in 1998, after we have lived the vision for many years, pilgrims from India, Sri Lanka, Malaysia, Singapore, Australia, Europe, USA and many other countries are daily enjoying the radiance of this darshan as it nears its fulfillment, which will be complete at the *kumbhābhishekam* of the carefully hand-carved golden-domed Iraivan Koyil, the final resting place of the multi-million-years-in-the-formation crystal Sivaliṅga. You, too, will be welcomed when drawn by a dream, a vision or inner impulse to come to have darshan as you perhaps did several *yugas* ago in another life. Sitting here on Kaua'i's eastern coast, looking out upon the calm Pacific Ocean, listening to the musical waves caressing the ancient coral reef and reminiscing the eventful days in which these scrolls were read, I wonder, as you also may, what other gifts of knowledge these great beings have in store for us. Maybe, just maybe, the masters of ages past and the age to come, within the inner world will open the doors of their *ākāśic* library again. The door nobs are on the inside and can only be used by them. We can only wait and wonder, wondering while we wait. Enjoy *Lemurian Scrolls, Angelic Prophecies Revealing Human Origins.*

Love and blessings ever flowing to you from this and inner worlds,

Satguru Sivaya Subramuniyaswami
162nd Jagadāchārya of the Nandinātha
Sampradāya's Kailāsa Paramparā
Guru Mahāsannidhānam, Kauai Aadheenam, Hawaii
Seventy-Second Satguru Jayanti, Tamil Hindu year 5099
January 5, 1998

A view of Kadavul Hindu Temple (opposite page), the spiritual hub of Gurudeva's Monastery on the Garden Island of Kauai, enshrining six-foot-tall images of Lord Gaṇeśa, Lord Muruga and Lord Śiva Naṭarāja.

I. WAYAN MARYA

Our monastic community, sitting with me in Kauai beneath a giant banyan tree. Back in 1975, as the *Lord Subramaniam Śāstras* were completed, all *maṭhavāsis* adjusted to the new flows outlined in these great volumes. Each monk became stronger and stronger through the years. As we release this second printing in the year 2000,
we have four *ācharyas*—Bodhinathaswami, Palaniswami, Ceyonswami and Kumarswami—ten other *sannyāsins:* Muruganathaswami, Arumugaswami, Natarajnathaswami, Sivakatirswami, Sivadevanathaswami, Shanmuganathaswami, Skandanathaswami, Saravanannathaswami, Guhanathaswami and Karttikeyanathaswami; one *yogī tapasvin:* Yuganatha, eight *sādhakas:* Jothinatha, Haranandinatha, Adinatha, Tyaganatha, Thondunatha, Jivanandanatha, Japendranatha, Nilakantha; two supplicants: Chundadevan and Nanthakumar; and one aspirant: Brahmachari Tejadeva.

S. RAJAM

WE NOW BEGIN THIS BOOK WITH HUMBLE PROSTRATIONS TO THE BENEVOLENT GOD GANESHA, QUIETLY SPOKEN OF IN THESE MANUSCRIPTS, WORSHIPED TODAY IN NEARLY every country of the world. Famed even in this decade for drinking all the milk in London, New Delhi and elsewhere and flattered in headlines in numerous countries on September 19, 1995, when He started the "milk miracle," unchallenged by scientists, He above all the Gods must be worshiped first. God Lono to the Hawaiians, ts'ogsbdag to the Tibetans, Prah Kenes to the Cambodians, Tot-kharour Khaghan to the Mongolians, Vinayaksa or Sho-ten to the Japanese, Saint Nicholas to the Western peoples, He is invoked in millions of shrines, outnumbering those of all the other Gods in the Hindu world. Quoting from our Hindu Catechism, DANCING WITH SIVA, We humbly introduce Him here: "Lord Ganesha is the elephant-faced Patron of Art and Science, the Lord of Obstacles and Guardian of Dharma. His will prevails as the force of righteousness, the embodiment of Siva's karmic law in all three worlds. Lord Siva, the Almighty Power, created heaven and earth and the God Lord Ganesha to oversee the intricate karmas and dharmas within the heavens and all the earths. Lord Ganesha was created as a governor and interplanetary, intergalactic Lord. His knowledge is infinite, His judgment is just. It is none other than Lord Ganesha and His mighty band of ganas who gently help souls out of the Naraka abyss and adjust them into higher consciousness after due penance has been paid, guiding them on the right path toward dharmic destiny. He is intricate of mind, loving pomp, delighting in all things sweet and enjoying adulation. Lord Siva proclaimed that this son be worshiped first, even before Himself. Verily, He is the Lord of Karma. All Mahadevas, minor Gods, devas and sentient beings must worship Ganesha before any responsible act could hope to be successful. Those who do not are subject to their own barriers. Yea, worship of Him sets the pattern of one's destiny. The TIRUMANTIRAM says, 'Five-armed is He, elephant-faced with tusks protruding, crescent-shaped, son of Siva, wisdom's flower, in heart enshrined, His feet I praise.' Aum Namah Sivaya."

S. RAJAM

THIS SACRED TEXT IS DRAWN FROM THE GREAT INNER PLANE LIBRARY OF LORD SUBRAMANIAM, ALSO KNOWN AS SKANDA, SANATKUMARA AND KARTTIKEYA, ONE OF the great Gods of the Hindu pantheon. This yogic master of the Great White Brotherhood is known as God Ku to the Hawaiians, Zeus to the Greeks, Jupiter to the Romans, Thor to the Norse, Taranis to the Celts, cherished as the eternal youth by over 60 million Tamil Hindus, protector of their culture and defender of their faith, and revered as the Deity of ayurvedic healing powers. Worldwide today there are over 100,000 temples and shrines dedicated to Him, and He is lovingly enshrined in our own temples in Hawaii and Mauritius. He is introduced in my Hindu Catechism, DANCING WITH SIVA: "Lord Karttikeya, Murugan, first guru and Pleiadean master of kundalini yoga, was born of God Siva's mind. His dynamic power awakens spiritual cognition to propel souls onward in their evolution to Siva's feet. Lord Karttikeya flies through the mind's vast substance from planet to planet. He could well be called the Emancipator, ever available to the call of those in distress. Lord Karttikeya, God of will, direct cognition and the purest, child-like divine love, propels us onward on the righteous way through religion, His Father's law. Majestically seated on the manipura chakra, this scarlet-hued God blesses mankind and strengthens our will when we lift to the inner sky through sadhana and yoga. The yoga pada begins with the worship of Him. The yogi, locked in meditation, venerates Karttikeya, Skanda, as his mind becomes as calm as Saravana, the lake of Divine Essence. The kundalini force within everyone is held and controlled by this powerful God, first among renunciates, dear to all sannyasins. Revered as Murugan in the South, He is commander in chief of the great devonic army, a fine, dynamic soldier of the within, a fearless defender of righteousness. He is Divinity emulated in form. The VEDAS say, 'To such a one who has his stains wiped away, the venerable Sanatkumara shows the further shore of darkness. Him they call Skanda.' Aum Namah Sivaya."

S. RAJAM

THE SUPREME BEING OF THE VEDAS, HAILED IN LEMURIAN SCROLLS, IS GOD SIVA, THE INNER, OUTER, ALL-PERVASIVE ENERGY AND DIVINE INTELLIGENCE THAT INSPIRES AND informs every part of His creation. Divine Dancer—that is He, and creation is His stage. He is the All and the Everything, and the underlying Nothing as well, "the God of Gods," Brahma-Vishnu-Rudra to Hindus, Kane to Hawaiians, Wakan Tanka to the Dakota Indians, Jehovah to Jews and Christians, and to the Buddhists the supreme nonbeingness. Yea, He is the supreme director of Sanatana Dharma, of all souls, their father, their mother, the creator of gravity, giving the consciousness of time and space and all that exists, as its glorious preserver and eventual absorber. But He is hampered by a single inability—He cannot take Himself out of you or me. DANCING WITH SIVA explains. "God Siva is all and in all, one without a second, the Supreme Being and only Absolute Reality. He is Pati, our Lord, immanent and transcendent. To create, preserve, destroy, conceal and reveal are His five powers. Aum. God Siva is a one being, yet we understand Him in three perfections: Absolute Reality, Pure Consciousness and Primal Soul. As Absolute Reality, Siva is unmanifest, unchanging and transcendent, the Self God, timeless, formless and spaceless. As Pure Consciousness, Siva is the manifest primal substance, pure love and light flowing through all form, existing everywhere in time and space as infinite intelligence and power. As Primal Soul, Siva is the five-fold manifestation: Brahma, the creator; Vishnu, the preserver; Rudra, the destroyer; Maheshvara, the veiling Lord, and Sadasiva, the revealer. He is our personal Lord, source of all three worlds. Our divine father-mother protects, nurtures and guides us, veiling Truth as we evolve, revealing it when we are mature enough to receive God's bountiful grace. God Siva is all and in all, great beyond our conception, a sacred mystery that can be known in direct communion. Yea, when Siva is known, all is known. The VEDAS state: 'That part of Him which is characterized by tamas is called Rudra. That part of Him which belongs to rajas is Brahma. That part of Him which belongs to sattva is Vishnu.' Aum Namah Sivaya."

Migrating to this planet

in their subtle bodies, many of our forebearers traveled through the Sun. The beginnings of mankind's mission on this planet came in a far-away time, when the atmosphere was dense with waters and gases. Flowers and animals were larger and more exotic than today. At first, the transformation from etheric to physical form was difficult, but ceremonies evolved which, using the fragrances of fruits and flowers, brought devotionally to special pedestals, assisted in bringing through beings who absorbed these organic essences to materialize a denser, earthly, fibrous body. These beings loved the many jewels and golden ornaments that were crafted to bedeck and help support their flexible forms. Human life did not evolve from lesser earthly species. Aum.

Attainment of life's ultimate goal had lapsed, the scrolls tell us, among quiescent souls inhabiting far-off planets in a time remote from our own, four million years ago. Understanding that stress and pain, love and caring are necessary to endow the soul with sufficient strength to attain realization of the Self, God, Parasiva, essence of all, souls set forth on humanity's greatest known journey.

Sivaya Subramuniyaswami
Gurudeva

Pilgrimage To Planet Earth

भूग्रहयात्रा

Chapter 1

1 ℭ Mankind migrated to this planet in his divine soul body during the Sat Yuga, the age of enlightenment. He had reached a final stage of evolution on his native planet. The risk in migrating to a fire planet was great, but so was the reward. They were, however, at a place in evolution requiring a planet with fire in it to catalyze them through new experiences into completing their unfoldment to the final realization of the Self. Souls came from the other planets to Earth for one of two reasons: either they came to realize the Self, because they had not previously done so and were just drifting in bliss, or were great beings who already had the Self realized and came to help the others. They came from everything in a state of status quo. They had come to this planet to get jostled around in the fire to continue their unfoldment.

The Need For a Fire Planet

2 ℭ When a planet becomes old, it cools. Everything becomes static in it and on it. The beings inhabiting it exist together like a flock of birds or school of fish, so peaceful they are. Souls, who need fire to realize the Self, could not do so on such an old planet, so the leaders pilgrimaged with their followers to perform the austerity of evolution on a fire planet such as Earth, a hot planet, a young planet. There will be other planets ready to be colonized at the end of the Kali Yuga. Inhabitants of Earth will be able to rapidly access them by traveling as a ray of their own inner light.

The Lush Conditions of The Sat Yuga

3 ℭ In the Sat Yuga, the air was thick and the Earth lush and tropical. The thick clouds of gases and healthful substances floating in the air were the materials the divine souls that came to the fire planet, as they referred to it, would use to materialize a physical body around the etheric body of the soul to express through while living on Earth. As more and more came to Earth in their etheric bodies, ceremonies were performed in a scientific way by those who had already arrived, offering food and flowers, cut fruits and other ambrosia before them so that they could absorb some of the organic essences into the etheric body and materialize around and through it Earth bodies. Their etheric bodies became dense, firm and more defined during these food-offering ceremonies in what were to later become the temples of the Tretā Yuga. They continued to absorb these food-offering essences until they

began to smell and feel and acquired a full physical form and could eat normally, as the animals did on Earth at that time.

The Arrival Of Various Races

4 ℂ The most highly evolved souls who arrived first on Earth during the Sat Yuga continued to bring more divine beings through into physical form from the other planets. It was part of their mission to do this. Lord Skanda came to Earth in the Sat Yuga. He was one of the most highly advanced souls. He came as the leader of the first group, and will guide them all along through into the next Sat Yuga. He was the celestial king of Lemuria. It was because of this most ancient practice of offering the essences of fruit and perfumed ambrosias to the soul's etheric body to absorb and thus create a denser body that this planet became inhabited in the Sat Yuga. As this planet moved through time and space, different races came from the various planets and settled on one area of it or another. During one phase of planetary configurations, ceremonies would be active in one temple to bring through into dense manifest form a group from a certain planet, and as the planets moved into another configuration, the place on Earth polarizing the rays and race of that planet would become inactive, and another race from another planet would come through at a different location through ceremony.

The First Temples Are Established

5 ℂ In order to bring these divine souls through into physical form during the Sat Yuga, great temples to each of these planets began to form in which these priestly scientists would make food offerings and bathe a pedestal-like form as a point of concentration. The celestial beings would stand on the pedestal and absorb the Earth's pungent substances and with it materialize strong physical bodies. In the beginning it took a long time to bring the etheric body of a soul into physical form so he could walk off this pedestal on his own in the Earth's atmosphere. But through the thousands of years that passed, it became a very rapid process, and the entire Earth became populated with celestial beings from several of the major planets in the galaxy. Thus, the souls arrived in full force to begin a long, tedious evolutionary pattern through the three *yugas* to follow.

Our First Earth Bodies

6 ℂ These divine souls who came to populate the planet in the Sat Yuga looked much like mankind will still look hundreds of thousands of years from now in the Kali Yuga, except there was no gender—no male and female—or such a thing as death or reproduction or even sleep. There was no concept of hunger or pain. They could fly easily and freely in their new Earth body in the Sat Yuga by mentally lifting up into the air by using the power within their spine and travel anywhere. These bodies were impervious to cold or heat. The air was so thick and healthy, they would become nourished simply by breathing in deeply. They didn't really need to eat then, as the air completely filled their bodies with *prāṇic* essence each time they took a deep breath. Early in the Sat Yuga, they had only but to smell the essence of cut fruits and flowers for a complete meal. Everything was so pungent, and because of the nature of their physical bodies this was possible. But toward the end of the *yuga*, they had to eat to become nourished and could not fly as far. The closest they ever came to the concept of death was when the physical elements just dissolved under the power of realizing the Self and the essence of their individuality returned to the planet from whence they came, fully matured, having completed their mission on the fire planet. There was a distinct sense of personality in each of these first transcendental beings that came to our planet during the Sat Yuga, for even the individual soul has an evolution, one different from another.

Great temples to each of these planets began to form in which the celestial beings would stand on a pedestal and absorb the Earth's pungent substances and with it materialize strong physical bodies.

Cosmic Cycles of Four Yugas

7 ℂ It is necessary to understand the nature of the *yugas* to acquire full knowledge of the continuity of mankind as he evolves in experience from his beautiful state in the Sat Yuga to the veiling darkness of the Kali Yuga and into the dawn of the Sat Yuga, the golden age that will again follow. During this entire process, the evolution of each soul will individualize itself as it merges toward its essence. The Sat Yuga, the Tretā Yuga, the Dvāpara Yuga and the Kali Yuga are the names of these four divisions of planetary radiation, and they repeat themselves in that order, with the Sat Yuga being the first and the Kali Yuga the last. To understand clearly how they work, observe the four major divisions of the day. The darkest part of the night is the great dream of the Kali Yuga. The cycles of Earth around the sun, therefore, are sim-

ilar to the cycles of this galaxy around a Central Sun, which are called the *yugas*, because of the radiant cosmic rays that are either released or hidden. The *yugas* are the way in which the Mahādevas calculate time and space.

When More Souls Will Arrive

8 ℭ This generation of souls started to arrive and live on Earth since the beginning of the Sat Yuga, and more will come through the Tretā Yuga. Then no more souls will come until the end of the Kali Yuga. When the next Sat Yuga arrives, those who have lived through the cycle of *yugas* will all finish their evolutionary processes and leave. More divine souls will come during that time as the cycle repeats.

Life on this And Other Planets

9 ℭ The fire planet is very young, having become habitable only a few cycles of *yugas* ago. There are planets in this universe much older than the fire planet. The inhabitants of these older and larger planets do not live on the surface of their planet. They use the surface only like a park and to provide their nourishment and live in underground places that may have been constructed millions of years ago. It is necessary to live for several of these *yugas* on Earth in order to earn admittance to those planets.

Duration Of the Yugas

10 ℭ The *yugas* are calculated by a span of vibration. Our Lemurian calculations of time will not be translatable into calendars of the Kali Yuga, so at that time there will be confusion about the length of time each *yuga* is supposed to contain. But it is discernable when another *yuga* is imminent by the changes that occur within the population.

Dawn of The Glorious Sat Yuga

11 ℭ The Sat Yuga is always the time of dawn, of birth, of awakening into the fullness of the soul. It is a time of total light, with no confusion of the forces as later begins to exist at the wane of the Tretā Yuga, and through the Dvāpara Yuga and Kali Yuga. Everything existed in its fullness in the Sat Yuga, with a total and open giving of all the world's goods, physically, superconsciously and intellectually, between beings. There was no feeling at all of personal ego. In the Kali Yuga, there will exist feelings of possessiveness or difference, one from another, resulting from the change in the great mind flow of the *yugas* as souls become caught in the animal and human evolution as a result of the shift

toward darker states of consciousness. They will suffer the constant acquiring of yet a more dense body, from birth to birth, in the darkness of the Dvāpara and Kali Yugas until the Sat Yuga dawns again in light and glory. As the galaxy rotates into the second relationship with the Cosmic Sun, the space and mind flows persisting in and through the Earth are those of the Tretā Yuga. Much of the refinement and superconsciousness of the Sat Yuga will still permeate through the Tretā Yuga. But later it will wane when the dusk of externalization of consciousness permeates as the galaxy slowly shifts again, cuting off some of the rays of the Central Sun.

Man Takes On Animal Bodies

12 ¶ Now, during the end of the Tretā Yuga, souls can no longer migrate to our planet the way they did through the Sat Yuga. Many of these divine, Earthly bodies, constructed from fruit ambrosia, herbal essences and the pungent air, could no longer fly and have been eaten by the carnivorous beings of the animal kingdom, the inhabitants remaining from the last Kali Yuga. As a result of having been devoured by animals, these souls got caught within the evolutionary cycle of the particular species that had eaten their original body. Then, through the cycle of birth and death, they emerged again, but were captured in the instinctive nerve system of animal bodies. Then, through the long process of mutation and reincarnation, they finally, after great struggles and help from the Mahādevas, cultivated a body similar to the first Earth body devoured long ago. This human body had animal instincts and was difficult to live in. This mutation began new breeds of animals that were not carnivorous. Beings still in original bodies, but now not able to fly much anymore, could ride these animals, fly upon and feed from the milk within some of them. For these new breeds of animals encased some of the celestial beings yet to acquire a human body.

Life During the Tretā Yuga

13 ¶ The Tretā Yuga is a wonderful period in which intense cosmic rays still penetrate Earth. This makes such evolution possible as creating a flesh body that appears to be like the original one for these celestial beings caught in animal reincarnation cycles to inhabit. These flesh-and-bone bodies will last through the Dvāpara and Kali Yugas until the strong vibration of the next Sat Yuga comes to cause their liberation and

Ceremonies will be performed through the Kali Yuga that will bring a soul close enough to the physical world to establish contact with future parents to effect birth. This process will begin refining many races and varieties of people on the planet in preparation for the next Sat Yuga.

permit many of us to leave this planet. These final humiliations and struggles within the instinctive area of externalized mind through the darker *yugas* will give the final polish sanctifying our divinity. It has been observed, now that we are approaching the end of the Tretā Yuga, that a sense of fear is being experienced for the first time as a result of eating wrong kinds of foods, along with losing some of the personal abilities to fly.

Engineering The Process of Reincarnation

14 ℂ Our laboratories cultivate species of animals in order to breed bodies similar to the original body, and when a soul had become caught in the animal kingdom, experiments were conducted in these laboratories, near the temple of the planet whence the soul had originally come, to release him from this bondage into a birth of a body he could be more comfortable in. Many celestial souls would be quickly released from the animal reincarnation cycles in this way.

Ceremonies To Effect Human Birth

15 ℂ It has been predicted that similar ceremonies will be performed through the Kali Yuga, but will not bring souls through into physical form as they did in the Sat Yuga, nor will they accomplish the release of souls as in the Tretā Yuga. They will just bring a soul close enough to the physical world to establish contact with future parents to effect birth. This process will begin refining many races and varieties of people on the planet in preparation for the next Sat Yuga. The few left who have original bodies will live in caves high in the mountains during the end of the Tretā Yuga to avoid being caught in the fleshy, hot body of the animal and to preserve the original bodies as long as possible. Here new metals will be found to work with, and large communities will grow as a result, through the use of them, our prophets tell us.

Cycles of Bondage in Animal Bodies

16 ℂ The cycle of getting out of the animal kingdom takes a long, long time unless help is given, and even to the end of the Kali Yuga and into the next Sat Yuga, souls will be seen still trying to escape from the fiery bondage of animal bodies. It will be during the Kali Yuga that a human kingdom will eventually fully come out of the different species of animals and form different groups on Earth, some of whom will be the predators of others, we are told.

Discomfort And Yearning For Release

17 ℄ The original bodies some of us still have are neither male nor female, nor do they sleep or experience heat, cold or fear. Therefore, the souls in flesh bodies feel uncomfortable experiencing these instincts and demands of their bodies and yearn for release. They will be found still striving through the Kali Yuga to adjust these forces. This is the evolution we had come here to experience.

The few left who have original bodies will live in caves high in the mountains during the end of the Tretā Yuga to avoid being caught in the fleshy, hot body of the animal and to preserve the original bodies as long as possible.

Yugas before mankind arrived on Earth, celestial beings in wingless spacecraft spread seeds from other planets. Souls arriving in the last Sat Yuga eventually formed monasteries in which experiments were conducted into the nature of life, designing forms it should take on this planet. Their flexible bodies were light and easily flew in the dense air. Occasionally, one would be devoured by an animal, thus capturing this soul in the incarnation cycle of that species. Through the long mutative process of repeatedly reentering these instinctive bodies, they finally cultivated a body similar to, yet cruder than, the first fibrous

bodies. To release a soul caught in an animal reincarnation cycle into human birth, ceremonial sacrifice was conducted, with the knowledge and silent consent of the animal. Aum.

Because each yuga is an advent in time and space, as these shastras explain, each differs in tone and tenor. We shall now watch what will one day be known as humankind makes the Treta yuga transition downward into the instinctive nature in order to grow, develop and then unfold the spiritual being. Thus the wheel of samsara spins in greater velocity in never-failing purposefulness on Earth.

Gurudeva

18 Only with the advent of the animal kingdom was there such a thing as *tapas* or *sādhana* to transmute the fires of instinctive desire. There will come a time, toward the end of the Dvāpara Yuga and into the Kali Yuga, when the soul will incarnate into a human body and be pulled back into the animal world, and then again into a human body, and be pulled back into the animal world, and then again into a human body, simulating a war between *devas* and demons. There will be families who live deep in caves, in the first evolutionary step out of the animal kingdom, who weren't reclaimed by the sacrificial ceremonies of the Tretā Yuga.

The Sublime Era Called Tretā Yuga

19 During the Tretā Yuga, the Earth has been lush and wonderful for those souls who avoided the animal world and continued to fulfill their evolution on Earth, without interruption, in their original bodies. All through this time we greatly perfected laboratory-like monasteries, working to help those who were captured. We all lived together in absolute, blissful harmony, and the world was a beautiful place. Everyone was creative and well occupied with various mental activities rather than those of a physical nature. All was ever in a state of total completion at each point in time, due to the nature of the *yuga* and our culture. Even when the original body was lost to a hungry animal, this did not disturb the inner equanimity. It will be only in the end of the Dvāpara Yuga and into the Kali Yuga that this completeness of culture and natural expression of soul will be lost, and the division between the inner and outer will become a great barrier, it is predicted. As others entered the animal kingdom, it was considered a natural participation in the evolution on this planet, though we all avoided the experience as long as possible. It was only those who came back from the animal herds, through mutation into the newly forming human race with bodies that mated, who knew a little of the duality of happiness and unhappiness.

The Ratio of Those Still in Original Bodies

20 As the Sat Yuga ended with the advent of the Tretā Yuga, the ratio of divine beings to those entering the animal kingdom was something like three to one. One half to one half was the ratio during the Tretā Yuga. But now, toward its end, the ratio is one in the original body to three in the others. Our prophecies read out that during the Dvāpara and Kali Yugas

every celestial soul will either be in an animal body or in a human body made of its flesh, fire and bones. And it will be at the end of the Dvāpara Yuga that all will see and remember the virtues of the Tretā Yuga and tell in great volumes its history and culture as it faces the looming gloom of the Kali Yuga. Soon man forgets those virtues and the proper way of moving in the mind and using its powers as he begins to work for dark purposes. It is during this time he will have mental battles with one another, and the black arts will be played with as games. It will be in the Kali Yuga that mankind kills one another. But in the Dvāpara Yuga still there is not yet the killing, no hand to hand combat as in the Kali Yuga, but one will hurt the mind of another in the dusk of his soul. It will be in the Kali Yuga, after the souls emerge in human form, with desires, passions and reproductive fervor, that racial and religious groups of many different kinds will begin. Before that there is only one religion.

Exercizing The Fading Ability to Fly

21℄ Our power of being able to fly is beginning to wane, and it is impossible to travel for long distances. And so we fly in games and for sport as we exercise this fast-fading faculty. Many are seen walking then flying a little and walking again, interspersing one with another, three or four hundred yards at a time. Those in the grosser bodies cannot do this at all and marvel at our ability. Children, however, can sometimes fly in the human bodies, and they lift them in the air and spin around as they dance and play one with another. They could fly long distances, but didn't really have the desire to go any place because their homes were so nice there was no need to travel anywhere. The sign of our losing our ability to fly, it has been predicted, is the official beginning of the Dvāpara Yuga's advent in space and time. Then vast substances will form and divide the land. Darkness will prevail and cloud the mind, they say.

Prediction About the Dvāpara Yuga

22℄ In the end of the Dvāpara Yuga is seen the destruction of everything that had been built in the Tretā Yuga in the dark area of the world. The races of light and the races of darkness become divided by water. The air becomes thinner. During this time there is inner darkness within man in one part of the world and inner light in another part, creating a balance of sorts. Monasteries form to hold the forces of light and keep the balance of the race. Whereas the races in darkness will not have any monasteries and just do agriculture and care for the body. Everyone will try to influence everyone else through the powers of his mind. People try to convert other people to their religion and philosophy. No one is left on his own. Thought becomes very important to everyone. Everyone tries to program everyone else's thoughts. The destruction of this civilization will begin the Kali Yuga. The loss of knowledge and the loss of the ability to evolve divine faculties in the human body will occur, they say. Great knowledge, however, will be forced through certain souls by the Mahādevas, who will speak it and write it through the Kali Yuga to stabilize the belief and the culture, the prophecy states. "During the Dvāpara Yuga many of you will be coming back into human form from the animal kingdom and feeling the power of reason and memory," our teachers tell us. Then man will separate himself from others to endeavor to seek control over the forces within him, with the object to arrive within himself at the state he used to be in, out of the wheel of animalistic reincarnation through procreation.

The loss of knowledge and the loss of the ability to evolve divine faculties in the human body will occur, they say. Great knowledge, however, will be forced through certain souls by the Mahādevas, who will speak it and write it through the Kali Yuga to stabilize the belief and the culture, the prophecy states.

Releasing Souls From Animal Incarnation

23 One of the major functions of some of the temples during this time of the end of the Tretā Yuga is to cause the release of the souls from the animal kingdom through sacrifice. Often the soul would be released from an animal body and be able to incarnate into a human family attending the ceremony. But later on, in the Dvāpara Yuga, people will indeed consider themselves fortunate to receive a blessing from a Mahādeva, we predict, because there will be too many in flesh-and-bone bodies at that point in time and space, and these kinds of sacrificial ceremonies will not be effective because the vibration of the Earth will not be conducive for this kind of transmigration of the soul to occur. At this time, many will begin to eat meat and fish as some animals do, and take on their characteristics of desire and cunning and live in the instinctive animal consciousness. Then, when the Sat Yuga dawns, these celestial souls who had been trapped in the instinctive nerve system, slowly working their way out of the animal kingdom as well as out of human bodies, will find liberation. Their human bodies then will still look similar to the few original bodies we have left among us now, but they will still have the heat and fire of the animal nerve system. In the Kali Yuga, humanity will follow routine blindly and their prophets completely. This will not be difficult, because the prophets will not be able to see well, hence not too far.

The Central Sun's Rays in The Sat Yuga

24. Cosmic rays from the Central Sun will become stronger and stronger, heralding the dawn of the next Sat Yuga. There will be a new vibration, and everything will change. Mankind will again understand himself and virtue will dawn as the Sat Yuga quickly unfolds its strength. Many who are not ready for the light of this *yuga* will perish. Those who are of the Sat Yuga will experience the beauty of its dawn, unaffected by the astrological and Earth changes which will claim the lives of the unenlightened bound by the fierce dragon of lust. There will be more atmospheric changes like heat and cold, gases and chemicals and things of this nature which will bring on the *yuga*. As the *yuga* progresses, people will know the nature of the planet and work with it rather than trying to control it, realizing what the planet needs and letting it go through what it needs to go through. This knowledge comes from the inside of man. This will be a time when people will change from the inside out. People won't think the way they used to. Everything will respond to the new inner and outer space vibration—cosmic rays getting stronger and stronger bringing in the Sat Yuga. This has to do with what's in space. As the *yuga* dawns everything on Earth will become clean on a mass scale through the media of a mass method of communication. When people again come from other planets in the way they did in the Sat Yuga, the change will be complete and the dawn of the Sat Yuga will have fully arrived. It will be a gradual change to a great intensity. It will seem as if time is speeding up in the beginning, and concepts of space will change. It will be slightly different, though, at that time, as the planet will be older and cooler. As time goes on into the Sat Yuga there will be less and less Earth changes because the planet will be cooler. Everything will set.

Cycles of Time, Mind And Space

25. The Central Sun is an unseen Sun, just the opposite of our Sun, as if it weren't, but everything revolves around it and the rays are felt like the rays of the Self are felt, but not seen. It is that brink of the Absolute consciousness. The *yugas* occur as a result of the revolution around the Central Sun,

which is likened to an intense hole in space. There have been several series of *yugas* before this one where similar occurrences repeated themselves. The *yugas* are time cycles of time, mind and space. Time travels in a circle in the inner mind, not a straight line. Space is a circle, too. Space, stars, planets, moons and time and mind all revolve around a Central Sun, our *śāstras* stress. There are planets similar to the Earth, but older than the Earth, that are way forward in *yugas* yet to come. This planet is not yet that far into them. But there are great souls on the Earth who have been in other *yugas* or other Earths and are now back again to guide.

The Central Sun is an unseen Sun, just the opposite of our Sun, as if it weren't, but everything revolves around it and the rays are felt like the rays of the Self are felt, but not seen. It is that brink of the Absolute consciousness.

Four Cycles Of Yugas On Earth

26℄ Each *yuga* is a cycle of time and a cycle of space. The end of the coming Kali Yuga will be the end of the third full cycle of *yugas* since this planet became habitable. The next Sat Yuga will begin the fourth cycle of *yugas*. During the second cycle of *yugas*, celestial beings arrived from other planets bringing with them vegetation. Their spaceships passing over the Earth's surface dropped seeds and foliage. Then celestial beings came en masse and hovered over the earth in their etheric bodies. Some became the birds and small and large animals because they couldn't bring through the duplication of the divine soul body strongly enough to live on Earth at that time. Due to the conditions of the Earth and the gasses in the atmosphere, a mutation took place among all the divine souls that started the instinctive mind on the planet. The animals at the end of the second cycle were big, beautiful and happy. Even during this *yuga*, the small animals from the second cycle of *yugas* are coming into human form. There will be many humans on Earth as it enters the fourth cycle of *yugas*, our *śāstras* have explained to us.

Devonic Races Within Birds And Mammals

27℄ Some birds are a race of *devas* that will never incarnate into anything other than birds. All egg-laying creatures are *devas* and stay in the inner world of this planet. This would include turtles, snakes, fish, lizards and birds. The large mammals of the water, however, that give birth will eventually take human birth. Most all of Lemuria will be under vast bodies of liquid during the Kali Yuga, protected by various kinds of these mammals swimming within it, they say.

Adjusting to The Vibration Of Each Yuga

28 ℂ At the beginning of each *yuga,* the celestial soul within each body will not immediately realize how to adjust itself to the external mind flow. But as the *yuga* progresses, the brain and intellect will adapt easily within the new forces that come into effect. The middle of the last Sat Yuga and the middle of the next, our seers tell us, exist simultaneously in one current point in time. The beginning of the next Sat Yuga will be similar to the end of the Tretā Yuga. During this time there will be similarities between the two *yugas,* such as mankind's ability to understand the true nature of himself, harmony between people, flying for short distances and the ancient orders of monasticism again flourishing on Earth. During the next Sat Yuga, knowledge of working with and through the rays of the Central Sun will return. Then man will live underground again as he did before he came to this planet, and then remember how to travel easily through space. He will never travel easily in space until he lives under the surface of the earth, our prophets clearly state.

Placing Books in The Ākāśa

29 ℂ We have a little *śāstric* book, small in size and quite thick, which describes the methods used in placing the manuscripts of all cultures and time during the latter part of this *yuga* into the atmosphere of the inner mind. It says that all manifest life comes from the forces within the inner substance of the mind and permeates out through all the other elements. All these elements exist within a seed. A seed is in direct connection to the *ākāśa.* Therefore, the oil from a seed is a direct tube into it from the physical plane. To place books in the *ākāśa,* they should be first soaked in oil and then burned, it states. It is through the method of soaking books in life-giving oils, then reading them aloud to imprint them in the memory *ākāśa* and burning them to put them into the astral *ākāśa* that all records of history, philosophy and prophecy are written. The books that are in the *ākāśa* were made out of the oil in this way, the exact same substance as Earth oil, but the inner part of the oils appear in any kind of manifest form in the *ākāśa* through this method. Oil is a form of odic force in a very condensed state. Anything crushed will turn to oil eventually, they say. Within the oil is fire and many other kinds of elements. Everyone who used the single eye had access to any or all of these books. Lat-

er, in the Kali Yuga, when this is not possible, books will be written and many copies of the same one will be made to be read by those who have the use of both or one or the other of the two eyes.

Original Bodies, First Flesh Bodies

30 ℂ Our original Earth bodies were boned very soft in the Sat Yuga. The bones at any place could bend as much as two inches or more. This was because of the atmosphere at that time, which was similar to the atmosphere under water at great depths. The atmosphere will change again in the Dvāpara Yuga and Kali Yuga, and the bones will harden. It will again change when the next Sat Yuga comes into power. The original bodies by the end of the Sat Yuga contained a high content of oil, whereas it is found that the flesh bodies have a high content of other kinds of liquids, and even the blood is different. This remains so through the Kali Yuga. Because of the high oil content in the original bodies, the bones were soft and springy, much like snake or fish bodies. All through the Tretā Yuga, we were able to maintain these fibrous bodies with a high content of oil and keep them soft and pliable. In these soft, pliable bodies, we were easily in touch with beings on other planets.

During the next Sat Yuga, knowledge of working with and through the rays of the Central Sun will return. Then man will live underground again, as he did before he came to this planet, and then remember how to travel easily through space.

Monasteries of ancient Lemuria were surrounded by thick stone walls designed to protect the inhabitants from fierce winds. Each artisan would enter with his trainees through openings at the four corners, as there was little mixing of monastic clans. In early days devas and Mahadevas would manifest and receive petitions from the monastery at pagoda-like temples at auspicious times, offering guidance and direction from the inner worlds. These beings would manifest in three stages, becoming more and more visible as they hovered over the pagoda until they appeared on the pedestals. All would gather to absorb the darshan, receive direction and be graced. Much of the communication in these days was through mental means, and there were many games and pastimes related to this art. Aum.

Could they have known the experiences they were about to have? The ruling grace of Him who oversees all, sustains all (later to absorb when experiences birthed forth their knowledge which when used rightly in timing and amounts became wisdom) keeps from them the future which was to be lived through to be known. They valued and invoked cosmic rays which enhanced the process.

Gurudeva

31 In the Sat and Tretā Yugas we lived and live mainly in our minds. During these *yugas* everyone came into the new Earth body, functioning in the eye at the top of the head. We go deeply into the development of the inner bodies and do not come further out in the mind than the fourth chakra. It was during the Tretā Yuga that the inner bodies of the celestial beings were so adjusted to the Earth atmosphere that when each one acquired a flesh body, the eye in the forehead could faintly be seen in the ether, penetrating through it. No distinction between the inner bodies and outer bodies was ever made, and each conversed freely one with another, through verbal and mental means—about their experiences at night while their fleshy bodies slept and they soared on rays of light and sound to visit friends on other planets—as freely as they talked of occurrences within the immediate surroundings through the day. The more advanced ones could leave the body into light and sound and go to another *yuga* cycle. If they wanted to go into a tenth *yuga* cycle, they would go to another solar system where it was occurring. No distinction was made between the inner and outer. One thing was as real or unreal as another. It is just the total mind we are experiencing. The mind is so clear at this point in time.

Assistance From Our Mahādevas

32 Mahādevas from other planets often visited us on ours and—through mental means in their etheric bodies—through helpful conversations guided and instructed the various avenues of our evolution. There were such a great number of these inner plane beings and they did all sorts of things to help us. In this way they would continue their own spiritual advancement without taking a body. These advanced souls were specialists in certain areas of the evolution of the elements of the celestial bodies inhabiting these original bodies or fleshy ones, for each celestial body was of the elements of the planet upon which it originated.

Easy Living; Traveling From Earth

33 There is no consciousness of time in the Sat Yuga, but our prophets say that by the end of the Kali Yuga, time will seem very important to the Earth-bound souls that still remain. We are advised that during the first part of the Sat Yuga mankind will spend his time overcoming the reaction of the night of the Kali Yuga. The fear will leave, and the memory of

it. It will become increasingly easier for everyone to live on the planet. He will live underground and travel to other planets with the grace and ease that he, in his celestial body, has always been accustomed to. Many of the celestial souls that came and are coming to the planet were transported on the power of more advanced beings, and once here they will not be able to leave the planet until the next Sat Yuga. However, many of us can freely come and go. Many souls that just barely made it to Earth were not highly evolved and once here lived in a consciousness similar to birds, living right on the vegetation they found on the planet.

The Need For Ego Armor

34 ℂ Man will have to protect his celestial body, as well as physical body, through the Kali Yuga by developing a shell around them both, except for a few who do not need this ego armor and will keep alive some semblance of our philosophy and too few strands of our culture. Toward the end of the Tretā Yuga, this division began to occur, and some of us separated ourselves from the population, along with others with fleshy bodies more sensitive to the harrowing feelings of change that were beginning to groom the external patterns of the population as we merged into the Dvāpara Yuga. This group of us who will carry the power through in the monastic tradition—and many of us will be the same but in different external forms—are able to hold within our minds the rays of the Central Sun of this galaxy that are diminishing due to the configuration of the rearrangements of the galaxy. We and we alone will have the powers to initiate others into having the ability to disseminate through their celestial and physical bodies these penetrating, life-giving rays of the Central Sun. During the next Sat Yuga, a synthesis will occur for the first time of all three cycles of *yugas* that have preceded it. All that has occurred since celestial beings first began to inhabit the planet will blend together, as man will then be consciously conscious of the forces on the planet.

The Molding And Weaving Of Gold

35 ℂ We cover the physical bodies and our original bodies with a shiny yellow substance that is a conductor of force, and in this way are more able to feel the rays of the Central Universal Sun. The arts of weaving and working in stone are quite advanced. Our laboratories and technicians wove this gold and silver substance into fabrics and other kinds of decoration for these bodies. By the end of the Dvāpara Yuga man will use other materials to cover the body. We have oils that if put on gold will permeate right through to the other side. While the oil is going through, we can mold the gold like clay. Gold worn on the body is also molded right to the muscle structure of the individual. In the same way, we have oils and medications to put on hard stone to soften and mold it with our hands. Some of our activities now are in writing great volumes of information as guidelines for our culture and the preservation of all of us on this planet, to establish patterns, systems and formulas to be adhered to through the Dvāpara Yuga. When the darkness comes people will begin to lose their inner knowledge and awareness of the chakras and their function. Though we have the wheel as a tool at this time, it will be lost in the Earth changes during the Dvāpara Yuga. Blind to the inner wheel, mankind will also become blind to the wheel on the outside.

It will be only through this cycle of *yugas* that we gain our own individuality and realization of the totality of the Self.

Various Patterns of Evolution

36 ℂ The group of divine souls that came to Earth in the cycle of *yugas* before the one we are in now became some of the animal kingdom that the extraterrestrial souls who came in the Sat Yuga had to face. Some of us in this *yuga* came to rescue them, along with others who came to experience the same evolution as they have done. These gentle *devonic* souls did not encompass the experiences of having to devour one another to further their evolution. Many of them came from the great star, the Sun of this solar system. The route most of us took to this planet was by first arriving on the Sun and then continuing on to this planet. One of the great amazements to the *devas* in the fleshy bodies was the feeling of the heat of the Sun and the inability of that body to cope with the rays of it.

Why We Came to Earth

37 ℂ The mother principle was not recognized on Earth until the race came into human reproducing bodies in the Tretā Yuga. Souls in their perfect state were in cellular evolution. They were in a complete state, as complete as a cell, and evolved within their own strata of evolution. Some of the most highly evolved souls would grow another body within them and then divide themselves into two. These then would divide themselves and become four. They would just slide out from themselves and one would energize the new one. Another soul would then inhabit the new body. In this way, soul bodies duplicate themselves in the Third World. This occurred on the planet that we came from, and this is why we had reached a pinnacle of evolution and become as a flock of birds or school of fish, because we were so similar to our originators. It will be only through this cycle of *yugas* that we gain our own individuality and realization of the totality of the Self. Then, when we are granted permission to leave this planet, with access to other planets in the universe, we will be the first there to divide our celestial body into two, then the two into four. And we will in that way spawn a new *devonic* group, through this method, who will later have to inhabit a fire planet to gain their evolution and attain their individuality. Those who realize the Self fully are in three phases of evolution, depending upon the advancement of the soul's evolution when they arrived on the planet. The *śāstras* explain that some are still here today by personal choice helping with the evolutionary process. Others of the second phase of evolution have since left this planet and are on other planets, and still others in the third group just became the Self. A soul's evolution is long and vast. Therefore, the animal kingdom, the human kingdom, the *devonic* kingdom are all seen through our wisdom as one and the same. The original intelligence is a cell, and many of those cells gathered together to make this celestial body which in turn divides itself. Our Mahādevas have several sets of arms, as they are always dividing themselves. The *devas* that surround them and serve them are of them.

Space, Time And Mind Are Synonymous

38 ℂ Our *śāstras* say that in the depth of the inner mind there is just a thin veil separating one planet from another—for space, time and mind are synonymous. In the external mind, created because of the animal kingdom, this thin veil is seen as billions of miles of empty space. Therefore, no one has ever really been separated, because in the inner mind the planets are not great distances apart. There is a yoga practice where one can go into the Self and come out at any point of time that he chose in the future "faster than you could blink your eye and be just as you were when you went in." And the *śāstras* say that, being That, you would then have realized the Self at that point in time. One could decide to come back to Earth in the middle of the next Sat Yuga and go into *samādhi,* come out and be there. These time cycles

will have nothing to do with the concept of time at the end of the Kali Yuga. The middle of the next Sat Yuga as well as the middle of the last Sat Yuga exist right now; as well as this current point in time exists right now.

Our *śāstras* say that in the depth of the inner mind there is just a thin veil separating one planet from another—for space, time and mind are synonymous. In the external mind, created because of the animal kingdom, this thin veil is seen as billions of miles of empty space.

Ceremonies To Call the Deities

39 ℭ During the ceremonies in our temples in the Tretā Yuga, when bringing another celestial soul through to the fibrous body to begin the evolution on this planet, we would all come together and vibrate our inner body so that the outer one would become as transparent as possible so the Deity would come. The object was to get into the Self. This is what everyone was striving for. The Mahādeva from their planet would assist us. Some of the most evolved would become so transparent that it would be almost impossible to see them with any of the three eyes, so great was the power generated by us. They would become like a shadow. This is when the ceremony started. Rays would emanate from the brain and other chakras, which would make the one from whom these rays were emanating a God himself for a period, as he sent out power from himself.

Releasing Souls from Animal Bodies

40 ℭ A similar kind of gathering was held to release a great *deva* from the bondage of an animal herd. Occasionally, and this happened rarely, he was able to manifest a second and, upon very rare occasions, even a third fibrous body, thus avoiding the reincarnation cycle. The Mahādevas came in full force to help this evolved *deva* create a second or third fibrous body. It was difficult, but they were very powerful and radiated all of their force through him, and he was evolved enough to contain it so that this could be accomplished after the advent into the animal nerve system. They will again perform a similar function through the Kali Yuga and into its successor, in helping these same universal spirits out of the bondages of the consciousness of flesh into the attunement to the universal core.

Mahādevas Came to Bless And Instruct

41 ℭ There were many pagoda-shaped temples with a high, raised platform in the center of them for the divine Deity, the Mahādeva, to come and stand on while blessing and instructing people. We stood on all four sides looking up at the platform. Everyone in the temple attended these ceremonies, which occurred quite often. They were periodically

timed, though the festival of entertaining a Mahādeva was very unstructured. The Mahādeva guided it all along. Many Mahādevas would come, one after another, to listen to the petitions that would be presented to them. The monastics would read the petitions and messages from the villagers who had sent them in to be read to the inner-plane beings who each did different things. As the Mahādeva heard something they could help with, they would just go and do it. The Mahādeva, upon leaving, would tell us when he was returning and what to have ready for him or who to have there. We would obey. This was the Mahādeva's way of communicating with us, not our way of communicating with them, because they were in charge. These Mahādevas were our friends that we knew and loved. We approach them as a ten-year old child does his parents. They are so beautiful in their transparent bodies, so strong as their rays of light pierce out as darshan flows into our minds. These same Mahādevas led us to this planet and we respect them, their will, their guidance and obey. Some of them we divided off from on the planet they live on before we arrived here. However, we do not have any desire to attain to being a God, for since we have been on Earth we have found that we are already totally complete and simply fill a space of service at a point in time, performing our duty. We are their helpers, and they help the planet and everyone on it. Our goal is to dissolve the physical elements and ascend—go back to the source of it all.

Helping Souls To Leave The Planet

42 ℂ During some of our ceremonies, the Gods would take one of us evolved enough to leave this planet onto the platform with Him and dissolve his elements so that he would not have to incarnate again, and have access to other planets in our universe, having totally completed his evolution on the fire planet. Once he became established in his new abode, he, too, would begin to duplicate his body there into forms similar to it, and he would visit us occasionally on the platform to administrate petitions and bring us news of his new evolutionary experiences there. When a Mahādeva appeared on our platform, He pulled the fourteen elements together and in doing so created a temporary body. Upon leaving this body, it dissolved and floated down to the floor into a small mound of sweet, airy substances which we divided up among ourselves and took into our bodies. Everyone present left after eating

it, filled with divine energy, for it contained radiations from the Central Sun. The eating of this gave us the strength to pursue our duties with vigor, and it often contained valuable information or messages for one of us. This message would only go to the one to whom it was intended inwardly to help in his craft, skill or personal meditation. Our Lemurian monasteries were at their height when more than half of the population in each one dissolved their elements into the essence of Pure Being.

Mankind's Divine Guidance

43 Our Mahādevas were the divine beings from the Sat Yuga who because of their power did not go into the animal kingdom and remained still active on Earth through the Sat and Tretā Yugas these many hundreds and thousands of years. Now, toward the end of the Tretā Yuga, the most prominent of them are the ones who were the leaders of major groups of us to this planet then. And they tell us they will incarnate into flesh-and-bone bodies during the Kali Yuga to help the celestial souls at that time, as contact from another planet or the inner mind of this one will be almost totally impossible. It is hard for us to conceive that this light will not remain in the minds of all of us as the Dvāpara Yuga begins. But our Mahādevas kept admonishing us to prepare and taught us how. They said that getting the physical body with the three lower chakras was our way to realizing the Self. They told us they would help us adjust and learn how to use our physical bodies in order to anticipate events and coordinate our lives. Toward the end of the Dvāpara Yuga, new magnetic forces will begin to develop so very strongly on the planet, as the gravity on the Earth gets stronger and stronger and nothing floats in the air anymore. These forces will be new to the people, and they will not quite understand them soon enough to protect themselves and will become vulnerable to the magnetic pulls and begin to become confused, one of our Mahādevas carefully explained to us from the platform. We listen but we do not understand all that we hear. Now the mental communication is excellent. All of us know everything that occurs. We have circular mental vision, and if some kind of out-of-the-ordinary experience happens to one of us, it happens to all of us. This is the way we evolve.

All of us know everything that occurs. We have circular mental vision, and if some kind of out-of-the-ordinary experience happens to one of us, it happens to all of us. This is the way we evolve.

Changes During the Tretā Yuga

44 ℂ During this time, all of our body structures, along with the Earth atmosphere, are undergoing a rapid change. So, in this *yuga* our basic challenge is to hold the vibration that existed through the Sat Yuga within a core group of us so that the others could continue their peaceful existence without experiencing drastic changes. We, one-third of the entire population, lived separately from all the others, as all but a few of us were in the original, fibrous bodies. The other two-thirds have now come up through the animal kingdom in this *yuga*, and we don't want the race to keep getting back into it. That's why we are trying to hold the vibration. Different races are forming at this time, coming back through the animal kingdom. They mate as the animals do, on a cyclic pattern through the year. We lived behind great walls to protect these bodies from the imposing forces, and within these encasements performed our function. In this way we held the full impact of the vibration of the Sat Yuga through the entirety of the Tretā Yuga.

Carrying Cosmic Darshan

45 ℂ When the Mahādeva sent one of us on a pilgrimage away from our accustomed surroundings, we were commissioned to carry a ray that He brought from the Central Sun with us to a place that was obscured from these kinds of radiations because of the Dvāpara Yuga vibration that was imposing itself upon us. When a pilgrimage of this kind is initiated, we are told of our exact destinations and method of travel. When on these kinds of pilgrimage, we draped our bodies in white and were recognized and cared for along the way, as this was the sign of the pilgrim. The Mahādeva Himself, from the inner world of our planet, could easily distinguish one of us draped in white and assist us along the way. We carried the rays of the Universal Sun that He prismed. This was His way of giving power through us to the celestial beings in their various and varied kinds of Earth bodies we met along the way. As one of the "carriers of the darshan," on a pilgrimage we all were charged with the responsibility to begin the darshan streams that began to run like a river close to the ground. This helped our Gods send their power through these channels. When our temples had festivals, the Mahādeva's power flowed through the established streamers, keeping all of us invigorated and stable on Earth in our desire for Self.

About Our Monastery Cloisters

46 ℂ Surrounding our pagoda-like temples are places where we live. These vast homes, in which we were alone and apart from the other two-thirds of the population of this planet, were monastic in nature and protocol. It was here that we set the pattern for the next million circles to come, the pattern of the gathering together in aloneness. The only company we keep is with those who live without the grosser bodies that we hold, live in, express through and carry the rays given to us by our Mahādevas, who gathered them together from the Central Sun, limiting them to the velocity of our capability and usage. We have divided ourselves into many of these monasteries, situated adroitly at various important areas around the planet. Monasteries were always located where they were needed most, and always within walking distance of another monastery. The reason for this was that our large monastery would hold a vibration of darshan for the surrounding area extending out for a radius of some fifty to 100 miles. The purpose of these Lemurian monasteries was to keep the total vibration of the Deity and the religion alive and vibrant through the cells of the people who lived in the vicinity. The monastics living together in these monasteries, totally devoted to their *sādhana* and religious practices, held this strong darshan vibration of the Deity steady, and it radiated out in a circle in a radius of fifty to 100 miles. The next monastery would be placed on the perimeter of the emanating darshan of the one nearest to it. In this way there was no break in continuity, and therefore they were always within walking or flying distance of each other as they spread out across the land. The preceptors who guided groups of us here a *yuga* ago are our teachers, our prophets, our gurus, and they are responsible for many of us who gather apart from all others in these monastic groups.

The purpose of these Lemurian monasteries was to keep the total vibration of the Deity and the religion alive and vibrant through the cells of the people who lived in the vicinity.

Piles of gold and silver brought by the inhabitants of the surrounding communities to the Lemurian monasteries served as destination markers for the devas and Mahadevas, as these glowing substances were easily visible from the Third World. Along some of the walls inside of the monastery were holes bored in which the Lemurians slept and left their physical bodies while traveling on inner planes of consciousness at night. At these times, they gathered before their guru to receive instruction and inner knowledge. During the day, they disseminated the revelations to family men by speaking through other holes in the wall. The senior minority group was calculated by the youngest among them all, known as the Vadivel, by studying the wooden sticks on which monastics kept track of their seniority age. Aum.

Deity and master guru were synonomous during this period. After all, the gurus were the chosen channels of the Gods. He who was, is and ever will be all pervasive lived within each soul, ever present and alive. All knew this as fact. But the soul encased within its many bodies needed maturity, evolving more and more into His likeness. Satgurus directed with infinite patience and accuracy.

Gurudeva

47 ℂ Our guru played a different part in the temple than anyone else. He was the absolute head of the monastery. Many times he would be entirely incognito to a number of his monasteries. No one, or only a few of us, knew who he was, and then we wouldn't tell anyone else unless we had his permission to do so. He would often come to the wall that surrounded each monastery to seek admittance into it as did so many others. In this way he would see to the general mood of the newcomers and how they were treated, or often he would serve in a monastery at some ordinary type of work with the monastics who did not know who he was. In this way he could train them secretly. For instance, a young monastic may be asked to teach the guru how to milk the animals that preserved our external form, but would not know it was his guru. The guru would fit in in all capacities if he chose to do so. Some of the gurus, though, chose to be well known in their monasteries. It depended totally upon them. All gurus would be incognito while traveling. Therefore, they would often meet and help us while on pilgrimage to another monastery seeking admittance. Anyone we might meet on pilgrimage might be the guru, and so we all kept a very reverent attitude toward everyone we met.

The Role Of Our Mahādevas

48 ℂ The great Mahādevas, our Lords, became deified during this time. They would sometimes go beyond manifesting a temporary body on the enthroned pedestal and would actually draw the elements together more closely and form a physical body that would last a moon or two. In this body, they would live in our monasteries that were generally so large and well populated that they could move freely about incognito, helping us all in one way or another as the force of their presence disseminated out through us to the gracious lands.

The Guru's Visits to a Monastery

49 ℂ Each guru headed many monasteries, and when he took up residence in one of them, and if he chose to let his identity be known, we would all stop everything that we were doing, gather around for periodic instructions in the deeper arts of meditation and *samādhi*. Festivities and celebration gathered the Deities and *devas* in great throngs, and our monastery began to become the head monastery of them all, depending upon the length of stay of our guru. The hosts of *devas* that traveled

with our guru from monastery to monastery intensified the core in all of us, and when he remained for lengthy periods of time, so did they, and the darshan polarized itself through our walls. When he left to go to another monastery, we felt his presence in the inner ethers. Sometimes he would leave and return a few days later incognito. So we never actually knew in which monastery he existed in his physical body.

Teaching Through Holes In the Wall

50 ℭ Long vigils were kept by us, sitting on the inside of the wall. This wall had holes in it through which we spoke when inspired. Many philosophical truths, prophecies and practical advice were disseminated through these holes in the wall, and if no one was there we spoke to the wind. This was our method of remaining unidentified and giving the inner teachings freely to the world. On these great vigils we would live alone in a solitary niche and write what came from the depth of our being. Some monastics just sit and write down what comes from the inside and put it away without anyone ever reading it. These writings were never signed, as this *śāstric* book is not signed. The one-third senior minority of the monastery, without reading these writings, would condone them solely upon their vibration, and they would be put into tremendous libraries which have accumulated over the years as the monastics developed them. When a family man became one with us, portions of the library were given to him. He would read, study and disseminate the teachings to the village folk. The libraries were always being replenished by us with single-copy manuscripts, and large numbers of these manuscripts were supplied family men periodically, who took them and opened schools for the people so that they could study the depth of their beliefs. Our libraries will in time disappear into the *ākāśic* ethers, our prophets say, to be copied down again by monastics of another era.

Our Secret Names or Soul Tones

51 ℭ When we all arrived on this planet, our history tells us, each one of us had emanating from us a certain combination of sounds or tones. This was the way we spoke, and as we thought, these tones radiating out from our body changed. The basic tones were our names. After we manifested the first Earth body, these tones ceased and the power of speech came. We always were called or identified by the basic tone of the inner body; but now, so many thousands and thousands of years later, that has been forgotten, and recordings of it only exist in our libraries and are remembered and spoken of by our scholars.

On the inner plane during the darkest nights, our entire order, which was the entire population of each monastery headed up by one guru, would come together all at once and receive instructions from the guru.

Changing Names Often

52 ℂ When someone comes to our monastery, he's given any kind of name. The name of the place that he came from becomes his name, or some significant story of an experience he may have had along the way. We would derive a name from this for him. Each one of us had many names, and generally if we pilgrimaged from monastery to monastery, quite often we would be known by a different name in each monastery. None of us had a permanent name. We only associated the permanent name with the history of the basic tone of the inner body that was explained to us by scholars and authority. Some of us knew the combination of our tones, and in speaking with ourselves we always inwardly repeated these. The *devas* and Deities, in speaking to us from the pedestals in the temples, would often call us by these inner names. That is how we came to know them.

Remaining As Pure Channels

53 ℂ Our concern was not for the individual members of our monastery but for the total functioning of the mission of the monastery. Therefore, we did not distinguish ourselves by attaching a personal history to our names. If this began to occur within the monastery, we quickly moved or were sent by the Deity to another monastery and were given another name. We have to do this to remain pure channels for the divine force. This was our concern and our custom.

The Fine Art of Meditation

54 ℂ When we meditate, we always do so lying down. Meditation was either merging in the Self or travel to other planets. The first thing that would occur would be disconnecting our inner body from the physical, and in this body we would enter the inner world and be taught deep things concerning time and space and *yugas* to come. Great Master Beings educated us deeply in the knowledge of the Dvāpara Yuga as a vast time span which brings this planet into the Kali Yuga. These teachings we discussed among ourselves during the day, and when the morning came, the inner body would connect with the physical and we would stand up. I remember being told that in the Kali Yuga vast numbers of people would sit up straight to meditate in an effort to simply calm

their thoughts. When we put the physical body into a state of meditation, we placed it in a hole in the wall of the monastery, or in the side of a mountain in a tube. Each of these tubes bored in the wall or in the rock mountain were spaced so that no one was ever directly above the other. This enabled our inner bodies to leave the physical without the obstruction of someone else's physical body above it. These tubes are just the size of our body, and we always entered them at the darkest part of the night. During full moon we did not sleep or meditate at all.

Grand Meetings on Inner Planes

55 ℂ On the inner plane during the darkest nights, our entire order, which was the entire population of each monastery headed up by one guru, would come together all at once and receive instructions from the guru. He would address his entire order. If he had 2,000 or 200 monastics in all his monasteries, he would address them all at night on the inner plane. We always saw him in his resplendent body. In his waking state he was not like this, and employed himself in simple kinds of activities, working with newcomers to the monastery, assisting here and there, except, of course, at times when he also instructed us on the physical plane. Each guru who had a monastery on the physical plane also had his own structures, vast halls and palaces, on the astral plane. In these we would meet, be together. The Deity never came during these times. The guru had his monasteries. He was head of them. The Deity had the temple. He was head of it. We took care of the temple. The Deity and devas took care of us.

Use of Gold For Power and Protection

56 ℂ We had a gold substance that came from the ground, and silver, too. Of this we made jewelry to decorate the physical body and make it look like that of the Deity and *devas*. This gold and silver could be seen, even in the Third World, glowing. The people in the surrounding countryside would dig it out of the mountains, find it in their rivers and streams and bring it to us. As was our custom, we kept one third of it in the temple and fashioned jewelry for their bodies from the other two thirds. We prided ourselves in this skill, of which we had many. This gold and silver jewelry made by us carried the darshan from the monastery wherever it was taken. Walking through the monastery and temple, one could see large piles of gold and silver here and there, and in the Third World, each monastery and temple could be easily distinguished because of the vast quantities of gold and silver it contained. It glowed there as a marker of the destination point so that Deities and *devas* would know where to come.

All these kinds of skills came from the many different radiations of darshan from our Gods, who live in the inner world creating new darshans in the *ākāśa* to rule the physical world.

Moving Objects with Our Minds

57 ℭ One of our skills was in moving physical objects from temple to temple with our minds with the help of the *devas*. This method was also used by us in building our temples and monasteries. Large stones were easily moved in this way. We could apport people also. All these kinds of skills came from the many different radiations of darshan from our Gods, who live in the inner world creating new darshan*s* in the *ākāśa* to rule the physical world. Our Gods constantly watched all of us, carefully giving out darshan in just the right amounts where it was needed most, using anyone of us at any time as a channel for this divine grace.

Dancing, Levitation and Mesmerism

58 ℭ Dancing and levitation were some of our other skills, as well as mesmerism. We could create a burning forest fire in the mind of another, but it would not actually be there, though he would see it. It was in this way we controlled the large and small animals and kept them away from us. All of these skills and many more were quite natural to us. Our prophets tell us that toward the end of the Dvāpara Yuga, when the body becomes more dense, we will have to begin developing these skills through intensive practice over a long period of time.

Writing Books for The Ākāśa

59 ℭ One such skill has to do with how a book was written. We would not write a book to be seen in the physical world, but to be seen in the *ākāśic* ethers. I am now writing this book in oil with a gold rod. A thin layer of oil is spread on a stone and upon it I am writing everything that is now being recorded, and it is going into the *ākāśa*. For all time, anyone who is sensitive to reading the *ākāśa* can read this record.

Novitiates and initiates seeking entrance stood before the outside wall during the day, begging admittance and performing service, like gathering wood or drawing water, while waiting to be interviewed. Often they were told of monastery life by the residents. They might remain by the wall up to nine months, endeavoring to adjust their vibration, both inner and outer, to those within the monastery so they would fit in transparently. Once admitted, they were given disciplines by the guru, such as carving large statues; then, to perfect concentration, carving them smaller and smaller unt they fit in the palm. They meditated

often, communicating with beings from their home planet. Some chronicled their experiences in books to be transported through fire into the vast akashic libraries. Aum.

Easy peacefulness and inner communications reigned in the early days on Earth. But toward the end of the Treta yuga, mankind eventually evolved two types of communities: those who lived in monasteries and others who settled in individual homes, large extended families of a hundred or more. These were days of merging the Divine and the instinctive, days of adjustment.

Gurudeva

60 ℭ Near the end of the Tretā Yuga, many *devas* were coming back up through the animal kingdom into human bodies, but with animal instinctive nerve systems. Some of us were still in the body brought through the original way. It is very difficult to bring anyone through now, so many of our bodies are thousands of years old. There are three kinds of beings on the Earth. Those of us in our original body, the *devas* in the human bodies and the animals. This creates for us a culture partly new and partly that which we brought with us when we came. We are in changing times. Some just go off by themselves to go deep within and try to stabilize the forces of the planet, working closely with the Gods. We found that being alone, which is new to us, for we are always with our kind, was very fruitful. Our elders developed this practice and taught many advanced souls how to live alone and polarize the changing forces of our time.

Emergence Of Individual Outlooks

61 ℭ The *devas* who emerged from the animal kingdom quickly learned the culture and religion of our times in our monasteries and temples, and then we sent some out on missions to teach it to others coming into human form. Small groups began to develop for the first time, and philosophies and individual outlooks emerged with the *devas* who lived in bodies with animal nerves, as they would sometimes call the teachings their own, which began to develop religions with different names. Our prophets tell us that one day everyone on our planet would have an animal nerve system in one degree or another.

The Core Group in Original Bodies

62 ℭ In the monastery, of course, all had to be in our original body and receive initiation by our guru. The *devas* in human form came in to study, and some were allowed to stay on, but not many, for they became attached to us. The most important thing for them was to not be magnetically attached to other people. We have always watched to see that this does not happen, for it creates an inconvenient pull of forces, inhibiting us from doing our work in the service of the Deities. When they found they were attached to someone in the monastery, they would go to the one to whom they were attached, and they both would beg for release from the Deity. The Deity would cut the sticky substance binding them together psychically. This was the same substance the Deity would make his temporary body out of. If these attachments

persisted—and it was always those in human bodies that responded in this way—it would finally pull so much on the senior group in the monastery that they would finally suggest that he do *tapas* by himself, then return to the monastery or pilgrimage to another monastery. Our guru always set the course of the *tapas* and gave his instructions through the senior group or directly to the *deva*. Our guru always administrated *sādhana* and *tapas*.

Involvement In Inner Worlds

63 ℂ Our life was a life of involvement with the inner worlds. We would talk to the *devas* and among ourselves rather than those of us who lived in surrounding areas to the monasteries. For our main service was to provide the vibration to sustain the darshan and religion through the nerve systems of the people who surrounded the temple, also to write our inner perceptions, clarifying the philosophy during our changing times, and giving these writings to the elders of the external community to share among the population or record them in the *ākāśic* libraries. Sometimes we did both. We would also make golden jewelry and prepare medicinal herbs. But our monasteries were totally introverted during this period in time. It was the elder men of the surrounding community that did the formal teaching and talking to the people, not the monastics, with the exception of our speaking to these elders through the wall, as previously described, without allowing our personal identity to be known.

Choosing Monks from The Community

64 ℂ Our guru would choose from the community those he felt would do well in serving in the monastery. The guru always did the choosing, and the training went according to what he wanted. The strands of inner lineage are still very clear. Our guru would know who was living in a certain body, and upon that he based his invitation or direction. The greatest austerity performed by those who entered the monastery from families was that of living away from home. The human families were very, very serene and peaceful. The entire atmosphere of the Earth at this time is lush, calm and sublime. It is easy to live, and family life was very close due to the animal quality of being attached to one another. So, when they come into the monastery, they suffer the breaking of this attachment, and then when it does break they feel alone. This feeling of aloneness is also from the animal world through the instinctive nerve system. But they know all about this animal nerve system, and this knowledge helped both the family and the monastic when these feelings emerged.

A Joyous, Healthy Life

65 ℂ We take our nourishment once a day, when the sun is high. The nourishment is always the same. It is a complete chemistry for our bodies. Those who have animal nerve systems eat somewhat differently, and it takes them quite a while to become used to the monastery diet. Everyone was quite satisfied after a meal. They really enjoyed their food. We were always happy and laughing. Often two of us would catch one another's thought and break out laughing.

No Room for Personal Identities

66 ℂ In our monasteries were great souls as well as some of the younger ones, but it was almost impossible to tell one from another, for the old souls helped the younger ones by outwardly appearing to be like them. If they had a strong darshan, they would always appear to have none at all and, in various subtle ways, deflect any attention drawn to them because of their unfoldment. Everything that we do within these temples is founded with the principle of the elimination and annihilation of our personal identities. The monastery and the temple is one place so integrated in our daily living that there is no room for one of us to be more outstanding than another. If one of the monastery-temples needed extra strength—perhaps because something in the surrounding area occurred and there was an excessive draw upon our darshan flow from the pedestal—our guru would send some great soul to us from another temple, one who had lived in it consistently for a long, long period of time. He would traditionally enter our monastery-temple as a guest and, unbeknownst to anyone, live and move around through our ranks and procedures while all the time working inwardly, filling the great need which he had come to fulfill. Because he entered as a beginner, his chores were light and his ego vanished, for he was in the process of qualifying himself to become a permanent part of our group. In this way, our guru worked silently, inwardly and unobtrusively.

Everything that we do within these temples is founded with the principle of the elimination and annihilation of our personal identities. The monastery and the temple is one place so integrated in our daily living that there is no room for one of us to be more outstanding than another.

How a Newcomer Is Evaluated

67 ℂ A newcomer in our midst would humbly beg admittance in asking permission to live nearby the temple. He would work inwardly to strengthen our vibration. Even if he were a younger soul, he would be expected to do this. We would watch him silently and inwardly as the moon became full and waned and became full again, until about two-thirds of us came to know him. Our new visitor seeking admittance would always be found standing by the wall that surrounded each temple-monastery, either on the outside of the wall if he were just entering, or on the inside of the wall while fulfilling his period of blending his vibration with the total vibration that existed. Sometimes we have many, many standing on the outside of the wall for long periods of time before they are invited in, one or two at a time.

Limitations Imposed on Newcomers

68 ℭ Newcomers would never attend any of our activities unless invited. They lived in small shelters close to the wall and did some useful service to occupy their time when they were not involved in trance. During the day, they would walk around close to the wall, the circumference of it, talking with monastics who would come and visit with them. They would tell of their travel, both inwardly and outwardly, and about themselves. If they appeared to be on *tapas*, nothing would be given to them to do, and they would be allowed to fulfill their intended practice. For upon entering, they would clearly explain the nature of the austerity, and the intended purpose to be accomplished by performing it, to the one representative of all of us who was responsible for initially visiting them and admitting them.

Mystic Skills, Sacred Disciplines

69 ℭ Sometimes we were given by our guru disciplines to strengthen our powers of concentration. Especially the younger souls performed these practices, but occasionally the older souls did as well. We would be given to carve a statue half as tall as any of us, and during the course of its completion, certain chants and meditative practices were performed. When it was completed, our guru would inspect it and the one of us who created it. If the inner change that he expected did not exist, brought forth from the carving, the chanting and the disciplines within meditation, he would order it destroyed and begun again. When finally the inner attainment had been made simultaneous with the creation of the statue, the next phase of discipline and carving upon the same statue commenced, and that would be to continue carving on the statue, always keeping it in a perfect state of completion, until it began to become smaller and smaller.

As this was being done, other kinds of meditations given by the guru were performed, as well as chanting and frequent visits from the Deity and *devas*. It took a long, long time, ten or fifteen years or more, before the statue, which began half the size of one of us, was in its perfect state of completion, small enough to hold in the palm of one's hand.

We would be given to carve a statue half as tall as any of us, and during the course of its completion, certain chants and meditative practices were performed.

Utilizing the Power of Such Projects

70 ℭ The dust from this constant working on the statue was considered sacred and used in some of our ceremonies, and the last remaining dust, after the statue had become so small it disappeared, was ceremoniously given to our guru as a symbol the discipline had been completed. Some of these statues were never completed, as during the course of working with the discipline, the monastic became so refined himself, he fulfilled his purpose on the planet and disappeared from here—back to the planet we all came from—in a shimmering subtle body. These statues were considered most sacred and hidden away in mountain caves, sealed in. In this way we take an entire mountain and infuse it with the darshan by placing here and there within it these emanators of darshan. Some of these mountains and the darshan coming from them will persist through the next four *yugas*.

Writing Books, Conveying Information

71 ℭ We also write books, and after a book is finished, it is burned at a ceremony that causes it to be imprinted in the inner ether, and old and young souls alike in other temple-monasteries can read it. News is also conveyed in this way. The inner and the outer are one. Our prophets tell us that toward the end of the Dvāpara Yuga, as the Kali Yuga begins to be felt, we will make a strong distinction between the inner and the outer. But now, through thought transference, it is easy to communicate with beings on the planet that we came from, those around us and in distant places on the Earth. It is difficult to conceive how it will be possible for us in the next *yuga* to refrain from doing what is so natural for us to do now. We experience the total mind.

Use of Thought Projection

72 ℭ Through the projection of our thought, we are able to make ourselves appear temporarily in other temples and talk with different ones within them. This art is reserved for the older souls, mature in their practice. We also could make ourselves appear in the minds of another and convey to them the news. During certain ceremonies when fire was used, the Deity or a great *deva* would take the smoke and create a temporary body and talk with us. As smoke faded, they would fade. Most of us knew everything to be known on a current basis. They tell us that through the darker *yugas* communication will become most difficult, knowledge limited, and we find this difficult to understand as it seems so natural to us now.

The Special Functions of A Monastery

73 ℂ We have a tremendous force of power that flows from temple to temple and can be directed where needed. But, they say—those who see ahead—that the surface of the Earth will change, and the divine energies that we work with will have to be stored away in mountains, to be brought out and used again when the next Sat and Tretā Yuga come to this planet. Each monastery-temple had its own kind of activity within it, depending much upon the location. Some wrote books for the *ākāśic* libraries. Other monasteries worked in gold. Still others were masters in the carving of stone.

Fruits, honey, milk, nuts and seeds formed the basis of the pure and simple Lemurian diet. A most delectable dish called Lemurian prasadam was prepared daily in large vats, made of various combinations of fresh milk products such as yogurt, along with several fresh fruits, dates, nuts, seeds and honey from the bees, all gathered from the forests and fields in large baskets—mixed together and eaten from natural goards. It was a sattvic and invigorating meal, especially for those who deeply meditated. This was all they consumed day after day. To help keep the body flexible and easy to live in, exercises were

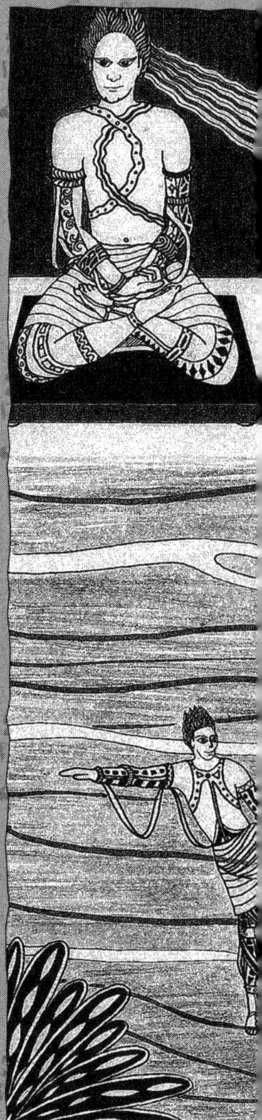

performed at dawn, noon and sunset. Working with mental powers, they provided equilibrium for the planet, and nearly everything could be done with the mind, even moving and lifting things. Aum.

Foreseeing the future was important in those days, as our main purpose was to prepare the planet for human life. Recipes for daily diet evolved, based on a system of health and healing. We, the select inhabitants living within ourselves more than in the outer consciousness, knew when a monastery no longer served its intended purpose and provided a way for it to become a power place of the future.

Gurudeva

74 ℂ The animals that ate the vegetables and gave forth milk were valuable to us. We recognize them to be one of us, caught in the animal kingdom on his way back to human form. We take this milk and with it fruit, seeds and nuts, the honey from the bee, mix it all together as our daily potion for the maintenance of the outer form. In large vats this mixture was made and each one of us had a gourd to hold it while it passed into our bodies, absorbing the energy from our hands.

Our Four Sources of Nourishment

75 ℂ Our nourishment is divided into four areas similar to the four great forces of this planet. The first area is the vegetable kingdom, consumed by the cow and other milk-producing animals. This provided the muscular structure with great strength. The next area is the life-giving seeds and nuts and tiny kernels within seeds that provided nerve strength and vigor to our bodies. The third area is the milk of the bee, derived from the subtle pollen of our flowers. This protects our bodies, as well as the entire combination within our nourishment, from deteriorating forces. This excretion of the bee protects against astral forces promulgated from the animal kingdom indigenous to this planet. The fourth area within our nourishment is the outgrowth of trees and bushes which can be picked without destroying the plant. Thus, fruit, seeds, nuts, honey and milk mixed together in proper combination compose our nourishment.

Variations According to Weather

76 ℂ The proper combination is as follows: when the wind blows from the north, more milk is used than amounts of honey, seeds or fruit. When the wind blows from the south, more fruit is used to enhance the combination. When the wind blows from the east, the sweetness of honey overpowers; and the west wind brings in an overabundance of seeds and nuts. Wind does not mean simply a breeze. Wind would be that which made waves upon our lake. When the air is cool, milk, seeds and nuts dominate, and extra honey is added to neutralize this combination. When the air is warm, fruit and honey, seeds and nuts and milk occur in equal amounts, none standing out over the other, complementing the temperature—the nuts appearing two to three inches apart, or measured out as a small handful for each of those of us partaking of this nourishment. On hot days, fruit, honey and little seeds; milk and

nuts are few.

Food Is Taken at High Noon

77 ℭ Though we eat when the sun is high and fill up fully our bodies with this nourishment, we take time and eat long. Should it at any time occur that later in the day or as the sun is setting our nourishment is taken, the combination is more of a liquid nature, light and easy to digest, for pure water and spice have been added to the leftovers from the noonday. Nourishment is never taken after dark, when you cannot see to move around and perform your chores, nor before the rising of the sun.

Herbal Remedies For Illness

78 ℭ When the body becomes frail or ill, various herbs that were brought with us from the planet we came from and strong spice were added to the nourishment and taken before nightfall. This did its work within the body during the night as we left the body for these herbs and spices to work upon without interference from the inner bodies living in the outer one. If the healing did not occur, no nourishment was taken at noon except for absorbing the rays of the noonday sun; and only the leftover nourishment—with pure water added, herbs and hot spices to stimulate the currents of the body—was taken at night until full health returned. These herbs are prepared in a similar way as the cow digests the vegetables and grasses. They are mashed and heated and boiled and brewed and presented to the evening nourishment in such a way that they blend right with it like a milk. Oils, too, were added for certain types of malcontent of the outer form.

Everything Needed Is At Hand

79 ℭ Our nourishment is a similar duplication of the manufactured external body the Deity leaves behind upon the pedestal. The combination of the four types of nourishment builds the body to withstand heat and cold and all types of atmospheric pressures from the outer world and makes it convenient to live in. We always use what is available to us to nourish these bodies. The residents within the surrounding area around our temple bring to us out of their abundance. We usually find what we have is the perfect combination and use it according to the formula, the blowing of the wind and the temperature of the day. On this we thrive and live and do our work. When we found a fruit or nut or seed not tasty and delicious to complement this combination, though nourishing in itself and vital to our health, we fed it to our milk-pro-

ducing animals, and they made the necessary adjustment for us.

How Milk Is Prepared And Stored

80 ℂ The liquid from the animal was prepared in various ways. It was hardened, made to be thick, or more liquid by adding water to it. The juices were crushed and molded into it, and all of this was always kept cool in our caves and clay and stone vats. Our nourishment was always served cool, as the natural heat of the body responded to this coolness and flamed up to warm it up. This aids in assimilation through our cells. Some of the temples are quiet inventive and others simple. In the colder climates, the fruit is dried and taken there, as are the nuts and seeds. The milk is hardened to preserve it, and it is mixed together with warm water to melt the milk and moisten the fruit and then chilled just below body temperature a few degrees. Herbs were also dried and oils were taken to these mountainous places. However, a consistency of our nourishment persists through all of our people in all of the temples, except for those who are just emerging out of the animal kingdom. Their instinctive nerve system causes them to eat, like the animals themselves, grasses and leaves, roots and plants and the outgrowths of these organisms. In training a young monastic to prepare our nourishment, any handful of it that he would take and place in fertile soil should begin to grow. In this way it was assured that the balance of life-giving seeds existed throughout the entirety of the mixture. The seed hidden in the nourishment that will fertilize the soil to aid in its growth as it decomposed would sprout and soon become more nourishment.

We always use what is available to us to nourish these bodies. The residents within the surrounding area around our temple bring to us out of their abundance. We usually find what we have is the perfect combination and use it according to the formula.

A Simple Exercise for Health

81 ℂ Apart from our daily activity, we would perform an exercise. This exercise was performed three times a day: at sunrise, high noon and sunset. We would hold the physical body immovable in certain difficult positions and breathe it strenuously. Breath pulsing through the lungs while facing the sun's rays, consciously absorbing them into every cell of the body, kept it flexible, healthy and easy to live in. Some of these positions in which we stand are: legs far apart, hands and arms stretched up high while breathing strenuously and very deeply until a tiredness comes to the body and leaves the body because of the new energy infused into it from the sun's rays and the breath. One leg outstretched and opposite arm, both raised, is another position we assumed. Still an-

other position: standing erect, arms to the side, heals touching, head thrown back as far as possible, facing the noonday sun.

Letting the Body Assume a Remedial Pose

82 ℭ If the body ails or does not function properly, stand in the rays of the morning, noon or evening sun, we are told, and move it vigorously to the count of three. On the third move, stop and hold the body in whatever position it naturally assumes, as long as possible. It will of itself learn to assume the complementary position that will cure the discomfort through vigorous breathing and the rays of the sun. The forces of the body itself will be more inclined to appreciate the morning sun as it rises, opposed to noonday or sunset, or the other way around, as the case may be. This natural method of exercise, along with our nourishment and normal movement of the body through the day and night, is enough to keep all of its counterparts in harmony, one with another. Our only nourishment taken in the morning was fresh spring water in any quantity, large or small, or the juice of a tart or sour fruit.

Preparing Earth for Future Yugas

83 ℭ We work with vibration more than physical things, for we are preparing this planet for human life during the next several million years. Vital rays from other planets have to be polarized here, hooked into this planet at various spots, so that the planetary balance will persist for mankind, of physical and mental equilibrium. This is our main purpose and activity during this *yuga*, and our laboratories in which we work within our minds provide this function. Nearly everything that we do is done with our mind, moving things, lifting things. This, too, we are told, we will lose during the next *yuga*.

Dismantling Entire Monasteries

84 ℭ When a monastery-temple completely fulfilled its purpose, the darshan rays channeled there from the other planets became so strong that it became inconvenient to live comfortably within it. And, when the time is right, the Deity or our guru would tell us to dismantle the entire monastery and seal up the caves, leaving no trace that it ever existed. We would then form a lake where the monastery once was, to polarize the cosmic darshan rays, knowing full well that in another *yuga* the vibration would be felt and the monastery and temple that was there in the *ākāśa* would form again on Earth. In this way these sacred spots were generated here and there over the surface of the Earth to sustain the coming trials and tribulations of mankind so that he would not, in the future, be completely lost for all time in the ravaging emotion of the animal kingdom.

We are preparing this planet for human life during the next several million years. Vital rays from other planets have to be polarized here, hooked into this planet at various spots, so that the planetary balance will persist for mankind, of physical and mental equilibrium.

Power Places of The Future

85 ℭ It will be in the future, a million years from now, that, on the shores of the body of water that this monastery in which I write will eventually become, souls such as myself, perhaps, will perform austerity in preparation for service to mankind. These areas, vast or small, in which we have been generating cosmic power since we came to this planet in the Sat Yuga, are beginning to become extremely strong. We have dismantled many of our monasteries, and we never will return, in our physical bodies, to the place in which they existed. We utilized the force field as training laboratories in the inner planes in helping new souls from other planets become prepared for a physical birth or a manifested body.

Monastic Redistribution; Devonic Guards

86 ℭ When we were given the order to dismantle the monastery, seal up the caves and prepare the flow of water to form a lake through detouring a river, a series of streams—or often the Deity would graciously help us by causing underground streams to occur—a portion of our population would be distributed into other monasteries, as when the work was complete the remaining monastics also divided into small groups and begged entrance into other temples. When the lake was formed where the monastery existed, polarizing the darshan to that spot through the nature of the substance water, we would plant trees around its shore to serve as homes for visiting *devas* who did not manifest in earthly bodies but could live in the fibers of the trunks and larger branches of the trees, feed from the leaves and communicate through the tree itself. Some were permanently stationed there as guards of this sacred place. These *devas* can move from tree to tree, and sometimes two or three would be found living in one tree. We were careful that no relic or article was left to be found before we left the area, never to return. The animals themselves would bypass these sanctified areas rather than walk through them, and through the power of our mesmerism, the animals would see the entire area surrounded by a sheath of fire. In this way, too, we protected our

monasteries and temples before a wall was built.

Continuity Of Monastic Duties

87 ℭ In entering a new monastery-temple, we were always given to do the same task that we were given before. What each one of us did was on the level of what we were able to do. We performed our daily routine with great care and precision, each one of us a specialist performing some particular part in the whole activity. If perchance we were to perform a different task, our guru or the Deity Himself would give the instructions through one of the senior members of the monastery. And so, when one monastery was dismantled and we moved on to assist in another, we offered all the skills and talents we employed in the previous monastery to the next one. It was in this way that we preserved our heritage without allowing too much earthly knowledge to jeopardize our purpose for serving the Deity under the guidance of our guru.

Training for priesthood began early, with emphasis on inner matters, visions and the quest for Self. Having sat for long periods at the wall and gained entrance as a first test of sincerity, young monastics were regaled with true-life stories of their tradition, told by elders. They had time to play, to fly and participate in music, art, drama, dance and noncompetitive games. The first months were a period of inner adjustment as they blended with the group vibration. Later they were taught to read in the akasha the book detailing the skill they would perform the rest of their life. Flying was always fun and laughter accompanied

it as techniques were perfected. After a few years, each one settled, with the guru's blessings, into an artisan's family group, serving there tirelessly for the duration of his stay. Aum.

Grand sons took it seriously, then to conceive, in desireless manner, sons for monastery service. Wisdom exceeded ignorance during this yuga. Each monastic who served provided added stability. Every year in a monastery changed a sadhaka's training and responsibilities. A sadhaka's spiritual capacity was recognized by elders to be limited according to his lineage, instinctive or otherwise.

Gurudeva

88 ℂ All young people coming into our monastery would be carefully taught over a long period of time, and when one had learned his skill well, he performed it for the rest of his life. We are concerned more about inner visions, interplanetary travel, precisions and communication and our quest for the Self rather than perfecting a multitude of external skills, going always deeper and deeper into the core of our Being. Taking care of our monastery and temple consumed all of our time, as we followed a strict routine. We are told that this routine has not changed for thousands of years, each one of us performing one small part of it.

Ākāśic Manuscripts Of Procedure

89 ℂ Every aspect of a monastic's training was written for him in *ākāśic* books. Every move of the hand in performance of his task, how and when to proceed was designated there. Therefore, we knew exactly how to perform each task, where and when to gather in the monastery in small groups or large. But for the most part each one was alone, as the map for running the monastery was so precise that two of us were rarely found in the same place at the same time, unless the task to be performed required the presence of two or more. The senior always taught the junior, and in his training he was taught to read in the *ākāśa* the book that clearly outlined the simple skill that he was to perform in his function within the monastery. If he were to leave on a pilgrimage or *tapas,* someone else would fulfill this exact function in the exact same way. In this way this vast machinery of beings worked on Earth, bringing through divine radiation from our other planets to this one.

Representative Lemurian Priesthood

90 ℂ The Lemurian priesthood contains all of the phases of mind powers represented by different groups of individuals, from the least evolved on into the highest evolved. Each must be represented, none neglected. In the Lemurian culture we tend to emphasize transcendental means as the mode of what we are all aspiring for, to set a standard for the ones of us coming out of the animal kingdom into human form. This cultural attitude should not exist in our temples and monasteries. Each one within the monastery should acquire a semblance of sameness, be he evolved or not evolved, be he in a manifested body or a body given birth to by a mammal human. This sameness should and

must persist for the monastery to perform its function and for the Deity to be able to do His work within the temple. We all know our Deity and Lords rule the temples. The gurus of our culture rule the monasteries. Each monastery of this great Lemurian priesthood blends so closely with the vibration of the darshan, that only one person, one other person than the guru, should be felt to exist within the monastery, while in the temple there is one person and the Deity felt, even though a thousand may be present.

Training From an Early Age

91 ℂ The training of the Lemurian priests begins at a very young age. A Lemurian becomes a priest in the monastery at the time he is initiated and begins his training, or assumes his position of service if he has already been trained in another monastery. To hold the force field strong so that the darshan persists when a group of Lemurian priests are together, each one must adhere to the dictate of grouping together in a line or a circle, always in succession according to the length of time each one has been in the monastery. Each one in the priesthood upon entering has direct contact with the guru, the band of *devas* in the monastery and all our monasteries and our Deity, the great Lord of the universe.

Priesthood Order by Seniority

92 ℂ When a circle of priests was formed, it too was carefully grouped from left to right according to the length of time spent within that particular monastery. The more time the Lemurian priest stays within a monastery, the more of the darshan of that monastery he's able to disseminate. There can be others within the monastery, not in the priesthood, but here to learn on a short or long tenure of stay. They must follow the same pattern as the priesthood as well as they understand it, but they do not have to adhere as directly, because this group of beings move more frequently from monastery to monastery. It must be well known that all initiation be kept secret between the guru and the initiate. Neither initiations nor secretly imparted teachings shall change anything in the daily lives of Lemurian monastics.

Training Community Elders

93 ℂ The elders of the community surrounding our temple must impart the teachings, raise the children and train some of them for entrance into our monasteries. Only in this way will Lemuria persist and be strong on this planet. The elders may visit and live in the monasteries, take written teachings back to their homes and learn to read from the *ākāśic* libraries. It is the responsibility of all Lemurian gurus to carefully choose young men to study with our elder men in their homes before entering the priesthood. This then will be the training for the elder himself, as he will enter the priesthood in his next life at a very early age. If this be the case, he should be taken into the monastery from his parents' home and be raised by the monastics, for he will remember the training he gave to many young monastics in his last incarnation.

Each one within the monastery should acquire a semblance of sameness, be he evolved or not evolved, be he in a manifested body or a body given birth to by a mammal human.

Calculating Monastic Age

94 ℂ Our time is calculated according to the moon circling the Earth. Therefore, an elder who trained monastics in his last life, entering the monastery at one circle of age in his present life, would grow up year by year. Every two moons form one circle while living in the intensity of the Lemurian monastery. Generally, one circle would equal twelve moons. In this way the monastic age is calculated accurately, and each one has the same starting point, be he one circle or twenty circles of physical age. When taken from the wall for the first time, the young Lemurian must be one circle of monastic age, and then increasingly every two months another circle.

The Second And Third Circles

95 ℂ During the second circle in the monastery, his training must be then similar to a child's training in the ages between six and twelve circles. During the third circle of twelve moons, he is looked at as between the ages of twelve and eighteen, and it was generally during this time he became initiated and entered the Lemurian priesthood. During this time, between the monastic ages of twelve and eighteen, more strenuous demands must be placed upon him, as he is no longer considered a child. Nevertheless, his elders must supervise him well. The elders would be those more senior. During the Lemurian monastic's fourth circle in the monastery, from the monastic age of eighteen to twenty-four, he must settle into what he has been trained to do and perform these duties for the duration of his time in the monastery, perhaps for the rest of his life.

Exceptions To Training Norms

96 ℂ Education, being a predominant part of our culture, changes this pattern and is the only way that this pattern within the monastery can be changed. Should the monastic begin to make tremendous literary contribu-

tions to our culture that begin to be become used by the elder men of our community, or if he emanates tremendous darshan as a result of his personal evolution, intensified by his disciplines, only then would he be released from some of his duties that he had been trained to perform within the monastery or temple.

Training as Outlined in Ancient Texts

97 ℂ Each Lemurian monastic's training is clearly outlined in *ākāśic* manuscripts year by year, according to the ratio of one circle equaling six monastic years, throughout the duration of his life. Some of these manuscripts are so precise and detailed in day-to-day description of inner practice for our Lemurian monastics of 100 years of age and on that only the most astute are able to follow these disciplines. It is our gurus who have access to the chartered course given within these manuscripts, which were prepared on the planet whence we came, carefully placed within the *ākāśa* there to be read here by the gurus of Lemuria.

Latitude For New Monastics

98 ℂ Through the first six moons within the monastery after coming from the wall, all should come to know the newcomer, and he must be taught through telling him the favorite stories of the monastery, by playing games with him and blending him into the group. Sports of all kinds have always been a part of our culture ever since we came to the planet. They keep our culture strong, as while we perform in a group we lose all external awareness of ourself. A new monastic should not be given much responsibility until he is well into his second circle, or between nine and twelve monastic years old. Up until that time, he should be told stories and taught the subtleties of conduct, which only by living in the monastery one can learn, and enter into the many physical and mental games that are played each day. It is in the third circle, between the monastic age of twelve and eighteen, that he should be given tests of will, strength and valor, a lot more recreation and stories about how positive accomplishments for our culture have been made in the past and will be made in the future. Still yet, during the ages of twelve to eighteen, little direct responsibility should be given to him, but shouldered by the senior Lemurian priests that are training him.

The Giving Of Personal Responsibility

99 ℂ Between twelve and eighteen monastic years old is the time that personal discipline is given to him and when he usually is initiated as a permanent member of the monastic order, the priesthood. It is in this third circle of his monastic years, between twelve and eighteen, that a personal interest must be shown in him by his elders as to his ability to remember the teachings and the stories by examination as to how philosophically astute he is. This attention should by given to him closer to the end of the third circle, between sixteen and eighteen monastic years. The outcome of how well he had performed his disciplines then becomes apparent, and he is placed in the appropriate permanent position of service within the monastery.

Each Lemurian monastic's training is clearly outlined in *ākāśic* manuscripts year by year, according to the ratio of one circle equaling six monastic years, throughout the duration of his life.

Allowances During the Third Year

100 ℂ The routine for a Lemurian monastic going into his third monastic circle must never be terrifically strict in any way. They must be given time to play, to be young and move here and there, or from monastery to monastery if they are helpers on projects that their elders have initiated. It is only in the fourth circle that they settle down to regulated activity.

Four periods of time

defined the first years of training within the monastery. After acceptance, the sadhaka was given half a year to adjust to his new-found life, to meditate and learn his mantra, all the while given the best of care. After two passages of Earth around the Sun, he was introduced to the culture of inwardness and taught about his animal lineage, how it influenced his future pattern and expressions of service and relationship in the monastery.

After three years had passed, he was guided in pragmatic individual training by a senior monastic. In his fifth year he received responsibilities of his own, being expected to perform his known duties productively. These days and months and years were those of training, discipline, learning and testing. Failure was not an option at all. Aum

How peaceful was life in the days when monastics ruled the Earth, the peace of greater understanding among peoples. The monasteries were abundantly populated. It was a custom to dedicate a son to live within them or to train to reincarnate to be a worthy resident. The training was compassionate yet strict. Games, philosophy and daily duties were considered necessary for well-being.

Gurudeva

Lemurian Sadhakas

लिमुरियन् साधकाः

Chapter 8

101 ℂ The *sādhakas* in our monasteries were considered by us to be of the utmost importance to our culture. Some came but for a short time to learn to live as we used to when we first arrived on the planet and to learn of the life and culture of the planet whence we came. Their *sādhana* was only to adjust themselves to the life and to do some kind of service when they were not engaged in reading the manuscripts within our libraries, listening to dissertations given by senior members for their benefit or watching visions projected to them in their meditations as a lasting teaching. These *sādhakas* are of two fold, some who come to spend a lifetime and others who only plan to stay six moons or more. And so, we consider that during the first six-moon period a *sādhaka* is with us, after his having sat with our senior group and expressed his desire to stay, having proven his ability to live as we do, he's allowed to perform a certain mantra. The repetitions of the mantra are performed during his quiet time as he fingers numerous seeds strung together, golden balls or gems cut in a similar way. In chanting the mantra, he perceives the subtle nerve force which each of these many, many beads represents. Thus the nerve system becomes calm and detached from the life he has formerly lived.

Adjustment In the First Six Moons

102 ℂ We look at a *sādhaka* in his first six moons more as a newborn child than an adult, for he is adjusting to a new environment both inwardly and outwardly, as well as contacting face-to-face in his dreams and visions our colleagues on the several planets whence we came. A certain area of his mind is more attached to remnants of the animal functions if, in fact, he was a *sādhaka* inhabiting a body evolved from the animal kingdom. However, all but a few of us on this planet in bodies such as I have, that did not become lost or did not evolve from the animal kingdom, make up the core of our many monasteries on this planet. And occasionally, still, we are able to bring through souls from another planet into an Earth body, constructed from the essence of fruits and flowers, odors, lights and sounds, until it is in manifest form and able to be used. The bodies constructed through the animal kingdom do not last as long as ours. Though some have acquired the ability to fly short distances, they do not lend themselves well in this way. But those inhabiting them can run extremely fast and swim both over

the surface of the water and underneath it with great vigor. Our new *sādhakas,* however, going through the healings of the animal nature are given time to consider well the teachings that they are absorbing in life with us here, for their major task is to bring their mind flow back into the same way that it was when they, too, had a body such as mine.

The Power Of Those in Original Bodies

103 ℂ Here in the monastery in which I am writing this record is to be found an abundant majority of us in original bodies and a minority inhabiting the animal Earth body. This and this alone creates the positive, powerful force through which cosmic rays are channeled from the planets we came from and the emanations of the Central Sun. This spreads out through us, stabilizing especially all of those struggling with the mutations out of the animal world back into a refined body.

Novitiates Made to Feel Accepted

104 ℂ During the first six moons, the *sādhaka* is treated as a newborn child, allowed to learn his mantra and experience his experiences. His coordination and the pressures he is feeling make him conspicuous at times, and he is not allowed to see his family, if he has one, and receives no visitors. When the six moons have expired, if his body is that of animal structure, he has a mother and a father, obviously, and is allowed to see them. But never again does he see or attach himself to former companions while he lives with us. During his first six-moon period, we care for him and give him the best of all that we have. We want him to feel most welcome and accepted, even though he may have been with us, serving in some capacity for a prior time of three or four moons or more, waiting acceptance. Now that he has been accepted, we feel he must feel that total acceptance from us all, in order to absorb the teaching he will hear, to read and comprehend the manuscripts in our libraries, and to dream and remember those dreams projected to him. And so, with loving care, we treat him as a young child during this time of his transition into a monastery of Lemuria.

The Value Of Lemurian Sādhakas

105 ℂ The Lemurian *sādhakas* were valued, as they were the promulgators of the force of the monastery. A stable, well-run Lemurian monastery had potential *sādhakas* clamoring to enter. And if a monastery brought more *sādhakas* into it than it could conveniently hold, this was considered a

great boon, as then many of the senior members left our monastery, directed by our guru, to form a new one in an area of his choosing. It was said, "For every one *sādhaka* who entered the Lemurian monastery, over 200 souls escaped out of the cycle of animal birth."

The Lemurian *sādhakas* were valued, as they were the promulgators of the force of the monastery. A stable, well-run Lemurian monastery had potential *sādhakas* clamoring to enter.

Training According To Lineage

106 During the first and second circles of the Earth around the Sun, our young *sādhakas* were educated in a formal way as to our culture and lineage, and their future patterns of life would be explained to them according to their lineage out of the animal kingdom. That is to say, if they emerged back into human birth from cows, buffalos, milk-producing animals, we would have them perform a certain function in the monasteries where they could get along and work most creatively in this chosen area among others of a similar animal lineage. However, if they came from the lineage of the animals that carried people on their backs, still another occupation would be granted them to do. And so, the major areas of activity, creativity and usefulness were cared for in this way, by placing these *sādhakas* into these various avenues of expression.

Apprenticeship Begins in the Third Circle

107 It was in the third circle of our planet around the Sun that he was chosen by a senior member of our community for individual training. This training was given to him as an artisan works day by day with his apprentices. But until he was thus chosen by a senior artisan he was considered by us as young, but a child, and allowed to play in our playground of the mind, experience, learn, absorb, break up previous patterns of his past by establishing new ones simply by being here. It was in the fifth circle, when a certain area of their training was completed, that we rested a great responsibility upon their shoulders, and depended heavily on them to begin to become productive and perhaps train new *sādhakas*. Prior to this time, they were on the in-breath. The fifth and sixth circles began the out-breath of productivity.

Training Complete in Circle Four

108 It was during these first years that they received the training that was to be satisfactory for the rest of their lives. Never again did a training period occur, and upon the effort they put in and the skills they acquired in the area of service they were given to perform in during these first few circles was the pattern indelibly established for the duration of their lifetime. For this was our custom in our monasteries, as our efforts were directed toward the circumference of the people just entering, getting them well established in a lasting pattern that took approximately four circles to bring into being for the duration of their lifetime in the Lemurian monastery. After they were well set in their external patterns, after their sixth year, our *devas* and Deities would begin working, directing and showing them how to be of deeper service, while they slept at night and during their meditations by day, to all inhabitants on our planet. Many of these things they learned from the *devas* and Deities and their guru they would write down, starting in their seventh and eighth circles, and these writings made up our libraries that the new *sādhaka* would study in during his first few circles with us. This training was called secret training and would come according to their abilities and evolution enabling them to receive it.

Announcing One's Monastic Age

109 ℂ When a *sādhaka* first entered the monastery and began his initial period of training, in order for us all to look at him and treat him as a child, we established over a period of time our curious system of Lemurian monastic age: "Two circles of the Moon around the Earth equal one circle of the Earth around the Sun." The *sādhaka* would always, upon speaking to any of us, remind us of his age in such a way that we would know our relationship. He would say, "My name is Sādhaka Oomena, and I am six circles old." Though physically he may be in a body that's been twenty-two circles on Earth, we would immediately know he had only been in the monastery for one circle and therefore relate to him accordingly and as graciously and helpfully as we could. Each *sādhaka* would take every opportunity to remind us of his age as it increased, as this is one way he solicited the proper help and assistance from each member of the community.

Trained, Mature and Capable

110 ℂ When he was young in Lemurian monastic years, we told him stories and taught him to read our scriptures. When he became older, he learned to read alone. When he became still more mature, we depended upon the knowledge he had accrued through his reading and meditation, his training and abilities cultivated out of having been trained as he entered the central hub as a senior member of our core, one fully capable

and able to transmit positive rays from the planets we came here from, and the core of the Central Sun itself, to all inhabitants on this planet, stabilizing their quest for the totality of their Being, the fulfillment of which is the reason they arrived.

Qualifying To Enter the Central Core

111 ℂ So, the *sādhakas* received the welcome and the training and, when they so qualified themselves, entered the central core. Some never did quite qualify, due to one reason or another. Most generally, those of a certain animal lineage could not sustain the power of the cosmic rays. Those who were able to sustain this power did so and served in this way. Those who were unable to sustain this power and function as an Earthly channel—one who collected certain cosmic rays, drew them close together and disseminated them evenly throughout the world—performed their function closer to the Earth while pulling their elements together and basking in these rays held tight by the central group of us.

Monastics Raised From Birth

112 ℂ A *sādhaka* from birth is one who was born and raised specifically for the monastery. The parents were carefully trained to show absolutely no emotion before or during conception. Therefore, they had little attachment to the child, and if in an animal body he would grow up with less emotion, desires and cravings, and his body would shape close to the original body rather than in any other way. These young ones, prepared for us in this way by these families, were taken into our monasteries at a very early age.

When one became still more mature, we depended upon the knowledge he had accrued through his reading and meditation, his training and abilities cultivated out of having been trained as he entered the central hub as a senior member of our core.

Powers were obscured, and knowledge of the Self waned in those days. Rules in this era were generous and unbending. When commodities such as gold were brought as gifts to the monastery, one third was kept and used by the monks and two thirds returned to the givers in a new and more useful form. Thus the villages and the monastery flourished, and the internal and external government of the senior minority group within the monastery and its satguru governed fairly and with great compassion for all. Religion blossomed as a gentle yet dynamic way of life. God, the Supreme, was love to them, pure love. The Gods were wisdom givers, and their many devas were helpers on the path to final liberation, of merger into the great beyond of the beyond of the beyond forever and ever and ever. Aum.

I will now describe where we now live and whence we came, to remind us of the far distant past, longer ago than all the agos put together, and then some. We shall learn of the uses of gold, of universes and the mysteries of Central Sun, exploring the varied bodies, original and animal, as well as the arts of giving back when given to, the primary act that offers release from selfishness.

Gurudeva

113 ℂ In our many Lemurian monasteries there are several different groups of us. Those of us who are in our original bodies are known by the lineage of the particular planet whence we came, and due to the nature of the substance of our body, we are able to still contact our associates there; and even still others of us have a manifested body on that planet, which when we project ourselves to it is there to be used. The other group within our monasteries, that is increasing—and our prophets tell us that during the Dvāpara Yuga the monasteries will be totally made up of this group of souls—are those living in the body from animal lineage. We call all of these in this group "the Lemurians." Great effort at this time is being employed to set patterns so that the Lemurians themselves can hold the force of cosmic rays and emanations from the Central Sun of our galaxy without our aid. For as we move into the Dvāpara Yuga, and especially toward its end, all of us who are now in our original bodies will be a cosmic essence of intelligence or inhabit a Lemurian form to travel and communicate in on this planet.

Ākāśic Books For Future Lemurians

114 ℂ These books, in fact, are being written by me now for our library and carefully sealed in the *ākāśa* for the Lemurians to read and be guided by many thousands of cycles hence. Formulas for living on this planet have been developed by us, and when adhered to enable even some of the Lemurians to recontact their ancestors on the planets they once inhabited, even though their abilities to traverse space have been inhibited by the density of the organism in which their soul resides.

Designing Patterns Of Living

115 ℂ Our laboratories set the pattern for all forms of living, fueling the form, and designate relationships between the groups of us here on Earth. These laboratories are the emanating intelligence put into manifest action by us and the Lemurians as a result of communication with the *devas* and Deities. Some of us will become powerful, as the *devas* are, when we step out of this original body, for we are only here to help on an extended stay, having fulfilled our destiny in realizing the totality of the Self long, long ago. When this occurs to us, we will have the ability to travel from planet to planet and communicate with the Lemurians, help and serve them through their temple-laboratory monasteries in a future time.

Significant Cosmic Shifts

116 ℂ We who are not Lemurians form the senior group within each laboratory-monastery, and I must relate that as the Dvāpara Yuga approaches, we are becoming more and more in the minority. Our prophets tell us that at the beginning of the Dvāpara Yuga we will even be taking a few advanced Lemurians into our group to keep a certain balance of force among the peoples on this planet. This will be interesting to observe, for as yet the Lemurians have not been able to sustain the radiation from the core of the Central Sun. However, the laboratory experts prophesy that there will be a shift, slightly obscuring the Central Sun and its radiations, and even those of some of our planets will not be felt as strongly on this Earth at the beginning of the Dvāpara Yuga. This will greatly affect vegetation on this Earth, and most of it will mutate to half the size that it is, they predict.

Galaxies And their Central Suns

117 ℂ Many galaxies are comprised of numerous solar systems within each one. Each galaxy has a Central Sun, which is an opposite force to each sun within each solar system. Therefore, there are many Central Suns also, each one slightly different than the other, depending on the age, nature and composition of the galaxy; yet, there is a great similarity between each galaxy in its composition, structure and force patterns, our knowledge tells us.

Healing The Inner Body

118 ℂ Our Lemurians' basic *sādhana* was to be as much like us as possible in their reaction patterns, speech, communication, perceptions, uses of the inner eyes; and through this tremendous effort some of them had to employ, the outer structure of the nerve system of their bodies was strengthened and reformed, and the inevitable damage healed which occurred as their soul tumbled and turned, rolled and churned through the births and deaths of the reentries and exits in and out of the bodies of flesh. We promised them that if they healed the subtle tentacles and refined their external form to be as much like ours as possible and dive deep into the Self, we would take them back to the planet whence we came and grant them divine office within the realms of this or another galaxy. The reward is great for serving well, and their service was well performed.

Seeking Ways To Preserve Our Knowledge

119 ℂ Earth fulfilled its function for us very well. The pattern and the reason for our coming was first completed long ago and is fairly well routine now. Intense work is being done now in our laboratories to find the way in which we can sustain our knowledge on this planet during the Dvāpara Yuga and its succeeding counterpart, during which time cosmic radiations may lessen to the extent that all extraterrestrial perceptions may vanish and only the faculties that the roaming animals now have will exist for all mankind. All of our findings are carefully being sealed in the *ākāśa,* and copies placed in our libraries, as it is felt that man may forget his divine lineage during these impending eras.

Playing and Making Gold Adornments

120 ℂ Now we shall view a day through a monastery courtyard of this place in which I inscribe these words. The Lemurians loved to wear the color yellow. Much gold was placed upon their body as a transmitter of cosmic rays. They enjoy playing games and running after one another: the chase, the catch. This is inherent in their nerve system, and during times of relaxation, when they are not being trained, these patterns manifest. As much as possible, we have them work with gold. They create the adornment for the bodies within the monastery and surrounding countryside. The designs come from those patterns they see adorning our great Deities as they stand in their temporary body upon the pedestal. Others, of course, are not quite as fortunate to work in gold, for it is mainly the Lemurians from the milk-producing mammals that work with the gold substance and are more able to sustain the cosmic radiation intensified by having it close to their bodies.

The Custom Of Returning Two Thirds

121 ℂ As is our custom, when the visitor to the monastery comes with gifts of gold or other commodities, we keep for the monastery one third and, in some kind of preparation, return the other two thirds to him. Therefore, through the process of the preparation and his receiving it, carrying it back to his abode and his usage of it, he is in direct communication with the cosmic rays and emanations from the Central Sun. These rays are conducted through the temple, the pedestal and the monastic who molds them to the preparation of golden adornment that he creates, or combinations of food. The cosmic radiation then extends through this physical form, which is two thirds of their original gift, into the

As is our custom, when the visitor to the monastery comes with gifts of gold or other commodities, we keep for the monastery one third and, in some kind of preparation, return the other two thirds to him.

dwelling. The one third kept in the monastery is the original battery or conductor. If it is food, it is eaten by the *sādhakas*. Should it be gold, it is stacked against the walls. Hence the Lemurian in a far-off place has a direct physical link of cosmic communication to the temple and monastery and our laboratories of the mind in his own personal nest. The Deities, in pulling within these cosmic rays, draw the forces of his soul into strength and assist him in refining the flesh to be as close to our original bodies as possible. Thus all Lemurians in this way keep in touch with the central core of our universe. This sustains their treacherous climb of the refinement of the human form through the processes of flesh, bone and fear reactions.

Giving to Conquer Selfishness

122 ℂ This custom of giving two thirds back to the giver is one of our most treasured. Our heritage from the high culture on the planets that we came here from has never left; whereas some of our other ways of proceeding, doing and acts of performance, while active and alive in the Sat Yuga, no longer quite apply, as this flesh-body unfoldment process of the soul now consumes most of the time for us, in seeing to the Lemurians' needs and their seeing to their own. But this custom of the handling of a commodity persists among all beings on Earth and keeps a stability of our people, open and kindly toward each other, as one of the greatest aids in conquering the greed and selfishness of the animal instincts. This obligation of returning two thirds prepared in a slightly different form than received is the first learning absorbed by a soul in his first human body out of a series of animal births and deaths. This brings back into his conscious activity in his sleeping terrestrial nerve system the remembrance of his divine heritage and stimulates the abilities of striving to manifest an exterior form to match the interior elements of his solar being.

Seeing to The Needs Of All Others

123 ℂ Through the many thousands of years since we first arrived, this two-directional giving custom saw to a stability of abundance among us all. Our *devas* and Deities also abide strictly by this custom, and when energies as well as commodities are given to them, they, too, prepare and transmit back two thirds. The one third is kept in the inner world. The storing up of the one third and the preparation for the return of the two thirds to the giver of the three thirds completely utilized the time and creatively occupied all of the inhabitants of the planet. Each one saw to the needs of all others. No one wants or desires. The animals take what they need. The Lemurians are trained, in emerging from the circumference of the fur, to give what is needed. Alas, this primal custom of living on this planet will also be lost in the blindness of the moment prior to the next Sat Yuga.

Each one saw to the needs of all others. No one wants or desires. The animals take what they need. The Lemurians are trained, in emerging from the circumference of the fur, to give what is needed.

The Colors Of Our Apparel

124 ℂ Those of us in our original bodies are mainly seen dressed in orange and red, representing to us and to all the Sun through which we passed on our journey to Earth. The natural color white was used by villagers, guests, visitors and those performing *sādhana* here under the direction of the guru for specific purpose and a given length of time. We are told by our prophets that nearly everything on Earth will be approximately a quarter the size that it is now toward the end of the Kali Yuga: the trees, the plants, the Lemurians, the animals.

Age, Wisdom, Continuity Of Service

125 ℂ The longer we persist within these bodies, the wiser, more knowledgeable and content we become. Veneration for the aged Lemurian body and the original body was adhered to by all in the monastery, the temple and outside, for the body age indicated how long the intelligence of the soul resided without a break of continuity. Those of us in our original bodies—which are themselves orange in hue due to the nature of their construction—rarely leave the monastery. Our duties both inwardly and outwardly so consume us, and it would be a tremendous break in continuity were we to travel from monastery to monastery or carry the darshan to strengthen areas of the surrounding vicinity. So, we travel mentally and gain knowledge through visions.

Moving Transparently In the World

126 ℂ When the Lemurian monastics left the monastery to carry the darshan of the cosmic rays, they would dress and move among the people and be as close to looking like them as they were able. They would never teach, simply keep themselves open channels for the emanations of divine energies. We would inwardly closely watch them in their journey so that no harm would come.

nstinctive impulses were harnessed in the monastery, where praise and respect were freely given but never accepted. Many were the ways monastics stabilized the planet, so souls could be free to leave it. Carriers of the darshan were on occasion sent out into the world on mission, dressing so as to move about incognito, uplifting the people. They traveled in pairs through the windy countryside, consciously carrying with them the power and presence of the Mahadeva, Siva Peruman. They preached, chided, lectured and consoled, but never told where they were from or what their mission was. Some knew, of course, yet pretended they were strangers to their village, offering them luxurious foods and drink and other temptations, knowing their dedication to the simple life would win out. Aum.

Just a few original bodies were left as the next yuga approached. Great sanga discussions arose on how to hand over the planet to the Lemurians in the next yuga. What a dilemma they faced in training new applicants who were ignorant of impending changes, teaching the joyous, impersonal life, making sure that all done was in line with the command of the Mahadeva of all Mahadevas, Lord Siva.

Gurudeva

127 ☾ Within each of our monasteries there are four divisions of service, and within each division our experts and artisans work and serve and train young Lemurians in our culture. A lot of our occupation was directed toward educating Lemurians into remembering their heritage and culture as they traversed the bonds of animal instinct, refined their bodies and began to become more like us, or the way they originally were. So, each monastery is a vast university where learning in all areas of art and culture, science and interplanetary configurations of travel and communications is taught. We are concerned with the perpetuation of the culture and the constant dissemination of the cosmic rays. We even train animals here prior to their release of the soul inhabiting the body. There is a certain language that is used to speak to the animal that the soul within it will hear. The impressions of the knowledge they acquire are carried over in their next birth in a Lemurian body.

Cleaving Together in Monasteries

128 ☾ Many thousands of years ago we realized that as we began to experience the fire of entering the animal chain of fleshy birth and death, we lost contact with our culture in returning to the human body. Those of us in our original bodies began, therefore, to cleave together in structures such as we have today, keeping in close, constant communication with our great Mahādevas in a never-ending effort to guide the soul back into human manifestation, but in a flesh body more conducive to withstand the vibrations of the Dvāpara and Kali Yugas and survive through them than our original bodies are. So, constant training of the old and young alike is necessary. Each Lemurian *sādhaka* entering the monastery is intricately trained in his first four circles in a personal skill to which he is best adapted, depending upon the lineage whence his body came, in philosophy and the inner arts and sciences.

When Sādhakas Departed

129 ☾ Occasionally a *sādhaka* left the monastery, and we arranged for him to mate so that the race would be perpetuated. He later would become a teacher and train young ones to enter the monastery as *sādhakas* at a very early age. This training took place in the dwellings in which they lived. The teachers of this kind were brought away from their families periodically and were trained by us to disseminate knowledge to all those who lived outside the monastery. They are the educators of our

time. The monastery, their university, provides systematic dissemination of knowledge to them which they spread out, first to their immediate family and then to all who will listen.

Various Avenues of Service

130 ℂ Within the monastery itself, the Lemurians were always of the male gender, and those who had never mated were chosen. They performed all of the duties, the ceremonies and carried out the teaching of our intricate and profound culture. They build the dwellings, make the repairs, but they do not grow our food or gather it. Those who mate and produce the species grow the food. The more elderly and more advanced carry out scientific pursuits and advance the culture through the constant adjustments they make within the culture itself through new findings as the forces of this *yuga* wane and the forces of the next begin. These monastics, priestly scientists, some among them Lemurians themselves, are highly venerated by us and their counterparts on other planets.

Lemurian Carriers of Darshan

131 ℂ Each time the configuration of the planets formed a straight line, the Lemurians would leave the monastery—this time not incognito, as they usually did as carriers of the divine darshan—and festively parade through the countryside as we used to on many of the planets before arriving here. Hence, the cosmic rays emanating through our temple—sustained by the surrounding monastery and disseminated to the surrounding countryside through the mind flows of the monastics—sustained the force of the entire community from this one central hub, our temple. Occasionally the darshan did not penetrate deeply enough into certain areas of the instinctive mind that were being developed through coming out of the animal kingdom back into human form. To counteract the force of the animal instincts entering the human realm, we send monastics incognito into these areas to be a temple unto themselves and channel a charge of cosmic ray into these mind flows, thus challenging and charging the very nature of the energies employed, thus refining that segment of the race. These carriers of the darshan are trained for this occupation and service. They are particularly strong and adept, knowledgeable and profound and wary that they are not captured by the forces they are sent to rechannel. These carriers of the darshan will appear *yuga*

after *yuga* in human form, our prophets say, to stabilize the mass of souls who will be in the morass of the feelings of the flesh and keep them reminded of their divine heritage.

Within the monastery itself, the monastics were always of the male gender, and those who had never mated were chosen. They performed all of the duties, the ceremonies and carried out the teaching of our intricate and profound culture.

Absence of Personal Preference

132 ℭ In entering a Lemurian monastery, a young *sādhaka* presents himself. He has no personal motivation or pre-determined idea, other than he presents himself for service. Occasionally one comes and is more delighted with one kind of service than another. He's not accepted and sent to the family for training of potential *sādhaka* which is given there. Each one here is here to serve our Mahādeva in the great divine plan and for the fulfillment of the reason and purpose of our coming to this planet, the one with fire in it, the fire planet. Oddly enough, the one thing we did not know when we came to this planet was that the fire which would kindle our evolution on Earth was the eventual obtaining of the body similar to the original body through the animal kingdom, a body with fire in it.

Initiation for Inner Plane Assignments

133 ℭ There is a willing joyousness, a children-like glee in awe and happiness here. Slowly working back through the flames of fire into the Self, the power will enable each soul to leave the planet and enter the others that require this maturity to be accessed. Therefore, when each monastic learns his area of service, he lives with it, and no one moves into another area of the four divisions of our monastery unless he deserves to do so by the virtue of his age. For after the fourth circle of training—and he is chosen by his artisan in his seventh circle—he's given inner tasks to perform by his guru and allowed to work within the strata of mental space. This great gift only occurred after initiation. Some of our gurus have given 18, 20 to 25 initiations, or various degrees of inner plane assignments. Powerful gurus such as these give their monastics guardianship of individual cosmic rays that permeate the temples of their monasteries, stabilizing the different mind flows. These are taught intricately and privately to them by their guru.

Blending in, Working Quietly

134 ℭ It is easy to tell whether one has had initiation or not, for the ones that have been initiated we refer to as the ones we cannot see, the absent ones. They never stand out among the others, but blend with and fade into their surroundings imperceptibly. In ever-increasing inner work and ser-

vice they are being trained and involved, keeping them thus occupied. Thus, this great priesthood of Lemurian souls, working together on many intricate levels of mind flow, channel through cosmic rays and the emanations of the Central Sun, stabilizing all the peoples of the Earth through the constant dissemination of this darshan.

Gurus Of Inner Groups

135 ℭ Our gurus of this time occupy Lemurian bodies as well as original bodies. They were some of the guides who brought us to this planet many thousands of circles ago. Some of them have fifty or more and others ten, still others five monasteries and temples, all run on a similar pattern that I have been describing. Each one contained a well-trained group performing their tasks so admirably that the surrounding countryside resided in peace and protection from the impending forces of the age to come.

Transferring Family Ties To the Guru

136 ℭ Many games are played in these monasteries, and a joyous atmosphere precipitated constantly through them. Since the herd emotion precipitated through the Lemurians, their main difference was to detach the long streamers of force that hung around them in the psychic atmosphere to the family that bore their body. They worked within themselves to do this by attaching this force to the guru and the Mahādeva. When this was accomplished, they were calm and content and joyous in the new surroundings of cosmic radiations, which was sometimes difficult for them to bear. They were careful never to attach these streamers of force, or any part of it, to another monastic, be he their artisan or simply a counterpart of the same herd whence their body evolved. This is the only basic personal area of struggle a new *sādhaka* inwardly goes through. An intricate training is given to him to help him in the replacement of this psychic streamer of umbilical-like force he must detach and reattach into his new place of service.

Precipitating A Sublime Joyousness

137 ℭ All correction and training was given to him so as not to enliven animal impulses within him. Therefore, artisans and experts in any one of the areas of our monasteries always take onto themselves the responsibilities for those apprenticing with them, so that this constant expression of childlike joy always precipitates and no animal emotion, therefore, is allowed to arise from any one of the Lemurians in the monastery, which would strongly inhibit the dissemination of cosmic rays. Psychic ties to the family were often immediately reconnected to the guru and Mahādeva by the *devas* themselves if they were asked in a proper way.

Deferring Praise and Respect

138 ℭ Great reverence and respect was given to a Lemurian monastic because of his accomplishment in one of the four areas of service, as well as his ability to train his apprentices to accomplish, for this is how one guru was able to acquire more monasteries, by sending these accomplished monastics to another vicinity, starting the same pattern all over again. As was the custom, no one accepted respect or praise, though it is freely given, for they felt it inhibited their direct channel into the mind flow of the Mahādeva. They would say, "Let the lion be and do his work. If you pet the lion in this way, he will stop his work, become hungry, and your hand might be too close to his mouth." Most of our stories were in accordance with the nature of the herd and species of animals the Lemurian bodies heralded from.

Our gurus of this time occupy Lemurian bodies as well as original bodies. They were some of the guides who brought us to this planet many thousands of circles ago. Some of them have fifty or more and others ten, still others five monasteries and temples, all run on a similar pattern.

Training—The Guru's Main Effort

139 ℭ Artisans and craftsmen were sent by the guru to other monasteries for several cycles to train others, and our prophets say this apprenticeship system of the dissemination of knowledge will be carried by the inhabitants of this planet through the Kali Yuga. The major work of our guru is to teach new *sādhakas* entrance into our monastery, disseminate knowledge to them for the fulfillment of their destiny, the maturing into the Self, and give them the grace of the ability to conduct good ceremony, contacting our Mahādeva, who gives inspiration and direction for the perpetuation of our race into the next *yuga*. We strongly avoid Lemurian monastics' acquiring too diverse a knowledge in the exterior mind. This is left for the Lemurians who live in the exterior mind who do not enter a monastery. "Those who mate learn of many things, but none too well of any," our guru recently observed.

Two Voices: Guru's and Mahādeva's

140 ℭ Our gurus are ordained by the Mahādeva to see to the proper running of the temple and the monastery. This ordination took place on the planet whence the guru heralded. Though the temple is the abode of the voice of the Mahādeva and His *devonic* helpers, the monastery is the voice of the guru subtly working through its many mind flows. In each monastery that a guru owned through his administration of it, there too was a temple in which his voice was heard, adjacent to the temple of the Deity.

Forceful elements

of the planet caused large, protective stone walls to be erected around monasteries. Within these, artisans and apprentices could be seen working side by side, and massive libraries of mystical knowledge developed over the centuries. The Lemurians were all tremendously skilled in their crafts, often spending an entire lifetime perfecting one particular skill, becoming more and more refined while working inwardly with the Mahadeva's darshan. When the monastery reached its fullness in intensity, assured by the Mahadeva that the power would persist through the coming yugas, it was carefully taken apart, and a lake was formed in its place to hold the darshan. When leaving, they equally divided themselves, setting off in all four directions to inhabit and strengthen other monasteries. Aum.

Karmas were directed in the monasteries of yore by the transmission of skills intricately conveyed from artisan to apprentice. The Lemurians and original-bodied souls coped with this in well-organized and remarkable ways, foreseeing the undoing of all that was done. Their being was to become the being of all beings, one with the Central Sun of the infiniverse. They served to become.

Gurudeva

141 ℭ Craftsmanship is long and tedious and sometimes consumes an entire lifetime of an apprentice, who perhaps never becomes an artisan unless he is sent by his guru to another monastery to fulfill this function. Each one is a specialist in carving some part of our rock-cave-city environments. An apprentice may be given to learn the intricacies of carving one flower in stone and perform the same function time and time again without variation for the totality of his ability to inhabit the same fleshy form, all the while working inwardly with the great darshan flow after initiation. Similar specialties occurred in each of the four areas of service within every Lemurian monastery.

Outer Knowledge, Inner Training

142 ℭ Knowledge about life on the planet which we inhabit, the planets whence we came and the intricacies of our stay here since arrival was always given to the young male by his family or an authorized family instructor prior to his entering the monastery. Therefore, this kind of training we did not disseminate, but interrogated him quite thoroughly upon his arrival as to the extent of his knowledge. The less he knew of these matters in their intricacies, the better he could serve the Mahādeva, it was felt, and he would be in the temple or close to it. The more he knew of the intricacies and involvements of the external affairs of our planet, and the nature and herdsmanship of various animals and peoples upon it, the more he would most likely serve in craftsmanship, dealing with materials of the planet itself, such as stone and the denser substances which constructed our environment and protections from the winds and elements that were treacherous to our bodies.

Qualities Of the Artisans

143 ℭ Monastic years kept an intricate balance precipitating between the artisan and his apprentices of about nine or ten monastic years difference between the artisan and his apprentice. An artisan is always chosen because of his power to convey and cause another to learn. In many of our monasteries there are many, many apprentices well qualified to be artisans, but not allowed to be because they have not developed the power to convey their skills to another who serves alongside of them systematically enough to cause him to learn to be as proficient as they themselves are.

Training In Personal Behavior

144 ℂ An artisan, ordained by virtue of his monastic years, after his seventieth year not only conveyed the skill to his apprentices, but trained them in other aspects of our culture, such as the abilities to relate one to another, to the guru and the Mahādeva, our Deity, as well as various modes of philosophy, behavior, games and dress. These artisans, the guru and the senior group of us always held ourselves fully responsible for the apprentices under artisans of thirty to forty monastic years of age; and they were carefully trained in other areas of the monastery-temple and in their personal deportment by senior monastics, especially trained to perform this kind of service, all of whom have accrued more than seventy monastic circles. When an artisan over seventy monastic circles fully trained an apprentice, he and he alone is considered mature enough to be transferred to another monastery and serve as artisan, providing he meets the qualifications of being able to convey knowledge and skill and cause another to perform.

Artisans: Mature and Responsible

145 ℂ Each artisan was the first to arrive and the last to leave in performing his task. This is our custom. He, too, is never idle, but on occasion walks among his apprentices, giving correction and advice. They were always together, artisan and apprentices; even in the temple they would be seen sitting together. They would play games together. Our artisans are the most mature of the Lemurians in all of these many monasteries and temples controlled by these many gurus on the Earth at this time. Often the artisan sits with his guru, receiving instructions and advice. They are seen sitting together, for each one is professional in his area of government, working under the greatest guidance of the guru and his *devas*. A guru presiding over fifty monasteries may also preside over five hundred artisans.

Emulating The Inner Perfection

146 ℂ The Lemurians were all tremendously skilled at developing a skill which manipulated the external form and refined it into being as much like the original body as possible. Therefore, what is produced in the form of artwork and carving was produced to refine the form rather than adorn our buildings, which, of course, was the result of producing many refined Lemurian forms, or bodies. We also have much embellishment around to appreciate, causing this world to appear as if it were the inner world within these many monasteries.

Coordinating The Four Divisions

147 ℂ The four divisions of our monastery each had some one being who worked directly with the group of beings who also divided themselves into four divisions as a channel to coordinate the monastics within the four divisions. The *devas* hovered over and through each of our monasteries, but serving within these four divisions were highly skilled *devas* who disseminated knowledge and direction to all of the artisans and experts. The one senior artisan in each division saw to the smooth adjustments of the force within the division itself. This coordination has the effect of training a senior Lemurian monastic to perform a similar function as we in our original bodies do, and in years to come, a new senior group will form within each monastery as the forces of this planet become too harsh for these original bodies in which we live to persist.

Our artisans are the most mature of the Lemurians in all of these many monasteries and temples controlled by these many gurus on the Earth at this time. Often the artisan sits with his guru, receiving instructions and advice.

Lemurians On Special Missions

148 ℂ Many of these advanced Lemurians are here on a special mission to stabilize these monasteries in their four aspects, direct from the planet from which they were sent. Therefore, they perform this function for us with ease and agility. They tell of receiving their instructions before arrival here which ring out in their memory of the inner mind clearly. These are the ones that chose the sites of our structures and established patterns of performing the different skills. They are totally given up to their mission. Our libraries, developed through the centuries, written by anonymous monastics inside, delve into the core of existence and the complexities of space. These are the nameless ones, and our names change frequently as we move from monastery to monastery. In each monastery we are known by a different name. The gurus of our culture and time meet, converse and discuss the future of our race. They meet on mountaintops and in valleys with a solitary lake.

Dissertations Through The Wall

149 ℂ In the wall surrounding a monastery many openings appeared, and a great hall was built outside it. Those who mated came close to this wall and listened to dissertations given by us out of inner states of mind through a hole carved in the wall. We never identify ourselves to them as being one species or another, as the animals do when they howl at each other. We simply speak through this carved hole in the wall our

knowledge and let it rest in the ear and mind of the listener.

Tubes in the Wall for Meditation

150 ℂ We also had large holes in the wall or tubes in mountain walls where the Lemurians slept at night, left the physical body and conversed in inner planes. None of these tubes is directly above another, so that they left the physical form with ease. Lemurian monastics sleep through the darkest part of the night, and during the full moon they do not sleep at all. We in our original bodies do not perform this function and have a consciousness which precipitates as long as this body does through the Sun and through the absence of light of the Sun. Full consciousness is permitted because of the nature of the structure of this form. Our guru, on an inner plane at night, calls all of us in his many monasteries together in our place in a great inner plane hall constructed for this purpose. This is where we see him in his resplendent form. These great palaces contain thousands who meet while their physical bodies sleep; whereas we in our original bodies are also there and fully conscious of the occurrences without leaving the body.

Two Mind Flows: Concise And Casual

151 ℂ Nearly everything within a Lemurian monastery is in two sections of mind flow, one highly formalized and concise. This bearing would comprise two of the four divisions. The other two divisions are generally more casual, relaxed. Within these were those who performed ceremony within the temple, prepared our nourishment, and those that, through the accomplishment of the destiny and the great maturation of their soul, sent through a tremendous darshan of their own as a birth of their own being.

A Monastery's Fulfillment of Purpose

152 ℂ When a Lemurian monastery reached its fullness of intensity and precision and we were assured by the Mahādeva that the darshan, cosmic rays and the emanations of the Central Sun would remain permanent and stationary through the temple into the next Sat Yuga, even permeate through the core of the Earth *yuga* after *yuga*, then and only then did the temple and monastery fulfill its purpose, reach its fullness. When this occurred, we carefully took the monastery-temple apart. A lake was formed in its place. We divided each of the four sections, who went to four different other monasteries, never to return to the spot again, allowing the Deities and *devas* to disseminate the darshan.

We worked with them to establish that particular place on the surface of the Earth for many *yugas* to come.

An Array of Remarkable Abilities

153 ℂ We value our abilities to perform this function, the creating of a great temple, a great environment, a great cosmic ray of putting this planet in tune with the core of the universal mind of great beings on other planets. We value our abilities of being able to train the Lemurians to be skilled enough to refine the form of their bodies, built through mating, that they will sustain the culture. These abilities accrue as this refinement persists while they carve a great statue that they will never look upon, write a great book that they will never read, weave a fine fabric that will never be worn, carve the divine image of our Mahādeva, keep it in a perfect state of being finished until it is carved so small that it disappears, to live a life so fully and skilled until they dissolved into the essence of their own reality. This is the heritage we leave the Lemurians as the forces of the Dvāpara Yuga dissolve these forms we now inhabit.

Lemurian monastics sleep through the darkest part of the night, and during the full moon they do not sleep at all. We in our original bodies do not perform this function and have a consciousness which precipitates as long as this body does through the sun and through the absence of light of the sun.

The God of Gods,

known as Siva, came to be recognized at the end of the Treta Yuga, as the intensity of the darker yugas caused the mind to see the form of God more so than the formless. Though all-pervasive at every moment in time, at every point in space, He was invoked here in His etheric body, drawn by the need of humans living on this planet through the impending trying times. Through the darshan of this Supreme One, which is of the same velocity as the emanations of the Central Sun, we abide within, shepherded by Him from darkness and blindness of fading faculties into the all-knowing light. Now that we are aware He is here and near, we dance with Him as we live with Him, ever looking forward in the far off, yet not-too-distant future of the many futures to come, to merge with Him, into Him as He Himself. Aum.

Lemurians gave rise to Dravidians, a new race on the planet. Oddly enough, Sri Lanka was called Lemuria, and South India Dravidians still live to this day. Tamil Nadu's land mass is said to have never been under the ocean's waters. How ancient is ancient? Only the Gods know. Here we explore Siva's advent, and the arrival of the next yuga, starting and ending with the killing of other human beings.

Gurudeva

154 ℭ As the planet becomes older, forces equalize themselves and new innovations in cultural procedures are absent. Systems remain status quo. Our *śāstras* predict that a million years after the beginning of the next Sat Yuga there will be great research into science and planetary travel as the fire deepens beneath the Earth's crust. Nothing new is created, everything is preserved and nothing is destroyed. There is no fire. It is just a big space station here. Nothing is growing. One of the biggest space stations in the universe. It will be like a nation that gets to the point where it fulfills its purpose and goes away and others move in. But now in the Dvāpara Yuga in which we live and have been living for thousands and thousands of years, the vibrations of the next are imminent, and slight adjustments of the cosmic rays are even now being felt. The onrush of the fulfillment of purpose has culminated, and change is imminent. It is only with a great upheaval of the *status quo* of this *yuga* will the next begin. Hence, in retrospect, some of the important manifestations of the preservation of the culture recorded and preserved in the *ākāśic* ether of the inner mind will lay a foundation for the continuity of the culture during the wane of the Kali Yuga many thousands of years from now, when cosmic rays once again pierce the veiling darkness and the Sat Yuga dawns.

Diminution Of the Central Sun's Rays

155 ℭ From the Third World our great Mahādevas tell us that they see time as a circle persisting through millions of years and that now, as we are coming to the end of the Dvāpara Yuga, the forces will begin to change so drastically as the configuration of the galaxy diminish the rays of the Central Sun through our solar system and on this planet. These rays affect vegetation, animals and the inhabitants on the Earth much more than the basic functions of the planet itself.

Compensating For Loss Of Vision

156 ℭ During this period inhabitants are beginning to lose the power of this inner eyesight, the single eye; and many are seeking solutions within the laboratories of the mind, our temples and monasteries, in order to adjust the thinking patterns of the population so that the instinctive forces of fear become inhibited from welling up and consuming their intelligence. And so, with every loss of the faculty inherited from the Tretā Yuga, knowledge of how to compensate for this loss must replace it.

That is the work the core of us in our many monasteries and temples must perform, through keeping in constant touch with the hierarchical Mahādevas who arrived on the planet during the Sat Yuga.

Śiva: Greatest Mahādeva of Them All

157 ℂ It was at the end of the Tretā Yuga that we became aware of the greatest Mahādeva of them all along with a band of celestial helpers, here to guardian and guide our galaxy through these trying times inherited by us through the Dvāpara, Kali and into the next Sat Yuga. Thus, Śiva, God, who guides us all into His essence, tramples 'round our globe, initiating, destroying, consuming, ignoring and rallying around the force comparable to sustain the population of this and many planets. By His law do we abide, and our temples dedicate their usage to His wisdom as He leads us through the Kali darkness into the Sat Śiva Yuga. This *deva* of the crescent moon that will be seen in the darkest night of the Kali Yuga, this God of sleep, guides all remnants of the inhabitants from the *yugas* of light out of the night into the morning rains. We trust Him. We love Him. Our Mahādeva reigns supreme. It is His darshan alone that consumes all others. Through channeling the Śiva darshan, which is of the same velocity, consistency and radiation as the darshan from the Central Sun, which is now waning, this Deva of all *devas*, Śiva, supplements our loss with His grace to sustain us through the night.

Prophecies Of the Next Kali Yuga

158 ℂ Our prophets tell us that toward the end of the Kali Yuga the inhabitants of the planet will begin to lose the sight of their two eyes, and that it will be a similar time as what is being experienced now as the powers of the center eye diminish and go dark. Our great books have been recorded through the passage of time and stored tightly away in the *ākāśic* ether of the libraries of the son of Śiva, who led us all here during the Sat Yuga for our realization of the eminence of his Father and to meet the transgressions of our *status quo* on the planets which spawned each one of us now wandering to and fro. It won't be long that we will not be able to read these books *en masse*, and translations must be stepped down to the two-eye level of those who live surrounding our monastery-temples through the land; for it is in these force-field hubs our culture is preserved and new tactics to embrace and stand up to the dimness of the coming hours that are foreseen accrue.

Sustenance From Lord Śiva And His Son

159 ℂ We read that during the Tretā Yuga universal planetary forces enveloped the fire planet. It flourished. But through the shifting cycles of our galaxy and solar system, this envelopment of cosmic rays which penetrated and permeated the Earth will subside. As the first ray was inhibited from touching the fire planet, we began to feel His influence. As we have come to better know Him and find him to be as a Universal Sun Himself within the veiling light of the Third World, the immenseness of His wisdom is now fully understood. Through the Sat and Tretā Yugas, the Mahādeva Subramaniam sustained, and through its wane and into the Dvāpara and Kali Yugas the Mahādeva Subramaniam works, and Śiva sustains. Thus our records tell of this imminent conclusion and harnessing of the sustenance of mind emanating out of the Central Sun.

It was at the end of the Tretā Yuga that we became aware of the greatest Mahādeva of them all along with a band of celestial helpers, here to guardian and guide our galaxy through these trying times inherited by us through the Dvāpara, Kali and into the next Sat Yuga.

Śiva: Central Sun and Form, Self and Mind

160 ℂ In all aspects of vibration, causing multitudes of form—existent when perceived by any of the eyes possessed by the fragments of or those closest to the same vibration of this Central Sun, who when mature enough in their elements realize It as their Self—Śiva is both the Central Sun and form, the Self and mind; and being the essence of the spirit of the universe, has the power to sustain this and other planets in the circumference of the vibration of His hand of Grace through these darker milleniums of the *yugas*. Therefore, in the Tretā Yuga, the innovation to the polarization of the rays of the Central Sun was brought through great monasteries. We now use these same areas on Earth to bring through the rays of our Central Sun, Śiva, and in doing so sustain the culture and mind flows through the darshan, in the same way the Lemurians did eons and eons ago. This continuity of the dissemination of the emanations of the Central Sun, as persisting for many, many *yugas* on this planet, we are vowed to keep ever flowing, as this *yuga* wanes and man stumbles through the next, guided only by the ray, well established in him since he's been on Earth, of Śiva.

Holding His Ray through Darker Times

161 ℂ There will be times, our prophets say, in the Kali Yuga that this ray of Śiva will be all but lost, so black the days of externalization and blindness; but it will persist in Him, though at times unseen, unfelt, to the glory of the doorway that the Sat Śiva Yuga opens as the eye within the middle of

the head begins to see again. This solar system is but His toy, and when the Sat Śiva Yuga again radiates and basks because of the natural rays of the Central Sun, He will give His toy to the Lord Subramaniam, His son, who will take His office as He dances through the universe.

Other Lords And Other Worlds

162 Lord Śiva has another son that becomes active in the intricacies of the mind of all the inhabitants of this planet through the Kali Yuga. He is vastness itself and understands the intrinsic values and balances, impending dangers and avenues toward success for the Lemurians, the planet, the solar system, the galaxy and the universe itself, so vast is His knowledge. What Śiva tramples upon as He dances through the universe, around the Cosmic Sun as the sun itself, this Lord understands. Our recorded knowledge tells us these working together with their Father through the dusk and darkness of our solar system will actually hasten our travels into their Father, our Father, through Him into the core of our universe, the Self, the Cosmic Sun, the reverse of all form that can be seen in each of the three worlds. For now a new world is forming in between the world of *devas*, Deities and lords alike. This world surrounds this planet in congested force, claiming inhabitants who cannot find a body or a birth; so they live in this world. At this time we now have three worlds.

Kali Yuga's Beginning And End

163 Our volumes say that during the Kali Yuga the Second World will become so strong that even animals that live there will persist in antagonizing the inhabitants of the Earth into forces that they employ when on the kill, and that man, celestial souls, will actually kill and devour one another. This Second World will form a barrier between the First and Third Worlds through the Kali Yuga. These books prophesied that when one of the first inhabitants of the fire planet is so antagonized by the building of these forces in the Second World that he destroys the body of another inhabitant, that will mark the point in time and space when the Kali Yuga will begin; and that when the inhabitants of the Earth are able to light the night with their own devices, this and this alone will mark the time that Śiva is felt in all His might by a predominantly large group of souls able to pierce through the Second into the Third World with their inner vision, and the Sat Śiva

Yuga will begin through this one advent in time and space. They further state that the dimming of the one eye marks the wane of our day, and we should, too, record our history and our inspirations in great records for the *ākāśic* library of our Lord Subramaniam so that at the end of the Kali Yuga the clear patterns that have persisted since our arrival in the Sat Yuga can persist and be adhered to by those who will read these books at that time. These *śāstras* are called the *Dravidian Śāstras,* stemming from the oldest race on the fire planet.

Now a new world is forming in between the world of *devas,* Deities and lords alike. This world surrounds this planet in congested force, claiming inhabitants who cannot find a body or a birth; so they live in this world. At this time we now have three worlds.

Dravidians: Formerly the Lemurians

164 ℂ Due to planetary changes, bodies of atmosphere have now congested, forming great bodies of water that divide the lands, and there are several groups of inhabitants who live only in touch with one another through telepathic means. With the fading of these faculties this, too, will become impossible. The race called Dravidian are those Lemurians that inhabited the monasteries and lived close to them through the Tretā Yuga. The Lemurians that became divided from the others through the formation of vast bodies of water, so great they were unable to go around them through the thousands of circles, took on other ways of living. The Dravidians, formerly Lemurians, formerly the first priestly inhabitants, the leaders, the guardians of the primal race, have never had a break in continuity. Hence, now we shall report knowledge of temple, our monasteries and ways of performing our function at this time.

Five great winds

of the body were a keen study within the laboratories of Dravidian monasteries, where constant research into the nature of varieties of herbs and healing potions occured. They knew well that when taking oils and herbs into the body, while at the same time centering awareness in the Siva-Sakti darshan flow through the five winds of the body from the three rivers merging at the medulla, many inner adjustments could be made, consciousness could rise above the planet, and miraculous physical healings would sometimes occur. These first ayurvedic doctors and jyotisha shastris together perpetuated their mystical arts, based on the knowledge contained in the great volumes within Lord Subramaniam's vast library in the akasha. Aum.

Many of the monasteries within an area formed the government of that domain. At this time the monarchs were the satgurus. The next yuga to come follows this same pattern, but familied royalty prevails. We shall learn of the gracious times that will return in a future yuga, their prophets explain, times of healing with oils and herbs, of levitation and strictly following the spiritual path.

Gurudeva

165 ℂ The Dravidian monasteries are all managed along the same pattern as the Lemurian monasteries were, and since the Central Sun was their total everything, Śaivites of this time experienced the dissemination of Śiva's darshan more than any of the other great *devas.*

Teaching and Keeping Inner Faculties Open

166 ℂ The Śaivite monasteries in the early Dravidian era concern themselves in bringing man forth from the animal kingdom, reeducating him in the rules of conduct and culture. This main concern, coupled with laying firm foundations of systems to preserve their heritage through the Kali Yuga, consumed their time. Śaivite gurus served according to the patterns set forth in early Lemurian history and ruled their monasteries, some of which became great universities. Carriers of the Śaivite darshan mingled freely with the masses, working with bands of unseen *devas* to alleviate veiling ignorance with rays of sustaining light. Hundreds each circle left the monastery and traveled to all parts of the globe, teaching, keeping open the inner faculties of mankind. Others of these teachers remained with their guru in the monastery, constantly working with and training monastics, from the beginning to the most advanced areas of the various schools of philosophy that had accrued during the *yuga.* To perpetuate this vast effort of education, following a pattern unique to this *yuga,* when the guru finally left his physical body, all the advanced monastics left the monastery and wandered forth as teachers. He worked through them all simultaneously. They never gave forth teachings on their own while their guru lived in his human body, unless specifically sent on a mission to fulfill a certain task of this nature, during which time the guru worked closely with them. Great efforts of this type were employed to prevent instinctive tendencies inherent in the race at this time from arising within the monastic.

Mission Instructions From the Guru

167 ℂ Each initiate received personal instructions for the duration of his life from his guru before he departed from physical form. This practice and this alone gave the Dravidian monastics great continuity in covering all areas of the planet that they were able to access with an equal dissemination of sustaining darshan and knowledge, for all gurus worked closely together with this end in view.

When a Guru Dropped His Physical Form

168 ℭ Our gurus now are the elders who lived, worked and served in their original bodies in the Lemurian monasteries toward the end of the Tretā Yuga, the great *śāstras* and *ākāśic* libraries tell us. The guru was the one closest to the Mahādeva, and his instructions given to the monastics in his monasteries were regarded as final law by the *devas* working within and through each of his monasteries. Therefore, since the Śaivite guru polarized these *devas* to each of the individual monasteries, when he left his physical form there was no need for the monasteries, except for the ones that directly polarized the great darshan of the Mahādeva, Śiva, and these became places of pilgrimage. The others were taken down, and the monastics scattered themselves according to the assignments granted them by him before he left. In the Second World and in the Third World, the guru himself, with the same band of *devas*, worked with and through each monastic on his individual assignment until he, too, dropped his physical form and joined the inner band of tireless workers. This is what occurred as a result of the vows given by the disciple upon entering the monastery.

Continuity After a Guru's Departure

169 ℭ Each Śaivite guru is answerable to no one but himself, his guru on inner planes and the Deity within him. Therefore, each Dravidian Śaivite felt extremely close to his guru, and none of these gurus ever left their physical bodies at any other time than the right moment according to the divine plan conceived with them in the Third World. Therefore, the Dravidian Śaivite monasteries fulfilled their purposes when each guru had fulfilled his purpose, similar to parents who leave their physical bodies, and the children all leave the family home, finding ones of their own, then enter their spiritual, intellectual and worldly experiences. Those close to the parents inwardly always try to live according to the principles and the culture imparted to them by their mother and father. Those demanding instinctive freedom ignore the inner dictates and feelings and transgress, for from the inner plane perspective, in this *yuga*, the guru can work more closely with the individual disciple who is separated from all the other disciples than in a collective group. While in his physical body he can work best with individuals in groups, because he uses the group to catalyze the individual and the individual to catalyze the group.

Sustaining The Flow Of Darshan

170 ℭ Occasionally when a guru leaves his physical body, even though he has given specific instructions, some of the monastics cleave together, and every effort is made by the Deities and *devas* to separate them and send them on their respective ways to fulfill their destiny their guru has set forth for them. Many of them fulfill these instructions in secret and incognito, and others instructed and taught quite openly. Each pattern was clearly set, for after his initiation, a new dharma began. This system of perpetuating the darshan through many constant separate channels fulfills the dharma accrued by the disciple before entering the monastery, creates a new karma and forms a fine dharma after initiation, according to the guru's instructions in the fulfillment of the great pattern manifest in the Third World. Hence, these great beings emerged from the monasteries and were never swayed by the conflicts and temptations they encountered, but quelled conflicts and turned the forces of temptation into the love of God and the desire to be one with Śiva. Thus, our culture is sustained, and through the Kali Yuga great temples will mark the places where profound inner happenings occur, thus perpetuating the darshan accrued by the existence of these monasteries.

This system of perpetuating the darshan through many constant separate channels fulfills the dharma accrued by the disciple before entering the monastery, creates a new karma and forms a fine dharma after initiation, according to the guru's instructions in the fulfillment of the great pattern manifest in the Third World.

Mendicants Of the Kali Yuga

171 ℭ In the Kali Yuga there will be wandering monastics then, too, many of them the same souls as speak and teach now; but no one will listen to them. They will beg their food to embarrass and disturb the population by their presence, especially from the ones who will not give. Some of our gurus who are even now leaving their physical bodies will be among these beggars, knowing full well who they are long before they are recognized by the Śaivites attending the great temples built upon the spots which are their monasteries now.

Testers Of the Pilgrims

172 ℭ To prepare individual monastics for their eventual task of teaching, they will be sent forth as pilgrims, carrying the darshan from place to place. The "testers of the pilgrims" would be also sent to harass them and put temptations in their way, take their belongings as well as to provide protection for them. These protectors and testers of the young Śaivites attempting to carry the darshan of the temple were highly skilled, some of them gurus themselves, instigators of new innova-

tions, who did not head monasteries in our time. This is performed to bring forth the strong divine tendencies of the young monastics and strength to overcome their inherent instinctive weaknesses. These "testers of the pilgrims" were comparable to a band of monastic bandits, ever ready to help or harass. Incognito and disguised, they often caused confusion great enough to sustain lengthy meditations in the monastic to gain his peace; and with renewed strength, and a strength and confidence he did not have before, he would proceed with the thread of darshan and draw it into a rivulet of power, dispelling darkness and ignorance wherever he went. This is our way in this *yuga.*

Study of the Body's Five Forces

173 ℭ The Dravidian monasteries developed around the five great forces of the physical body, following closely the pattern of the four divisions of Lemurian monasteries. We find this system to be understandable and easy to follow, as the study of the physical body was of paramount importance, as constant effort was made to keep the refinement process of it going at a faster rate than the heavy pulls of the Kali Yuga, even now being felt, causing animalistic drives to appear, whereas previously they could easily be transmuted. Research constantly went on in herbs and various kinds of healing potions, and the knowledge of the five great forces, like liquid bone flowing through the body, is quite common. This liquid bone appears in the Second World as a solid and can be seen. There are five varieties of it, and it is constantly flowing through the inner ether. It is a carry-over from the animal kingdom and through refining its consistency through foods and the uses of various oils and different types of exercise of the physical body, a health and vigor and refinement and translucency of the physical body occurs. This is, of course, when all of these five flowing substances of liquid bone are in absolute rhythm. But when one of these flowing forces impinges itself upon another, pain occurs in the physical body. When oils and herbs are applied to adjust the liquid bone, the pain disappears. It is with this that research is constantly being done to set patterns to last through the Kali Yuga. Lord Subramaniam has given forth great knowledge from His libraries within the inner ether of the mind to aid in the refinement of the physical form so that occasionally Self will be realized on the planet now and again through the Kali Yuga.

Adjusting The Five Winds

174 ℭ These five forces of liquid bone flow through the body as does the wind through the vegetation in the forest, as do thoughts through the mind, as does the basic emotion through the nerve system. Therefore, they are called winds of the body. The darshan from our Lord Śiva can be received into the liquid bone substance of the five winds, and if they are ailing, in pressures one upon the other, the power of the darshan received into and flowing through the winds adjusts them to a natural ebb and flow. For this to occur, the awareness of the individual is totally centered in feeling the Śiva darshan flow through the winds of his body for long enough periods of time so that the inner adjustments can occur; and even miraculous physical healings sometimes result. Focusing awareness in this way is similar to holding a crystal in a certain position before the sun whereby it can intensify the heat and create fire. The sun shines forth its radiance as does Śiva by His existence send forth His great darshan; but the crystal or the awareness channels the Sun or the darshan and intensifies it to fulfill certain purposes.

The Means of Our Ability To Fly

175 ℭ Through this means we are able to lift the physical body off the surface of the Earth, as the pull of the inner gravity becomes stronger than that of the outer world. This is simply done through the adjustment of awareness of the Śiva darshan coupled with several of these winds within the body. Our body in the Second World is made up primarily of these five great winds plus the life force itself which enables us to fly through the inner atmosphere when not in the physical body. This power will exist in some through the Kali Yuga.

Lord Subramaniam has given forth great knowledge from His libraries within the inner ether of the mind to aid in the refinement of the physical form so that occasionally Self will be realized on the planet now and again through the Kali Yuga.

Knowledge of sound formed a singular science in those early days. It was known then what has been forgotten now, that everything has a sound, that even emotions create sounds that are "heard" by others. All through the Dvapara Yuga, devas of the inner worlds served and helped the inhabitants of this planet through birds. If one were ill, he could go into the forest and by concentrating and riding awareness in on the tones of singing birds, the physical body would be healed. Meditation was performed for practical reasons, not only for Self Realization, which was of utmost importance. Meditation drew one closer to the satguru's mind and invoked the help of beings behind the veil between the two worlds. Meditation was pursued for healing, arts, culture and myriad other sciences of that day. Aum.

Now we are led to understand
the origin of today's Sivacharyas
and how they have come into power
as Siva's ordained priesthood. We
also learn here of sound's potency,
of the sacred order of magic-makers,
of the sapta rishis and the many
great souls who existed and still
exist as great intelligences, lords
of karma, makers of the future,
Gods of destiny consciously guiding
the evolution of mankind.

Gurudeva

176 ℂ It was through the Dvāpara Yuga that we began to learn to live on the planet quietly and productively, following closely the principles given to us by the first race of Lemurians and their predecessors to avoid catastrophe. We live in small groups. Each is totally self-contained. No one travels much from one group to the other, and these herds of people stay together, following closely also the pattern of the animal kingdom. Keeping the physical body active and alive was one of the major concerns. The prophets with advanced knowledge about the Kali Yuga warned that this complacent contentment would change later on in that *yuga*, and vast groups of people would live together in their own kind of jungles. But now, if one is ill he can go into the forest, and the sound of a bird concentrated through one or more of the winds of his body will heal him. As the light of the sun can be halted by a single leaf on a tree, the sound of a bird can penetrate to the Second and into the Third World if it carries man's awareness with it.

The Sacred Science of Sound

177 ℂ The *devas* work and serve and help us through birds all during this *yuga*, especially when the Second World formed in greater and greater intensity. We relate to the animal kingdom and *devonic* world through sound as an everyday thing. The knowledge of sound is one of our sciences, and our writings are astute and thorough. Here now is a quote: "Placing awareness into different currents of the body produces sound. This sound is inaudible but allows others to feel how you are faring. If someone is angry, their awareness is going through certain currents within them, and it is felt by others. It is noisy. Sound currents from the soul have a darshan that can be felt hundreds of miles away even stronger than in their immediate vicinity. One can hear darshan with his inner ear. If one is able to hear the sound of darshan hundreds of miles away, he totally hears that sound with his inner ear. But if he is in the same area where the strong darshan is coming from, he might also hear the other sounds of that area, and the darshan would not be heard as strongly with his inner ear, as his outer ears are also active. Therefore, the darshan would not be felt as strongly. A guru gives off his darshan as a certain sound. Therefore, people can feel his darshan like a direct beam, for only one sound radiates out all over. Each guru has his own combination of tones, so their darshan can be

distinguished one from another. Being in complete harmony with the guru means hearing his darshan, being in tune with the power of his darshan through which knowledge and unfoldment are given and the individual is naturally stabilized."

The Four Monastery Groups

178 ℂ With this basic principle our carriers of the darshan worked and served in the small communities when they left the monastery. The monasteries were arranged exactly as a physical body. Each group within it represented a wind of the body; the guru himself, the fifth wind, the *ākāśic* wind. The monastics in the Śaivite monasteries of the Dravidian era related to each other according to the flow of the wind of the total body of the monastery that they were in. They were naturally closer to those within the flow of the wind they were in, as they came from the same tribe, had the same skills and served systematically and similarly in the same area throughout their lives. Each of the four groups within the Śaivite monasteries were careful not to press upon another group and cause pain and strain within the monastery, thus inhibiting the Śiva darshan which flowed through it out to the surrounding communities.

Unfoldment, A By-Product Of Service

179 ℂ The attitude of the monastics at the end of the Dvāpara Yuga is similar to the attitudes held toward the end of the Tretā Yuga. They entered the monastery to serve their guru and help him fulfill his mission in the great interplanetary plan. Their personal evolution was intensified and procured only because of their selfless, egoless work. The guru's mission was always the same: to establish many positive channels for the Śiva darshan to flow out and stabilize the mind flow in existing communities. This was done through *devonic* souls now inhabiting physical bodies made of meat and bone who were able to channel this darshan through the various mind flows and structures, thus stabilizing each soul on this planet in his quest for Self. Because of this, culture flourishes and new patterns are able to be set at the end of each *yuga* as guidelines for the next.

Refining The Physical Form

180 ℂ To make ready to enter the Śaivite monastery, these *devonic* souls worked diligently to refine their external physical structure so that they, as the internal inhabitants of it, could escape from it while it slept. The monas-

tery duplicated a form within an area of the newly formed Second World, which formed an area comparable in vibration, structure and action to that of the Third World. It was through this new area of the Second World, which existed in and around and through each monastery, that communication to the Third World was able to continue. Only when they had actually accomplished this refining process of the external form were they admitted into the monastery.

The attitude of the monastics at the end of the Dvāpara Yuga is similar to the attitudes held toward the end of the Tretā Yuga. They entered the monastery to serve their guru and help him fulfill his mission in the great interplanetary plan.

The Yoga of Being a Pure Channel

181 ℂ All of these monastics related one to another as divine beings did during the Sat Yuga. The only seniority was that of monastic age, and physical age being respected and appreciated in wisdom. Each potential *sādhaka* worked diligently with himself to be sure his motivation for entering a monastery was truly that of the old Lemurian monastics in the Tretā Yuga, for he knew that divine unfoldment into the Third World, knowledge and the final realization of Self would reward his having performed his *devonic* mission, and that only agony and mental remorse would accrue if indeed his motivation and refinement was not astute enough to be selfless enough to carry the force of darshan. For the monastics fear the rays of Śiva darshan, for this same force through the refined soul can heal and bless himself and others; but when animal motivations accrue and are not dismissed, that same force flowing through the bone marrow of his five winds will cut and heat and distress the nerve system. So, he guards himself well by seeking his area of service within the monastery, outside its walls or a respectful distance away, according to the nature of the animal instincts he has accrued and exhibits in his personal life and behavior, which, according to our practices at this time, must be dismissed through each one's building within himself a *devonic* channel strong enough to occasionally pierce into the Third World. This yoking the three worlds together was performed by a system of skillful practices, both physical and mental, which will develop into great schools through the Kali Yuga, when our monasteries performing the functions that they are today will no longer exist.

Seeking Oneness with The Guru

182 ℂ Our gurus of this time set the pattern for each monastery, and each monastic carefully works out this pattern through all of its intricacies. Each one, therefore, works to weave his awareness into the same area that his

guru is in so that each area of the divine pattern—of yoking the three worlds together at specific areas on the Earth and building within the Second World a counterpart of the Third, thus channeling the Śiva darshan through and out to dispel, break up and destroy the darkness and confusions that are beginning to well up as the Kali Yuga approaches in all of its imposing dimness—is accomplished. So, each monastic in each monastery that a guru owns works intricately to weave his awareness with that of his guru, so that each pattern within the conglomerate of patterns grows simultaneously one with another. These patterns have been told to a guru by his guru, who educated his guru's guru in the intricacies of the mission. The Dravidian Śaivite monastics are but the helpers. Their rewards accrue as the pattern becomes fulfilled.

Law One: Obedience to The Guru

183 ℂ These Śaivite monastics are beings of momentum, having prepared themselves in the skills of refinement before entering the monastery. They full well know the impending problems of souls on this planet during the next *yuga.* They are inspiration itself, and their untiring loyalties to each of our many gurus are renewed each day by their service and responses to the direction given to them. They adhere to one vow over all others: the obedience to the guru.

Feared and loved,

extreme in their actions—such were the remarkable gurus of those days who held Truth in the palm of their hand. They were magicians, mendicants and monarchs. Some were seen dancing in wild enstasy. Others wove intricate carpets by hand, then patiently unraveled them until only piles of yarn remained. A few consciously froze their bodies in remote, glacial mountain caves, while others became lawmakers and kings, immersed in the world yet fully detached from it. These masters of the karmas on this planet and lords of dharma on all planets where human types of evolution reside met privately and unobtrusively by regular telepathic communication. At auspicious times they gathered in secret conclave in the inner worlds to guide humanity on the right path. Aum.

Orders of remarkable souls, called rishis, walked the Earth in those days, knowers of the unknowable who held truth in the palm of their hand. Their behavior was not always understandable, so full of magic and divine capacity were they. Their purpose was to assist in the evolution of souls on this planet, which they did incarnation after incarnation. They met in council regularly in the Second World.

Sundera

184 ℂ Not all the gurus owned monasteries. There were others that banded together to perform a different kind of function. This is told of in our great *ākāśic* volumes but briefly. But in some small pamphlets there is elucidation of a secret order that not even inner plane beings were totally aware of except for the fact that each member of this order is known to one another. These small but skillfully written pamphlets carefully stored in the *ākāśa* explain the activities of many of the gurus who had many vast monasteries during the Tretā Yuga but now serve in a uniquely different way. Each has his own individual powers, *siddhis*, and uses them wisely for the good of all inhabitants on the planet.

Ṛishis in All Walks Of Life

185 ℂ Each was very individualistic. A few took unto themselves one or two disciples only. The others walked alone. They did not group together but spread themselves equally apart over the surface of the planet. Each one, however, behaved and lived in a similar way as every other. They were absolutely unroutined and would move freely through the world, yet they followed a very strict *sannyāsin* code, more strict than any other order. They would be the ones to establish the caste systems, some of the languages or establish some temple Deity. Some of these *ṛishis* were beggars, others kings on the side of the planet that did not disseminate the darshan through monasteries, and still others in the courts of kings as fools. They could be found in all walks of life, this order of sacred gurus, only known by the members included in it who each one actually was. Through their great telepathic powers they met in council most regularly, in an area of the Second World which they owned. Each one is very extreme in his actions. They were a very lonely type, yet were very busy and full of what they were doing. They were either loved, worshiped or feared. Their purpose on the planet, after the dissolving of their monasteries at the end of the Tretā Yuga, has been to set new patterns and innovate systems. Their help comes from the Third World. They will persist through the Kali Yuga, living, dying, living again, moving from body to body, known by many who sense their existence as "the body happens."

Secret Agents Of the Lord Subramaniam

186 ℭ Some would perform magic. Others could materialize a physical body and step out of the Second World, disguised as a monastic in one of the monasteries, harshly chastise one of the members, step behind a pillar and disappear. Another would sit and carve a small statue, then let it stand and make it grow big. Like this, they would do things backwards. There was a psychic game that involved seeing which pegs inserted in a box with holes at the top were longer than others. Instead of playing the game as it was supposed to be done, by breaking off the longer sticks, one of these *ṛishis* would break off all the short ones. Another would teach a lesson, would patiently loom an intricate pattern in a carpet and then as patiently extract each thread until nothing appeared but a pile of used yarn. They will be the ones, some of them, in the Kali Yuga to establish a system of reincarnation which will be orderly and complete. Each group will work in harmony with all the others according to their mentality. Each one worked directly with Lord Subramaniam in setting patterns anew. They are His agents in a human birth. This was an order of the *kuṇḍalinī*, and their secrecy holds the power of it.

Adjustments To Sustain Culture

187 ℭ They never met on the physical plane, for the *kuṇḍalinī* of each of them is so strong that the force would become so great, should they meet in the First World, it would prematurely excite *kuṇḍalinī* power of all in the vicinity. If, to fulfill a certain mission given to them by the Lord, one of these *ṛishis* needed the full force of the power of the entire group, it would come to him as an avalanche, not as the gentle, flowing, sustaining darshan, but as the piercing fire of darshan; and in this way this mystical Śaivite band of *ṛishis* plunder through the hundreds of thousands of years, from one *yuga* to the next, making the necessary changes and innovations masterfully and on time to perpetuate the culture, the life on this planet, to sustain the mission of all beings.

Mankind's Ancient Guides

188 ℭ These were the leaders who brought to this planet these same beings in their etheric bodies eons of time ago. They received their training and did their *sādhana* outside this galaxy to prepare for this tedious mission. These were the ones that knew the nature and quality of each of the four *yugas* and what was involved within them. They were the first ones

to realize that things were changing towards the decline of the Tretā Yuga and problems were coming. This became cherished as secret knowledge, as in the first three *yugas* the souls inhabiting the Earth are basically to be content, and they could never conceive of life and existence being any other way. These *ṛishis* are to lead all deserving beings from this planet in the Sat Śiva Yuga, thus completing their mission.

These were the leaders who brought to this planet these same beings in their etheric bodies eons of time ago. They received their training and did their *sādhana* outside this galaxy to prepare for this tedious mission. These were the ones that knew the nature and quality of each of the four *yugas* and what was involved within them.

Distributing Themselves Globally

189 ℭ Some of them freeze their bodies in deep mountain caves in glacierous areas of the planet and act as a pulsating powerhouse of constant, radiant darshan to fortify their individual darshan in another body that they are inhabiting. Early in this *yuga* they lived high in all the mountainous areas on this planet so that, when the condensation of our atmosphere formed great bodies of water that we could not traverse, they would be well situated to work in and among the inhabitants. In this way they equally divided themselves around the planet. On the other side of the planet, some became kings, some lawmakers and others founders of countries. On this side of the planet, those of them among us see to it in unseen ways that the monasteries persist in the same way they did during the Tretā Yuga.

Innovators, Instigators of Evolution

190 ℭ They assist with the evolutionary pattern of the inhabitants on this planet as parents assist and nurture their children to maturity. They carve the future as casually as one would cut a piece of fruit. Some are quiet on the inside of them, and could hardly be felt, this other pamphlet explains, and others so fiery and full of noise that it is difficult to be in their presence. This great power enables them to throw themselves totally, without reservation, into the fulfillment of their mission. That is why they never failed. They thought nothing of leaving their physical vehicle to decay when they were through with their particular assignment and getting in another somewhere else on the planet to begin the next. When changing times persist, these *ṛishis* give explanation to our Śaivite priesthood in all the various monasteries. They do this in various unseen, overt, subtle and sometimes upsetting ways. We take heed and begin to change our patterns through their instigation. The inhabitants surrounding our monasteries begin changing their patterns.

Effects of The Kuṇḍalinī Force

191 ℂ This then explains the function of the *ṛishi* gurus of our time. They are now performing a great service in our monasteries, for many of the Śaivite monastics have done so well in their *sādhana* and austerities that the *kuṇḍalinī* force is dissolving and causing to disappear the physical bodies, and they are gently leaving the planet, having fulfilled their mission. Due to this same *kuṇḍalinī* force, the instinctive animal impulses are carving deep pits into the minds of the population, and whereas seasonal mating generally occurred, now it is almost daily for some. Our *ṛishi* gurus of this secret order appear to be realizing that few new monastics are qualifying themselves strongly enough to enter our monasteries and that the population of our Śaivite priesthood is beginning to dwindle. Some of these *ṛishis* are even now supervising the closing of large monasteries and guiding the Śaivite monastics into new patterns.

The Closing Of Obsolete Monasteries

192 ℂ When the population of a Śaivite monastery diminishes to the point where the monastics are unable to maintain the vibration of the constant flow of darshan along with their chores, a *ṛishi* comes to guide them into dismantling the monastery. The order, of course, comes from the guru himself. The *ṛishi* usually appears among the monastics themselves and helps implement this order. He stays with the project until the lake is created, forests are planted around it and all of the monastics involved in the project are divided and moved to neighboring monasteries to increase their population.

Future Orders, Temples and Monasteries

193 ℂ Our *śāstric* manuscripts tell us this will continue until there are only a few monasteries left, and then the *ṛishis* will have those Śaivite monastics that are left mate and reproduce themselves, causing a new priesthood that will perpetuate the temples that they will found during the Kali Yuga. It is this priesthood that will carry on the Śaivite tradition through the process of reincarnation into itself through the process of mating and raising families and serving the Deity in the temple as an occupation. It will not be until the end of the Kali Yuga that a new Śaivite order, similar to the Lemurian order of the Tretā Yuga, will appear to fulfill the purpose of holding the vibration and darshan of Lord Śiva strong and steady, during which time a new cul-

ture, a revival of the original culture, will arise among the population that surrounds those monasteries. It will be the time that the last few monasteries became temples under this new priesthood and the first being destroys the body of another being that the Kali Yuga will have begun.

The Ṛishi Mission Is Immutable

194 ℂ And in conclusion, the mission for the order of *ṛishis* was set for these four *yugas*. The pattern has never changed and never will. No one has ever joined it since its original conception, nor will anyone of them depart from the others, it is stated at the end of this little pamphlet.

Many of the Śaivite monastics have done so well in their *sādhana* and austerities that the *kuṇḍalinī* force is dissolving and causing to disappear the physical bodies, and they are gently leaving the planet, having fulfilled their mission.

Mating instincts

and encounters were known to profoundly effect a seeker's journey and were assessed in detail. Brahmacharya, continence, started at the last mating experience. To facilitate healing of the inner bodies, distraught through mating, raja yoga meditation and bhakti yoga were performed. New monastics who were virgins, naishtika, cared for the animals, picked food and prepared prasadam in huge vats. Those who had mated, and perhaps lost their spouse, worked in the fields, as physical tasks softened the process of brahmacharya. Monasteries enshrined Siva Nataraja and other Gods, such as Ganesha. Two kinds of ceremony predominated, one quiet and meditative and the other akin to today's puja rites. Potential monastics were trained in the homes of mature, celibate families. Aum.

Patterns of constant mating arrived, bringing with them the loss of harmony and family. The knowledge of sexual forces and their restraint evolved. A new science called yoga emerged to enhance their abilities and continue their spiritual unfoldment on the path through the Kali Yuga, until the next Sat Siva Yuga blossomed. Patterns were unfolded for those who had mated, as well as for those who never had.

Gurudeva

195 ¶ The monastics of this era followed closely the pattern of the Lemurians in the Tretā Yuga in working within the general activity, never putting forward any bit of their personality, though they sought oneness with whomever they came in contact. They were always conscious, as fine Śaivites, that the great darshan of Śiva, the primal, all-pervading force of this universe and the next, flowed through all and all alike. So, they sought complete annihilation of the ego to be the perfect channel of this darshan.

Guiding From Behind The Scenes

196 ¶ They were always trying to please their guru and the *devas* in the Second World on the inside of their mind by performing all worldly tasks exceedingly well. As Śaivite monastics, they worked strictly behind the scenes of external life, leaving all overt activity to the *brahmachārī* family men who were responsible to disseminate the Śaivite scriptures, conduct philosophical discourses among the elders of the community and train the young prior to entering the monastery. They wrote anonymously and spoke through the holes in the walls, never identifying themselves as author or speaker. They were intent on doing their work and doing it well to prepare the population for the coming of the Kali Yuga, and they knew full well that any kind of personal personality built up would eliminate them from the opportunities to express the Divine and be of service through these trying times as the forces change and the shadows appear on the horizon of another era.

Employing the Wisdom of Celibacy

197 ¶ They were never conscious of physical age so much, as the age of the physical body, as well as monastic age, represented wisdom. As the forces of the Kali Yuga drew closer, the fire of the *kuṇḍalinī* rose stronger, and the homes were difficult to maintain in the harmony and serenity of which they knew nothing else for so long. This is because of the desire to perpetuate mating constantly as the Earth circles the Sun. Though the animal kingdom still mated in season, those in human form do not. This brings into our midst many different types of personalities; and for Śaivite monastic living, the practice of cessation of the mating instincts for those who have mated began to occur. This knowledgeable practice of *brahmacharya* began to come into being as a result of the change of the forces. Each circle of *brahma-*

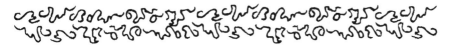

charya was kept careful track of. *Brahmacharya* age began at or near the time of the last mating experience and at the time conscious effort was made to cease the pulsating animal emotional activity of mating and contain within the body what was known as the sacred seed. This seed, when contained, marked circle after circle the vibrating forces of the emotional body of each of these monastics.

Seniority, Wisdom, Humility

198 ℭ Those of great monastic age, physical age and *brahmacharya* age had wisdom that was supreme and was regarded as such by all the monastics. But he does not hold himself out as being better because of these accumulated calculations of years. He works even deeper, "behind the scenes," as a loving parent, helping the younger ones grow in just the right way.

Research into Developing the Astral Body

199 ℭ Great research is now being done by those who never mated and are great in *brahmacharya*, monastic and physical age. These Śaivites are called *brāhmin.* This research is in preparation for the coming Kali Yuga, and we found it to be quite necessary to quiet the animal nerve system before the new body in the Second World began to develop—as the Second World developed around the planet—and could mature unhindered. This constant tearing down, through promiscuous mating, of the Second World body was as if someone were constructing a dwelling and while building one side of it tearing down the other, so that it would never become a total dwelling place of peace, contentment and happiness for the soul.

Quieting The Nerve System

200 ℭ This system being developed is called yoga, and it predominantly is a method for quieting the pulsating forces of the animal nerve system so the body in the Second World can mature and the deeper forces within it, which are called chakras or spinning discs that motivate the body into the Second and into the Third World, are again activated in their fullness. This method prescribes total supplication, dedication and devotion to the personal Deity and to Śiva. Along with the forming of this method, they are making a new language to encompass the laws of it, for the language that we use has little vocabulary to explain the happenings that are occurring now and will be occurring then among the population as they become more instinctive than the animals are. Our prophets say that this time will repeat itself at the end

of the Kali Yuga, when mating will be abundant and the planet will be heavily laden with people, and that this system, called yoga, will gently lead the greater souls out of the morass as heralds of the Sat Śiva Yuga.

Healing by Bhakti and Breathing

201 In the Lemurian times, all going into the inner world and traveling close to the surface of this planet was performed through the night. This new system commands a practice of going within oneself after the devotional mellowing of the forces has been conquered, which is called *bhakti yoga.* It was through sitting straight up with the legs tied in a knot that the slow and tedious practice of inhibiting the breath was performed to feed the body in the Second World and heal it, for in many cases it has been torn apart and damaged through the processes of mating in the First and Second World. Those who mated much performed these practices for many years and did the most physical of service in the Śaivite monasteries before the body of the Second World matured enough to contain itself in the peace and calm of the soul.

Duties of The Mohan Artisans

202 When the inner body of the Second World repaired itself, the *brahmachārī* became *mohan* and was permitted to speak philosophy and, as artisan, train young apprentices in the same way he had been trained. But he would only do this kind of mental training of his apprentices in the philosophy and other inner practices if he had attained the sanction of his guru, for it was important that his awareness flow perfectly with that of his guru's in order to take on and fulfill such a responsibility. And after many years, the *mohan* became as a *brāhmin*, having fully matured, healed, and the living channel of the three worlds. An apprentice only became an artisan if he was moved to another monastery to take over some project there that no one else could handle. But after serving as *mohan* artisan for many years, he moved into the temple to serve Śiva and the Deities and *devas* there.

Duties of The Priestly Brāhmins

203 Our *brāhmins* are always in charge of the Śiva pedestals. Our *mohans* who became *brāhmin* served as helpers at these Śiva pedestals, but are in charge of shrines of other Deities. The young *sādhaka brāhmin*, as soon as he entered the monastery, began helping with the animal population, in preparation of *prasādam* and serving in the temple. It was only after

When the inner body of the Second World repaired itself, the *brahmachārī* became *mohan* and was permitted to speak philosophy and, as artisans, train young apprentices in the same way he had been trained.

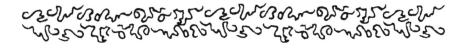

initiation that he was allowed to touch the Deity and serve during all the ceremonies as an apprentice.

Invocation And Worship In Samādhi

204 ¶ Our temples at this time conduct two kinds of ceremony. The first is a precise ceremony calling the Deities and *devas* to assist us in our daily activities, to give knowledge and to steady the flow of Śaivite darshan. Secondly is what is called "worship in *samādhi*," a highly simplified ceremony that was never performed during the periodic days through the circle that the Deities, Lords Śiva, Skanda and Gaṇeśa, penetrated most strongly their darshan through the intricate network we have devised to disseminate it. Worship in *samādhi* was performed when the Deity was quiet, as "Self," and the priest who was conducting the ceremony was experiencing "Self." This was best performed at the time when the darshan was quiescent, hardly felt at all, as quiet water upon a lake. It was during the in-breath of the darshan that the experience "Self" was best felt; and the slow-moving ceremony, performed by the priest in slow motion, continued for great lengths of time. On the in-breath of the darshan, the chanting was performed extremely slowly.

Performing Each Task Perfectly

205 ¶ In developing this new science, yoga, it was found that those who sat straight for meditation could not perform it well and avoided doing so if they were not perfectly obedient as an apprentice and careful and concise with how they handled their physical body and what they were given by their artisan to do. Therefore, even more than was the custom of our culture, the art forms and our work within the monastery became more and more precise, especially for the *brahmachārī*, for it was found that this concentration of energy, performing physical tasks perfectly, intensified *brahmacharya* and healed the body of the Second World more rapidly toward the *mohan* state of being.

Determining Maturation of Brahmacharya

206 ¶ It was the Deity who told us when a *brahmachārī* became a *mohan*, for the body in the Second World was looked over carefully by Him as to its structure, buoyancy, abilities and the comings and goings within the different areas of the Second World, which were carefully observed. Therefore, the perfecting of the skill and being able to convey it to another who worked by the side of the artisan is only the first qualification. For, to be fully accomplished he must be astute philosophically, have a mature body in the Second World and the grace of his guru to convey the deeper skills of philosophy and some of the practices of yoga—that are just now beginning to be tested out in our monasteries—to the apprentices.

Special Skills Form the Hub Of Culture

207 ℭ All Śaivite monastics have always prided themselves on their skills, as did the Lemurians. This was the hub of our culture that monastics are dedicated to preserve. From mental skills to the dissemination of the darshan to the base physical accomplishment, all these are carefully taught our young *brahmachārīs* and *brāhmin* alike. It was to be in the Kali Yuga that these skills would be forgotten, and men would live an entire lifetime within a body performing poorly every action. But now, our skills and power of concentration in acquiring these skills move us powerfully into maturity in the Second World and away from this planet after Self is realized and this physical body is needed no more. Many of our artisans, matured in all worlds, continue their training in the Third World, ordaining new innovations for the population to enjoy. These beings are always easy to recognize, because of their great skill and enthusiasm, ability to train others and produce on the physical plane what they have pulled through from the Third World.

These artisans are always easy to recognize, because of their great skill and enthusiasm, ability to train others and produce on the physical plane what they have pulled through from the Third World.

Duties of Sādhaka Artisans

208 ℭ Sometimes *sādhakas* were artisans and had initiated monastics under them as apprentices. When this occurred, the *sādhaka* did not train any of the monastics in their personal behavior, nor did he give them philosophy, even if he were able and well qualified to do so. Usually it was the artisan who was responsible for the personal behavior and training of his apprentices. But for the *sādhakas*, who were not initiated, there was always a *brāhmin* assigned to help—or a *mohan* who had become *brāhmin*—in these areas of philosophical training and personal behavior.

The Working Together of Three Worlds

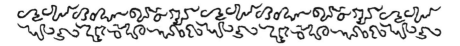

209 ℭ It was due to the flexibility of our culture—guided by the *devas* of the Third and Second World working so closely with us, as if they were also in the First World, and we so closely with them through our days as if we lived in the Second World and not in the First—that the great Lords of the Third World were able to send great shafts of divine light and cosmic rays and new innovations and inspiration with the stabilization of all mankind through these many thousands of Śaivite monasteries, which toward the end of this *yuga* are more and more becoming the only hub of culture which is looked to by the populace as the stability of the race and the tradition.

High stone walls

protected the monasteries. Those who sought admittance sat for long periods there, humbly begging entrance. Expert devonic guards watched over the process, and it was to them that seekers prayed for permission to enter. Monastics passing by on journey to another monastery sat by the wall, facing out, for short periods. They were lovingly served prasadam as they basked in the sunlight and darshan. It is "by the wall" that the destiny of the birth karmas of each was evaluated. The gurus and senior minority group considered well who, why and when one entered. While one was admitted, another was sent here, and another there. All this was preceeded by thoughtful study of their patterns of behavior and accomplishments since entering the first wall as young novitiates. Aum.

Quelling worry about the future, people in these days were well organized and happy, having evolved a sustainable life. This chapter explains how those monks who had mated ate fresh vegetables, which when mixed with oils and herbs healed every illness. Many strict rules governed the massive walls around their monasteries, providing physical as well as psychic protection against intruders.

Gurudeva

210 ℂ *Brahmachārī* family elders of our communities train the young men for *sādhaka* life in our monasteries and come to live with us as *sādhaka* themselves a certain amount of time each year to acquire the strength and direction for the mission of training the young *brāhmins*. These young *brāhmins*, when they entered the monastery, were not required to practice any austerities such as the *brahmachārī* who entered at a later age were given to do. Their greatest austerity was living away from home. Their families were so attached, and the umbilical-like psychic odic tubes connecting the young *brahmin sādhaka* to his mother did not dispel themselves until his full physical maturity of about twenty-four years of age occurred.

How Unique Śaivite Groups Will Form

211 ℂ Our prophets tell us that in the Kali Yuga great austerities will be performed, and the groups that perform them will each centralize on a different aspect of Śaivism. Each aspect will form its own particular group in the Second World to assist those in the First World governing it. The aspects will have different names and sometimes fight with each other. If all of the austerities were the same, everyone would be the same, but the changing forces of the Kali Yuga will not permit this. This *yuga* is ruthless in its way, and the one great austerity will be for us all, our Third World Deity states, to live completely through it and come forth triumphantly into the Sat Śiva Yuga.

Diminishing Psychic Tubes

212 ℂ Though our diet followed closely that of the Lemurian monasteries, the *brahmachārīs* who mated much with many different ones—that ordinarily would not have been entered into the monastery but for the fact that too few were inclined to enter at all—varied their diet from Lemurian *prasādam* to entering spacious gardens of the monastery and picking their herbs and vegetables that grew above the ground and eating them a short time thereafter. It was found that by "pick and eat" the actual life force of the growing plant was taken into the body. This revitalized the physical body and in doing so helped to diminish the pulls of the psychic tubes connecting to each one they had mated with. This revitalization, along with sunshine on the outside of the body, the practice of aloneness and inhibiting the speech, withered away the psychic entanglements that devitalized the physical body and inhibited the Second World body from healing.

Picking and Eating

213 ℭ Each of these different kinds of herbs and the vegetables should be eaten with the time it takes to pick them; dip them in spiced oils, which are carried in a little gourd in one hand, and place them in the mouth, one piece at a time. The posture for picking and eating in this way was that of sitting on one's heels with the knees up underneath the arms, which freed the digestive tract and aided in the intestinal flow. The other position was sitting on the heels and knees. The morsel picked, dipped in spiced oil and placed in the mouth, not too rapidly yet not too slowly, was chewed thoroughly, and a mental effort made to lift the life force of the growing plant up into the head. This form of eating was usually performed just before the setting Sun, after the green morsels and vegetables had absorbed the Sun's rays all through the day. There was usually enough sun left to hit upon the body and open the pores so that the Sun's rays, simultaneous with the life force within the plant, would meet and merge. No nourishment was ever taken when it was too dark to see to move around and do the things that one did when it was light. It was considered quite a treat if one were to pick and eat just after a gentle rain or if it rained gently during that time.

Herbs For Every Ailment

214 ℭ Our spiced oil, in which each morsel was dipped, was flavored with herbs, sometimes hot substances, that invigorated the body. All who practiced this *sādhana* became so in tune with scientific physicians in the Second World that they began to know the exact quantity of the different kinds of herbs and vegetables to be eaten for their ailments or for the continuation of their vibrant health. These *devas* of our gardens were well schooled in assisting the *brahmachārīs* to loosen themselves from psychic entanglements and mental foes, for they were so needed when they became *brāhmin* again in our temples. Many a *sādhaka brahmachārī* is inwardly instructed in dreams by the *devas* as to what to grow in his own circle of nourishment, in the center of which he sits on a small board, with spiced oils in one hand, picking and eating, picking and eating as the Sun's rays penetrate his back or chest and head.

The Wall in The First and Second Worlds

215 ℭ The walls around our monasteries were high and well protected by *devonic* guards in our Second World. It was only through the admittance first into the Second World could someone seeking permanent residency be admitted. Those monastics and newcomers seeking to become monastics sat by the wall, on the outside of it, and were observed as to their comings and goings as they slept at night quite carefully by our inner order of *devas* in the Second World.

Begging Admittance As a Resident

216 ¶ The monastics traveling from one monastery to another often returned to the monastery that they came from at night during their sleep. Until this ceased, they were not allowed in ours. It was only when during their sleeping hours they sought entrance and then were first entered into the Second World with blessings and sanction from the Third that our senior minority group was allowed to take them into the First. We have to be extremely strict in entering new monastics, and some stay by the wall many moons and are seen there chanting, in conversation with the Second World, begging admittance, telling the Second World inner order what they will do for the monastery, how well they will carry the darshan if given the privilege to do it, giving their qualifications and trying to blend their inner force with that of the monastery itself.

Not Begging Entrance

217 ¶ There are two kinds of monastics who sit by the wall: one actually seeking admittance and the others who simply are passing by from one monastery to the other, who stop and rest awhile for taking of nourishment and darshan. They distinguished themselves in two ways. Those begging admittance into the monastery from the Second World governing body of *devas* are seen sitting or standing close to the wall, facing the wall, chanting and mentally talking with the *devas,* asking for help and support in early entry. Those who are just passersby are seen standing or sitting with their back against the wall, facing the countryside, chanting and talking one with another, basking in the sunlight, the darshan and enjoying the *prasādam* that is served at regular intervals. They may sing songs telling of their journeys and the activities of the monastery that they came from and the ones they're going to and courteously and completely ignore those facing the wall.

Conversing With Those By the Wall

218 ¶ Only one member of the senior minority group speaks with them, sees to their needs and is arbitrator between them and the senior minority group and the

There are two kinds of monastics who sit by the wall; one actually seeking admittance and the others who simply are passing by from one monastery to the other, who stop and rest awhile for taking of nourishment and darshan.

Second World *devas*. Other monastics who are permanent residents going and coming from the monastery, who are not in the senior minority group, stop and talk with them, telling them how welcome they are, what a fine monastery it is and how happy they will be. They assure them that they hope the Second World *devas* will allow them entrance through the senior minority group at an early time. When their comings and goings during their sleep are minimal and centralized around the particular monastery they are trying to enter, the Second World *devas*, of course, begin to take them seriously, knowing full well that once they enter they will work with them as they sleep and not escape through sleep from the monastery, bringing back opposing forces from the exterior world and having to go through the harassment of meeting the *devonic* guards of the wall and the severe *tapas* that would have to be imposed to quell this mental and Second World behavior.

The Wall's Fierce Devonic Guards

219 ℂ Our great walls are established as psychic barriers as well. The guards in the Second World torment an intruder many months after his intrusion; and he'd know full well not to enter unbidden again. These guards are strong and fierce, well trained and in the Second World itself; and it is not uncommon that Second World *devas* would allow a *sādhaka* to enter because perhaps he was sent by the guru, but the guards would oppose this as they could see, even though he did not travel at night away from the monastery, his vibration around him and through him did not enhance the vibration of the monastery, but was different from it. So, the guards would be seen growling and objecting to the entrance. The Second World *devas* would be seen standing on the opposite side of the wall facing him, and the *sādhaka* facing them, the wall in-between. They would chant to him, begging him to adjust his atmosphere so that he could enter and the guru's wishes be fulfilled.

Keeping an Arm's Length Apart

220 ℂ Occasionally, more senior monastics would come to the wall, face it and talk through it of deep philosophy and of travels into other galaxies to the *sādhakas* facing the wall, to educate them prior to their entrance as to the current research, function and activity of the inner part of the monastery they were seeking entrance into. When a speech began from a monastery on one side of the wall, many of those on the other side seeking entrance were seen crowding around the niche in the wall to listen. They observed our protocol of never standing closer to one another than a distance of one arm raised by each of them, fingers touching, or two arms' length apart. This kept the shell around the aura touching, and the auras did not intermingle, thus draining force from one to another, inhibiting the divine work each one of us in these monasteries has to do during these trying times when the Kali Yuga is imminent. Its shadows are seen in the distance within the inner mind.

Our great walls are established as psychic barriers as well. The guards in the Second World torment an intruder many months after his intrusion;
and he'd know full well not to enter unbidden again.

Wars in the Second and First World

221 ℂ Our prophets are alive with their factual information as to how the Kali Yuga will cease our travels off this planet into this galaxy and to the next. They tell how this planet will be isolated through the Kali Yuga and that at times within the Second World around it there will be great wars between the people of conflicting forces, and at other times in the First World similar forces will conflict, sending those there into the Second World rapidly, that at times there will be more in the Second World than the First, but toward the end of the *yuga* more in the First World than the Second. And it will only be then that greater souls from other galaxies and this will be able to come to the Second World of this planet, live and help make the adjustments in the Second and in the First World that will be necessary at that time to bring the Sat Śiva Yuga into fulfillment.

Guarding Sacred Sites

222 ℂ Our prophets tell us that long after our monasteries cease to exist, even through the Kali Yuga, our well-trained *devonic* guards will protect the same areas, harassing and tormenting all intruders, and that only through secret mantra codes will former monastics of our time be allowed to enter those areas with no confrontation from the guard of the wall. They further say that all residents of the particular monastery that they are guarding will be allowed to come and go over that area of Earth even at the end of the Kali Yuga without torment or entanglement, mental and emotional frustrations that these powerful Gods, as they will be called in those days, can accomplish in protecting the great darshan flow generated by each of our monasteries and held fast to the Earth through it and hooked into a mountain on the other side.

In all Saivite monasteries, one law presided over all others: the strictest obedience to the guru. Through adhering closely to the word of the guru, and even to the unspoken thoughts projected telepathically to the artisan by the guru, and moving immediately with the direction, the monastics endeavored to capture the power behind the guru's instruction, a power aided by inner plane devas specially commissioned to work with each guru. In this way, the mathavasis, or monastics, were able to work intuitively and effectively in the external mind, fulfilling and communicating any mission bestowed on them with ease. Those who could not capture and work with their guru's power were considered of a beginning nature and performed day-to-day mundane functions until they matured. Aum.

Rains condensed upon Earth at the beginning of the Dvapara yuga to form a large body of water, previously held in the atmosphere, dividing once-connected lands into continents. In the absence of the guru's appointing a successor, the monastery would be dismantled and the monks dispersed. The power within these sanctuaries came from a profound source, obedience to the preceptor, a power that would wane in the Kali yuga.

Gurudeva

223 ℂ Though our planet now is divided by a great mass of matter that has condensed from the atmosphere and now sits turbulently on the Earth, hitting the Earth where it touches, we are told of another culture forming and changing quite rapidly on the other side of the planet and that Śaivism is becoming different according to the nature of these tribes and what they are now facing. Since we are on the side of the planet where most of the strongest Lemurian temples existed, our culture is more similar to the Lemurians than theirs is who live on the other side of the planet.

Reorientation Of a Guru's Monastics

224 ℂ Our gurus, of which there are many, have many monasteries, and when one of them lets his physical body down because he needs it no more, his monastics close their monasteries, take them completely apart and take down the wall, leaving the darshan to hover on the great lake that they installed. All work on this—even the surrounding population of the monastery—and then the monastics move into the monasteries of another guru or gurus, dividing themselves up into small numbers. They seek entrance by their wall. They seek admittance as beginning *sādhakas*, and when they are admitted, they are always beginning *sādhakas* and can never be initiates, even though they may have been initiates in their guru's monastery, because initiation is the seeing of one's guru in his resplendent form while looking at his physical body, and then the knowledge which is the guru enters the disciple. This can, of course, only occur with one's own guru, so in their entering the monastery of another guru, they do so only as servants and take a most humble position to live out their destiny in the physical form. Proportionately, they bring to the monastery some of the *devas* of the inner order, and they become servants to the *devas* there who hover around the presiding guru of that monastery.

The Guru Overseers Of Śaivism

225 ℂ Proportionate to the population, gurus do appear, and proportionate to the number of monasteries one guru is able to manage with his transcendental powers. This is arranged by the band of gurus themselves in the Second World as they govern Śaivism in our land. Our prophets say that in the Kali Yuga, this band of gurus will divide itself into smaller groups, as the Earth will be divided into smaller groups due to this condensation of our atmosphere into solid mass which we cannot cross over.

The Guru's Power

226 ℂ In working within the monastery, one law presided over all others, and that is the strictest obedience to the guru. This was called, "Working with the power of the guru." His direction and the force he gives along with the direction must be captured, and in being captured, the direction is accomplished with ease. Our greatest initiates were those who were able to capture and use the power that accompanied the direction the guru gave. Even the Second World *devas* worked in this way with the guru. Those who could not capture the force and move immediately with their guru were considered simple servants of a beginning nature and performed the day-to-day mundane functions. One who captured the power of any direction given to him and performed it in immediate obedience to fulfill the mission bestowed on him and then after a while ceased to fulfill this function and work with the direction given long after the power had waned was awarded strong *tapas* without explanation from his guru, and he had problems within himself finding his guru; and when he found his guru within himself again, another mission would be bestowed upon him, and if he captured the power of it, his *tapas* would have been ended. It is only in this way that the Śaivite guru works and serves and fulfills his mission, for he and he alone knows the preordained pattern that must be woven by all initiates and *sādhakas* within his monasteries to create a collective force strong enough to send them, as individuals off the planet, when the time is right and their bodies are needed no more, into another galaxy.

Guru's Constant Presence

227 ℂ Our gurus constantly moved from place to place. We never knew when they would arrive or when they would be with us. It is almost impossible to feel should they leave. Therefore, each monastery feels the presiding guru is always there, feeds him daily, and all is in readiness to meet his needs. Often, and more than often, he did not make his presence known except to the senior minority group. But occasionally he would give special instructions to the initiates and *sādhakas* alike, and all activities of the monastery halted to listen, to learn and to receive missions, personal instruction and great blessings, concluded with festivities and celebration.

The Guru's Dynamic Presence

228 ℂ Many of these monasteries are so large that the guru can travel through areas of the monastery and be incognito, as the *sādhakas* had never met him. He

would work with them in milking the animals or sitting by the wall, mingling in and through and among them. If those who knew him saw him doing this, they would not call attention to him in any way, but pretend they also did not know him, for it was known that each guru made himself known to a *sādhaka* or aspirant when his time was right. In one or two of his more senior monasteries, each guru took a prominent position, especially at the monasteries from which the strongest darshan emanated. These monasteries were generally small and more intimate in nature, and their primal function was simply the generating of darshan in disseminating it to all the other monasteries, whereas the other monasteries disseminated the darshan to the population at large.

Our gurus rarely taught except by instruction that was to be carried out in the strictest obedience and immediate spontaneity.

Fulfilling Assignments From the Guru

229 ℂ Our gurus rarely taught except by instruction that was to be carried out in the strictest obedience and immediate spontaneity. The teaching came from the *devonic* world within on the power of the guru that was issued when the instruction, direction or mission was given. It was through this method that we were able to perform many functions in the external mind for the population that surrounds our monasteries, without realizing that we are effectively working within the external area of the mind at all. This we call grasping, owning and working with the power of the guru. Our gurus, basically, only emit this one power to fulfill the mission. It is for us, without putting our personal mental structure in the way of it, to grasp it, to use it and to fulfill the direction of the assignment, for this is why we are in the monastery and this is why the monastery exists at all.

Disobedience Predicted in The Kali Yuga

230 ℂ Our prophets say there will be times in the Kali Yuga when the mind force will be so dense that the guru will give direction and the monastics will not heed either the direction or the power of it, and turn their monasteries into more ordinary places than those of the population which surrounds them; but at the end of the Kali Yuga this will change and be again as it is now, and that our monastics will appear again, as will our guru be obeyed, the power caught and the mission and direction fulfilled in issuing in the Sat Śiva Yuga, and that Śaivism will flourish 'round the world.

Meeting in covert conclave, the senior minority silently governed the flow of activity within each monastery, and when they met in private their very bones became as a chakram through which the Deities and devas would work to polarize that ray of light and love from within known as the darshan. The four divisions of the monastery were taught to function as the four major currents within the body. The north wind took care of all religious activities, holy ceremonies and milking animals. The east wind monastics headed the religious education, both within the monastery and to the elder family men in the community. The south wind monastic was the craftsman, gardener and caretaker. The west wind group handled all business. The senior minority anonymously governed this flow of activity. Aum.

Subtle was the regulation of the group, impersonal and unobtrusive, revolving around the satgurus, who in those days were self-effulgent and in supreme command. They ruled subtly, remaining in the background of their many monasteries, working through one person, the Umaganesha of the senior group. Their governing of the four winds and methods of atonement were unfailing and fair.

Gurudeva

The Senior Minority Group

वरिष्ठाल्प संख्यकवर्गः

Chapter 19

231 ℂ In each of our monasteries, the senior minority group silently governed the flow of all activity and polarized the darshan. Each wind was governed from a distance by one member of the senior group who was other than our guru's assistant in the monastery and his two helpers. Appointed by the most senior member of the group, each of these members who were closest in connection with one of the four divisions inwardly edited the darshan flow of that division, and if it was not correctly handled, the artisan or artisans were called to meet the senior group, sit, meditate and harmonize the vibration. In our smaller monasteries, the senior group took an active part in all the affairs, and if the group was small, perhaps one would be appointed to oversee the inner flow of two of the divisions. It was only in our large, well-established monasteries that the senior group could sit back and totally work within the inner force field of the monastery, because the monastics were so well trained, artisans so efficient that automatically, without effort, each one doing his part, the external and internal activities moved in perfect synchronicity. It was only in these monasteries that the senior group remained the same, with few fluctuations and changes. They are elderly and wise, cautious and strong and converse quite openly with our guru.

The Four Winds of the Monastery

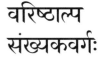

232 ℂ The guru looks at each of his monasteries as he would one person. If there is anyone who stands out apart from the others, it shows a problem is imminent and more training is needed. So, since there are four major currents in our bodies, carried with us fully intact from the planet that we came from, the four divisions are taught to function as these currents do. We relate them to the wind from the east, the wind from the north, the one from the south and the west wind. Our guru, of course, holds council mainly in the *ākāśa*. He is the *ākāśic* wind, along with anyone he might appoint to work with him for a time on specific innovations. Therefore, each of the four members of the senior group is not in charge of the division or wind of the monastery. He simply feels the flow and observes the physical plane activities, keeping himself, of course, incognito, as does everyone in the senior group. It was always considered a break in the flow of transparency to be discovered as a member of the senior minority group, especially by young *sādhakas,* who had to be trained to inwardly approach the *devas*

of our monastery for their help and stabilization rather than personalities within our monasteries.

North, East, West & South Wind Duties

233 It is the north wind Śaivite monastics that take care of all religious activities, special *pūjās* and ceremonies, preparing the *prasādam* and milking the animals. The east wind monastics are in charge of religious education within the monastery itself and provide a continuing education for the elder family men in the community. It is the west wind monastic group that handles all business in relationship to the surrounding community in the acquisition of goods as well as the disbursement of them, and the south wind monastic is the artisan, the craftsman, the builder. He produces all that is to be produced to sustain our culture.

The Duties Of the Senior Group

234 Each monastery enacted the divine play. The guru, Śiva Himself, dancing through the *ākāśa*, speaking only with the most senior of the monastery, His divine son of wisdom, Umāgaṇeśa. The Umāgaṇeśa has two helpers. One is Śiva's servant, Hanumān, whose great mission is to bring souls to Śiva. He is the host of new guests, the overseer of the wall. He addresses the entire monastery and voices the guru's words whenever necessary. The least senior, the Umādeva, the carrier of messages, was often seen during a gathering of the senior minority group of the monastery, running out, finding and bringing someone to sit with the group, an artisan perhaps, a newcomer who had been living by the wall. He was always at the right hand of Umāgaṇeśa; and, in the circle, the *deva* sitting next to him was his assistant, too, as was the one sitting next to the Hanumān the assistant Hanumān. Their assistants shared some of the responsibility, especially if the monastery was new, for at this time the senior minority group assumed an administrative function, as the core of the new monastery was made up of members of the senior group of another monastery or monasteries, and they knew all that had to be done in building a new, strong, fine Śaivite monastery. As the training persisted and as fine artisans were brought in and the winds all became strong in their function, this group retreated more and more within the inner core—having to authorize less and less innovations of new growth—and concerned themselves mainly with the comings and goings of *sādhakas* and guests.

The Great Calendar Of Activities 235 ℂ The Umāgaṇeśa efficiently reported all that occurred to Śiva, his guru, each time they met, and kept close followup on all important events, activities, monastic discipline in the great calendar log of the monastery. According to the formula by which the senior minority group was chosen, if a new member entered into the vibration of Umāgaṇeśa, this calendar of our future was passed over to him, losing no continuity of the most minute of events.

The guru looks at each of his monasteries as he would one person. If there is anyone who stands out apart from the others, it shows a problem is imminent and more training is needed.

Gatherings Of the Senior Group 236 ℂ Each time the seniority minority group gathered, it gathered secretly, and all were present at this holy event if they were within the monastery walls. Occasionally the inner forces were found to be strained or taut, and the Umāgaṇeśa would hold special vigil; and they all sat together for long periods of time in prayer and meditation in an area apart from everyone else. Occasionally Śaivite gurus would ask that the senior minority groups in all monasteries hold vigils together for long periods of time, in prayer and meditation in an area apart from everyone else. Occasionally Śaivite gurus would ask that the senior minority groups in all monasteries hold vigils together in silent inner workings with the forces to cause fusion of these forces, thus strengthening the darshan flow in his chain of monasteries which he worked with himself quite regularly by traveling from one to another.

Cleaning Is "Āśrama Sādhana" 237 ℂ It was the Hanumān's assistant that sought out the guru, if the guru could not be found, to handle important issues. He arranged meetings with the guru, and the Umāgaṇeśa and saw to all the guru's needs, when arriving in the monastery, during his stay and upon his departure. During this time, he was relieved of all of his other duties. It was the assistant to the Umādeva who was in charge of the great *sādhana* of our monastery, that of cleanliness and beauty. This *āśrama sādhana* brings contentment and life to the doer as well as the viewer of beauty, an intrinsic part of our culture. By keeping our monasteries in absolute order, a physical plane magnetism occurred, drawing others to our walls. If no one sat by our walls or came up to them to be lectured to through the holes in the walls, if our crops failed and the abundance of our needs did not enter our storerooms, we always worked diligently to increase the magnetism through the perfection of our culture, bringing love, harmony, cleanliness and beauty into each minute area.

Those on Tapas Are Six Years Old

238 ℭ The divine family—Śiva, Umāgaṇeśa and the Hanumān—was not without the other son, Bala Muruga, who was represented in many faces and forms by *devas* wearing yellow on *tapas* of a nature that changed their monastic age to that of six years old. Each one in yellow is treated as a six-year-old, and when the senior minority group was computed by the youngest member of the monastery whom we called the Vadivel, the third son of Śiva, the age of six years old is always taken into consideration. A *sadhāka* in white accumulated his monastic years, but when performing *tapas* of a certain nature he is six years old as well. He, too, could wear the 108 *rudrāksha* beads on *mahā tapas,* and as the yellow *deva* on this *tapas,* he would be taken completely out of the monastery flow as in the *ākāśic* wind, working with his guru. Coming out of *mahā tapas,* he would go through a reentry period in the monastery of living by the wall for a moon, a philosophical test given by the senior minority group, along with a welcoming ceremony entering him into the monastery again.

Customs and Attitudes of Mahā Tapas

239 ℭ When a *deva* is wearing yellow, on *tapas* as Bala Muruga, he assumes the attitudes of youth and joy and happiness, spontaneity. But even though his monastic age is adjusted during this *tapas,* his resident time within the monastery is not, and remains the same. However—on *mahā tapas* in our monasteries when the 108 *rudrāksha* beads of our Lord Śiva are worn—after the reentry ceremony, residency time begins to accumulate as if he has just arrived from another monastery. This only applies, however, if the *mahā tapas* has lasted one full moon or more. During *mahā tapas,* food is given to him where he lives, and he lives alone. He does not speak. He looks within and sits for long periods of time at the foot of the pedestal in our temple. He is ignored by everyone and left alone, by himself with his guru and the Deity, who works silently within him. To begin the *mahā tapas,* a ceremony is conducted before the pedestal under the direction of our guru. The Deity and *devas* are informed that this *tapas* is being commenced. No time is set for the duration of the *tapas.* It is the guru who begins the *tapas* and ends it; and when it is ended, a ceremony is held at the

threshold of the pedestal. Deity and *devas* are informed that the *tapas* is ended.

Special Care of The Youngest Monastic

240 ℭ The youngest member of the entire monastery in physical age and *brahmacharya* age, as well as monastic age, is carefully sought by the Umāgaṇeśa, and constantly reports are given to the guru as to how this Vadivel is faring. He is given favors, gifts, love, care and attention. He is Śiva's third son, represented by the trident. He is the one who is trained to calculate exactly who is a member of the senior minority group each time there is a change in the comings and goings of the monastery population. He is the youngest and most blessed and is always taken care of by the Hanumān's assistant, as well as cared for by him as to his rest, his food and his training.

Vadivel And the Umādeva

241 ℭ A young *deva* would only become a Vadivel—and each monastery has one—after one moon by the wall, philosophical test and entrance ceremony. He's invited to sit with the senior minority group after this only at times when everything is going well within the monastery and the darshan flow is perfect. When he joins the circle, he sits directly opposite the Umāgaṇeśa. When the guru joins the circle, he sits between the Umāgaṇeśa and Umādeva, for the Umādeva helps the guru as well, with his assistant, carrying special messages, and is always at the guru's right hand, when he visits the monastery, to run errands for him.

Not the Head of the Monastery

242 ℭ The senior minority group is able to hold the vibration of the entire monastery because they've lived in it the longest and have been monastics in one monastery or another longer. This group is not the head of our monasteries. Our guru is, and they take a most humble position of obedience under his radiance. Occasionally the worldliness of the externalities and over-involvement in things or people allows one to take the position of heading up the monastery, especially if the guru has many monasteries and his visits are rare. When this is discovered, he is always placed on *tapas* or asked to pilgrimage to another monastery. Thus the gurus of our race and time stand upon the head of the serpents of our ego.

The senior minority group is able to hold the vibration of the entire monastery because they've lived in it the longest and have been monastics in one monastery or another longer. This group is not the head of our monasteries. Our guru is.

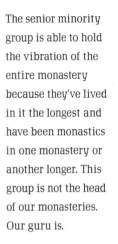

Overseeing Timing and Sublimity

243 ℂ It is the artisans—those highly skilled, trained beings—and the executives of the west wind and north wind monastics and the teachers of the east wind that actually keep the monastery productive. The senior minority group sees to the overall darshan flow, that the timing is right, that the artisans are performing correctly and, through the great calendar log, that not too much occurs at one time and that all major occurrences happen in line with similar occurrences in the Second World and sometimes deep in the Third. Our guru accepted each of us into the monastery through the senior minority group. We are, therefore, all here because of his grace, and when it is time for us to leave this spot, taking down our walls and leveling it all into a lake, he will tell us, and we will do so without question.

Harmonizing Negativity In a Wind

244 ℂ The senior minority group is not the head of these Śaivite monasteries. They carry out the edicts of our guru. They are the receptacle of the vibration. All positive power is channeled through them, and negativity, too. They read it through their nerve system. They determine which wind a negativity might be coming from and call in an artisan or executive, *brāhmin* or *mohan* or *swāmī* so that he can report as to the problem he is experiencing. The forces within him are harmonized by sitting with the group. If his problem cannot be solved through the *śāstric* rules governing the monastery, the solution is sought for through the Umāgaṇeśa to the guru himself, for it was important that the Umāgaṇeśa keep in constant contact with his guru. Most of the time he was the only one in the entire monastery, including the senior minority group, who knew where his guru was.

The Guru's Secrecy and Immediacy

245 ℂ The whereabouts of the gurus of our time were always kept in the strictest secrecy. They were the ones who traveled alone. No one knew when they left or when they came or at which monastery they would be next. Through this strict secrecy of the guru's whereabouts, his life in his physical body was preserved into great longevity. All Śaivite monastics were taught to look within themselves for their guru and to always feel him living in the monastery where they were. They were always discouraged in looking for the guru as a physical person outside of themselves. And, so, he is always discussed among them as be-

ing a part of their monastery, living in their monastery, and never discussed or thought of traveling from one monastery to another. This is strictly adhered to, as all monastics are trained to think within the monastery walls, not outside of them. Only in this way can the work of the alignment of the three worlds be consistently performed. The gurus, however, within themselves, carried each monastery constantly within them as one person, and within their minds they lived in each one simultaneously through this method.

The senior minority group is not the head of these Śaivite monasteries. They carry out the edicts of our guru. They are the receptacle of the vibration. All positive power is channeled through them, and negativity, too.

The Guru's Unified Perspective

246 ℂ Therefore, there was no individual head other than the guru, who is absolute head of many monasteries, constantly in touch with one Umāgaṇeśa. Though he may be speaking with one Umāgaṇeśa in the form of one monastic in each monastery, to him it is only one Umāgaṇeśa, one Vadivel, one Hanumān, one Umādeva and one senior minority group, one artisan, one executive, one *brāhmin,* one *mohan,* one swāmī, one darshan; and he holds this within him wherever he is. This is the secret of the gurus of our era and one of the main ways in which a guru was able to be head of and administrate forty, fifty, sixty monasteries, allowing the Deity, Lord Skanda, to manifest the culture, teachings and the new innovations in science through the darshan and the monastics from deep within the mind. Lord Śiva governed the great darshan flow through the guru, and often for long periods of time the only one contact a guru had on the physical plane with his monastics was through the one Umāgaṇeśa. Often, in the guru's inner mind, if he had fifty monastics and forty of them were in a perfect flow, the entire forty would represent one person to him, and sometimes the entire fifty. This was the ideal state for a Śaivite guru to manifest for his monasteries.

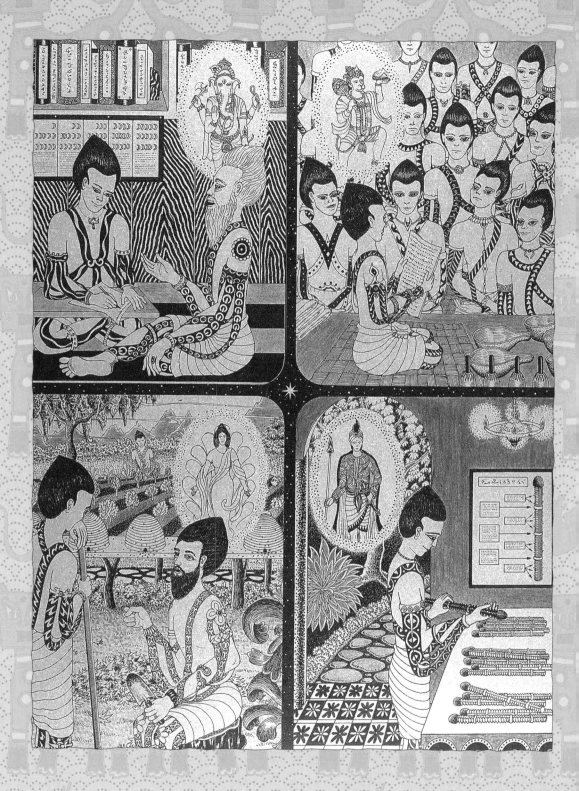

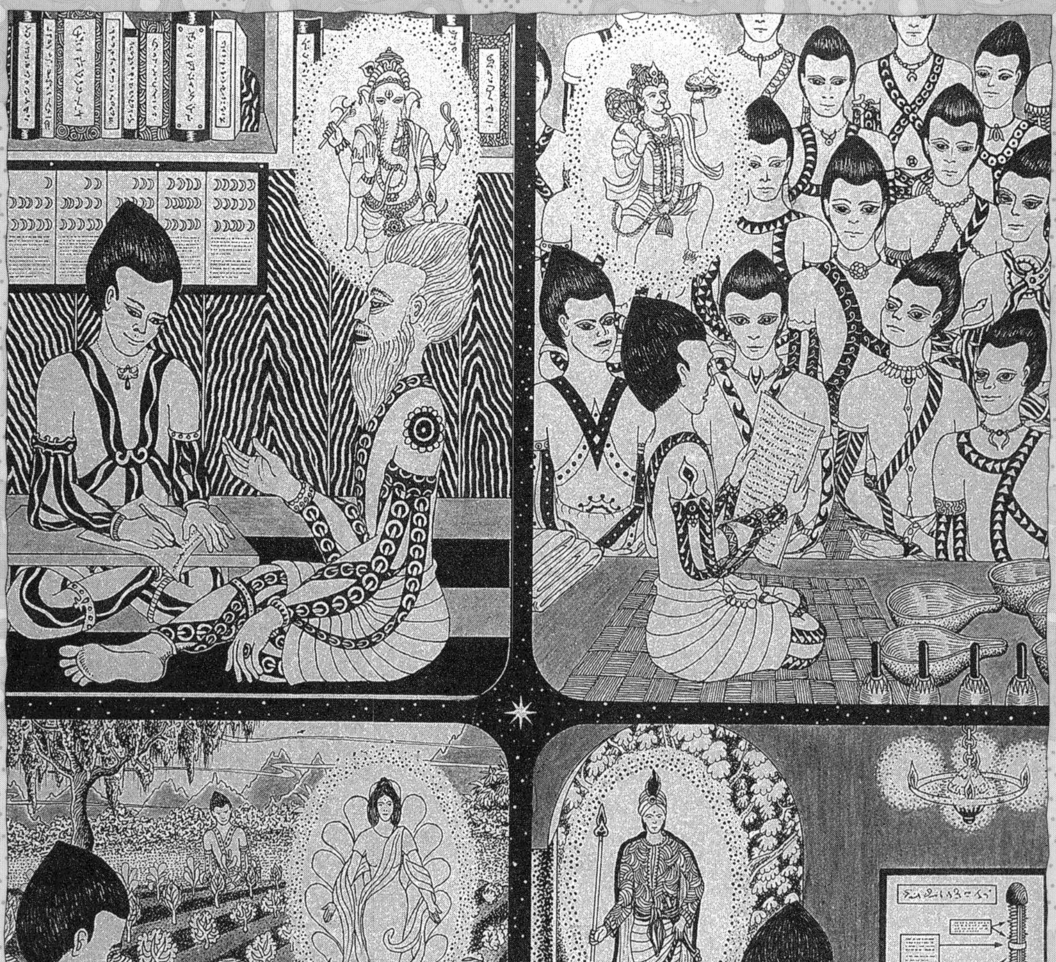

The swamis and mature brahmins, inspired by Lord Ganesha, worked personally with the monks, enlightening them in the philosophies and guiding their writings. Lord Hanuman empowered the senior group member, known himself as the Hanuman, commissioned to speak with groups and the entire monastery. Goddess Sarasvati, Lord of Learning, was ever-present as the Umadeva humbly inquired of artisans regarding the training of their apprentices and how the various divine services were being fulfilled. The youngest within the monastery, the Vadivel, guided by Lord Muruga, worked alone through the night analyzing special wooden sticks the monks carried, determining their seniority in the monastery and their place on the almost invisible governing group called the senior minority. Aum.

Thoughtless and immature were some monastics in those days. Others were advanced enough to guide, and these the gurus worked through. Discipline came from the guru, but the senior group monitored spiritual patterns and helped him resolve worldly challenges. When a monastery was well balanced in energy flows, the community around it enjoyed peaceful solutions to all their problems.

Gurudeva

247 ℂ The senior minority group always kept themselves a little apart from the other members of the monastery and sometimes even lived together in a separate area of the monastery. They kept apart mainly by their attitudes, and this enabled them better to understand how the inner force fields of the monastery were behaving.

Constant Philosophical Discussion

248 ℂ In the larger monasteries, often some of the most senior monastics of the senior minority group would all the time be walking through it, engaging others in philosophical discussion. Philosophical discussion was important in all Śaivite monasteries, as when the harmony of it began to occur between two or more, many *devas* on the inner planes would hover around and send blessings through these Śaivite souls, and often the discussions would be heard by others at great distances through their inner ears. The inner darshan of the *devas*, the Deities and the guru himself would merge as one great darshan flow out through the senior minority group in the totality of the monastery, its population and to those who lived surrounding the monastery. The darshan, as well as the *kammaba*, rested equally and was shared by each member of the senior one-third minority of each monastery.

Sticks Indicating Seniority

249 ℂ Each monastic kept track of his monastic age by placing notches in the stick that he carried with him. His physical age, *brahmacharya* age, and time in our individual monastery would be kept in this way through notching the stick. Each time he entered a new monastery, while sitting by the wall he would prepare a new stick and discard the old one. One could actually tell by the age of his stick whether he had lived in the monastery a long time or not, as he carried it with him all of the time. It represented to him the ray of the light he traveled on while coming to this planet, and he was always seen with it in his hands, meditating on this ray of light which emanated back into the Central Sun. Occasionally monastics would dance and clap their sticks together.

Vadivel Calculates The OTM

250 ℂ Whenever there was a change within the monastery's population, someone came or left, each monastic would leave his stick, together with all the others at a certain place, so that the Vadivel could separate them through analyzing the monastic age and duration of his time within the monastery walls to find the one-third minority of them all. This often took

the Vadivel far into the night, preparing the next senior minority group, and in the morning each one would choose his stick again and carry this wand away, knowing full well whether he was to polarize the darshan or not.

Formula of Residency & Monastic Age

251 ℭ All kinds of activity that would lift the ego in the Vadivel were given to him, for the ego comes from the animal nerve system, whereas nothing would be given to the rest of the monastery that would lift the ego in any way. It was subdued but not suppressed. And so, it was the Vadivel that calculated the senior minority group, chose the Umāgaṇeśa, the Hanumān, the Umādeva, each time the comings and goings within the monastery and *devasthānam* occurred. He used a simple formula to calculate and determine who they were. He would first determine how many were living within the monastery and *devasthānam* and then subtract one third of that number. That would tell him how many sticks represented the resident seniority in the monastery. His next calculation would be to choose one half of this remaining group, and this would be determined by monastic age. The most senior in monastic age would be the half that represented the senior minority group. If there was a tie between two members, the *brahmacharya* age would be looked at. The most senior would be chosen. If there was a tie here as well, the physical age would be looked at, and the oldest would be chosen. Occasionally, but not too often, the Vadivel made an error in his calculations. If it was discovered, it was always overlooked as divine providence of the trident.

Residency Determines Duties

252 ℭ The Umāgaṇeśa is chosen through the arrangement of the circle. The seating occurs because of the resident age within the monastery itself. The oldest resident is the Umāgaṇeśa, the youngest, the Umādeva. The one on the left of the Umāgaṇeśa is the second in residency. If there were a tie in the Umāgaṇeśa or any one of this group, then the monastic age would settle the question. The most senior would take precedence. If this also tied, then *brahmacharya* years and physical years were consulted.

Applying Tapas Instead Of Discipline

253 ℭ The senior minority group never disciplined anyone, though they did correct to try to bring each one into line with the *śāstras* that governed our cul-

ture. If someone was out of harmony within the monastery, he was out of harmony with his guru, and it was recommended through the Umāgaṇeśa to the guru that one kind or another of *tapas* be given to him. *Tapas* and discipline always came from the guru. The senior group always approached the entire population in the monastery from the perspective that each one arrived on this planet in a perfect state, and if anything was askew with anyone it was because of some external thing that came to him from this planet. It was not inherent in themselves, but simply had to be dealt with. And so, if problems occurred, they would recommend certain prescribed kinds of *tapas* as remedies, and if the guru acquiesced, *tapas* was given and the matter righted itself.

If someone was out of harmony within the monastery, he was out of harmony with his guru, and it was recommended through the Umāgaṇeśa to the guru that one kind or another of *tapas* be given to him. *Tapas* and discipline always came from the guru.

Three Kinds Of Dravidian Tapas

254 ¶ Three of the basic kinds of *tapas* given are called Dravidian *tapas*. Sitting alone by oneself for long periods of time, breathing and waiting while the *devas* in the Second World heal and harmonize the forces was one. Another was walking for long periods of time alone, with the *devas* in the Second World running along beside him, breathing and refraining from thinking but simply feeling the forces of the body. And the other was called, "the quest for the guru." A monastic would be sent away from the monastery to find and travel with his guru. The gurus of our time worked with this *tapas*, trying to always avoid them, hide from them, until such a time they let themselves be found. Then he would travel for a time with his guru and be left alone at one of the monasteries.

Senior Minority Meetings

255 ¶ Every member of each senior group were all of one area of the mind. They would rarely discuss anything, just look at each other, know and nod. Each individual spokesman of the winds would just speak out. The Umāgaṇeśa, in a quiet, humble way, would guide the meeting along, and when they met, everything was there—the darshan was there, the problems were there, the Deity was there, the *devas* were there, the guru was there. They were amazingly of one mind. When *tapas* was given, it was always given by the guru and ended by him, either in person, but more often through one of the spokesmen of the senior minority group. He instructed the Umāgaṇeśa; the Umāgaṇeśa always conveyed the guru's instructions to the entire group and then, either privately or in the group, told the Umādeva, and the Hanumān, how the guru wished his instructions to be carried out. And so we see that the Umāgaṇeśa, in his wisdom and compassion, was the spokesman of the guru and nothing more.

Routine, Simple and Easy-Going

256 ℂ In large monasteries the senior minority met regularly, at least four or five times each moon. In small monasteries they would have to meet for long periods each day. Sometimes twice a day. Meetings were always scheduled by the Umāgaṇeśa under the instruction of the guru, who would set the pattern for the formula each monastery was to function under. All monastic problems were handled by the *devas* or the guru, and it was only those who performed good *sādhana* by the walls who were allowed to enter the monastery. And so, the daily routine was easy-going, simple, yet lively, with a lot of force for the fulfillment of the mission, but no real complications or congested forces ever occurred, because of the immediate residency, and everyone had enough time for everything. The senior group never made decisions on previous flows or routines that had been established or tried to alter them in any way. Each one was so highly trained, this was not necessary. In the larger monasteries they just gave approval or disapproval to the timing of events and looked after how these events were being handled, especially if they were ones that did not occur too often.

The Main Duties of the Hanumān

257 ℂ It was the Hanumān and his assistant who coordinated—from the core of the monastery out way beyond the wall into the *devasthānam*—all of the activities and events of various and varied natures, especially those that were not in the total direction of an executive, artisan, *brāhmin*, *mohan* or *swāmī*, and he would fill in for anyone of them to see to the smooth flow of their duties if they were transferred from one monastery to another. He performed his work in an unseen way. No one knew who the Hanumān was, and sometimes, in an important event, the Hanumān would form a committee of other members, and there would be under his direction four or five Hanumāns within the monastery, handling the event.

Hanumān's Flow of Information

258 ℂ Those within the *devasthānam* seeking entrance were closely watched by the Hanumān, and their needs were always met in unseen ways. Occa-

sionally he would work with the Umādeva, and groups would be spoken to and individuals simultaneously—after the group meeting—in this way. But, of course, they never initiated anything. His instructions came from the Umāgaṇeśa, who in his wisdom, received his instructions from the *śāstras* and our guru.

Speaking Out, but not Being Known

259 ℂ In a large Śaivite monastery, *mohans* of the east wind would speak to the entire monastery occasionally and talk of monastic life and occurrences and activities within other monasteries. *Swāmīs* of the east wind would speak of the philosophy, as well as mature *brāhmins*. The Hanumān would also speak, as well as the artisans would address their apprentices as well as others. In monasteries such as these, it was not difficult to speak, as well as not be known. And in these large monasteries, no one knew or cared actually who was in the senior group. The activity and attention was placed elsewhere.

Adjustment Of OTM Members

260 ℂ Our Śaivite gurus could change, for reasons of their own, different members of the senior minority group by simply moving a few new *sādhakas* into the monastery, taking out a few or putting someone into *mahā tapas* or reducing, because of another type of *tapas*, monastic age to six-years old. In this way they could balance the forces if the senior group or any member of it were becoming out of harmony with the responsibility of polarizing so much of the darshan or for any other reason. These were such humble souls and inwardly expressive, that their gatherings were inspirational to each and every one of them. On rare occasions when they met, the many within the monastery would feel the vibration and sit and meditate. To eliminate more of the animal nature in this great priesthood, many kinds of different names were given, names with and without meaning to the individuals, and these names would be changed occasionally, especially during the time they lived by the wall.

Training Young Monastics

261 ℂ The senior minority group was primarily concerned with the training of the monastics, and through the great calendar log at regular intervals, the Umādeva would be sent on tour through the monastery to inquire from the artisan and the new monastic himself as to how his training was being attended to, making his own observations as well. He would al-

The daily routine was easy-going, simple, yet lively, with a lot of force for the fulfillment of the mission, but no real complications or congested forces ever occurred, because of the immediate residency, and everyone had enough time for everything.

ways do this incognito, of course, and in a very humble, quiet way. If the training was not properly being done, the artisan or executive would be called to meet with the senior minority group to seek solutions to the problem. They knew that the first three moons after entering the monastery were the most important for a new monastic, and if he was tended well during that time, everything would go well with him from that time. The Umādeva or his assistant hovered close to new monastics for their first three moons, sometimes giving daily reports as to their proper orientation. However, no training or concern was given to anyone within the *devasthānam* seeking entrance into the monastery.

Orienting Monastic Newcomers

262 ℂ Regularly, the Hanuman or his assistant would speak to the entire group, as would others who spoke to groups. Most of the monastic orientation has already been given to those who entered the *devasthānam* from the family they had been living with, studying, learning and preparing themselves with. It was felt that a newcomer into the monastery may be a guru or a God in disguise. The gurus of our time were often traveling around, entering the monasteries of other gurus as new monastics. They did this in order to allow themselves time to work inwardly and to help the guru whose monastery they entered, as all of these gurus gathered together in inner conclave in the Second World to plan their strategy.

Among the Broader Community

263 ℂ Senior minority groups in the monasteries faced other kinds of problems as well. Acquisition of land, building of buildings all had to be taken care of without upsetting or disturbing the darshan flow. Many tribes were forming at this time, and it was necessary to send *swāmīs* into these tribal areas to teach the most outstanding leaders, so that they could pass it on to those about them. Other problems, too, such as negotiation for water, seeing to the flow of food and gold—which was very important and helped to hold the vibration of the darshan in the temple—existed. They also had to prove themselves to the tribal community, that they could maintain the monastery in good order so that the community would come, sit by the wall and listen to the dissertations of teaching through the holes in it.

Forming A New Monastery

264 ℂWhen these monasteries were formed, it was the most senior one third of the senior minority group of each of the guru's monasteries that would become the new residents of the new one. This might occur every three or four years. This selection of monastics would give all of the power necessary to form a new monastery, because they took with them some of the power from all of the other monasteries. The guru may work within the new monastery, or never enter it until it's well established, but work with them from a distance. Also, their most senior monastics knew how to prove themselves to the surrounding community for the first three or four years, as well as bring in new *sādhakas* into the monastery. In four years, when the monastery was well founded and artisans had been brought from other monasteries, these senior members would begin to leave, allowing the growth to come from those who had been entered into the monastery during that time.

Many tribes were forming at this time, and it was necessary to send swāmīs into these tribal areas to teach the most outstanding leaders, so that they could pass it on to those about them.

Prudence was the hallmark of each member of the monastery's senior minority, striving to be perfect in his personal life, behavior, craft or area of service. Perfection was that which can be carried into the inner world for a lengthy stay. Elders realized this more than the others, for they conclaved in deep togetherness, supervising every artisan's training of his apprentices and observing closely the results. Correction was freely given and deemed necessary even by those who received it. Yet, the attitude that nothing was amiss always preceded all others. While others were trainees, seniors were the monastery itself, wisely watching from afar as artisans made corrections. They had a responsibility to become, remain and thereafter be the perfect examples of the guiding shastras. Aum.

Unremitting training was highly valued in the monasteries, all toward protecting and strengthening the darshan, which encompassed the sight, the feelings which sight produced and the divine energies thus transmitted. New monasteries were carefully begun, with senior members from established monasteries helping. Always the senior group monitored the energies without correction.

Gurudeva

265 ℂ Occasionally a group of devoted *brahmachārī* men would gather together and obtain the blessings from their guru to live the *śāstras* and form a *sādhaka* monastery. Their guru would occasionally visit, encourage and instruct. He took this as his personal responsibility and worked with it until it was well established. This is the second of the two ways a Śaivite monastery could be begun. As the Śaivite *śāstras* contain all the controls necessary so that each aspect of monastic living was performed correctly, in adherence to the definite pattern, and our tradition and culture blended easily into this, it was not complicated for a group of sincere souls to begin a Śaivite monastery as *sādhakas* in white.

Senior Monks Entering New Monasteries

266 ℂ When a *sādhaka* monastery became fairly well adjusted to the intricacies of the Śaivite *śāstras*, their guru might send a delegation from the senior minority group of several of the surrounding monasteries to live by their wall, seek entrance, blend into and later help and serve in the new *sādhaka* monastery. Because of their monastic years, each one in this delegation would soon be in the senior minority group, thus effecting a balance of force. The number sent from each monastery would depend upon the number of *sādhakas* within the new one. It may be one monastic from each senior minority group, two or more, but rarely if ever exceeding more than one third of the count within the *sādhaka* monastery. Often their guru would go and live with this sincere group of *sādhakas* and personally help them with every phase. And while he was there he would assist his senior monastics from other monasteries with their entrance through the wall, who would later represent him in the senior minority group when he left.

Routines And Divine Innovations

267 ℂ As the monastery flow was handled according to specific routine—which when learned was always performed in approximately the same way, for no new innovations were entered into it unless they came directly from our Deity or the guru himself—the gurus of our time never discussed anything with anyone, except possibly the Deity. Their dictates were activated as carefully and precisely as was possible through each monastery, and the senior minority group was held responsible to this by the guru, the Deity and *devas* in the Second and the Third World. So, it was because of this that a new monastery was easy to form. In the beginning of the formation of a new *sādhaka* monastery, the guru himself would talk personally with each *sādhaka*, adjusting and explaining the attitudes that he was to hold, but as soon as the senior minority group became stable and strong, he would speak to the monastics through his Umāgaṇeśa, who would in turn employ the services of the Hanumān and Umādeva to disseminate his word.

Training in Precision for Sublimity

268 ℂ The senior minority groups were very careful that each member of the monastery was well trained and that each innovation their guru made was carried straight through in full, immediate cooperation from each member of the monastery. And when each one was expertly trained in his duty and chore, it was a rare occurrence that this did not happen. The senior minority group would use hours in explaining and training new monastics, as well as supervising artisans and executives in their procedures of training and observing closely the results obtained. For they well knew that the well-trained intellect did not inhibit the darshan flow and that when each monastic was well trained it would last within him, develop within him, year after year and flow through his life in the monastery he was trained in or he would enhance any monastery he pilgrimaged to. Once trained, he was never trained again, and after approximately fourteen monastic years had passed, he settled down to a precise routine, always remembering that the dissemination of the darshan as a pure channel was his major chore.

Preparing for Impending Darkness

269 ℂ We are all aware at this time that the darkness of the mind is nearing and about to encompass the population of this planet through the Kali Yuga, and how important it is to preserve our message and our culture for as long as possible and impose these notes into the *ākāśic* ether to be read at a later time when the darkness begins to wane. It was because of this that, at every opportunity, our gurus founded new monasteries, and *sādhaka* groups gathered, upon their own motivations, to assist them in their work.

Assistance For Personal Difficulties

270 ℂ When a Śaivite monastic had a problem within his mind, or a misunderstanding while he adjusted to his training occurred, his artisan or executive, along with all of the other apprentices, would go within the temple, and

before our Deity a ceremony would occur to lift the vibration of darkness that surrounded him into one of light. If anyone other than our gurus ever lectured to correct it or disciplined some one of us, it was always done in private through the artisan or the executive, if they were qualified to correct, or through the Umādeva or the Hanumān.

The senior minority groups were very careful that each member of the monastery was well trained and that each innovation their guru made was carried straight through in full, immediate cooperation from each member of the monastery.

Our Innate Perfection

271 ℂ No discipline or correction ever came in the presence of the senior minority group toward any monastic. Interviews of this nature were always privately held and in secrecy. This was to avoid too much thought force by the entire group upon a single monastic; and if he were out of harmony with his guru, *tapas* was simply given to him to make a part of his life and correct the situation. The attitude of arriving back to our original state and that nothing was actually amiss always preceded all others, for we were perfect when we arrived on this planet to evolve. Most of our difficulties are because of the nature of the external nerve system and the motivating forces of these bodies that we currently inhabit. Some of us have never evolved through the animal kingdom.

Refined Living In Mature Monasteries

272 ℂ After a monastery established by either one or two of these methods was smoothly transformed from a training school into a way of life by the senior minority group, and the artisans and executives had been well chosen within the monastery itself and brought together from neighboring ones, the senior minority group had little to do other than concern themselves with those coming from the wall into the monastery and upgrading the philosophical precision and way of life, in adherence to the *śāstras* within the monastery itself.

Surprise Philosophical Exams

273 ℂ Occasionally a monastic resident would be asked without warning to sit with the OTM and receive a more intricate philosophical and *śāstric* examination as to his personal life and knowledge as to how he should conduct himself under the many possible circumstances that could arise in his present surroundings and his future life while on the mission for his guru or pilgrimaging from monastery to monastery. The intricacies of his training, as outlined in the great book of Śaivite monastic attitudes, was well taught through this method. And it was before a monastic was transferred to another monastery that he

was also given ceremony and blessing by the senior minority group, as well as an examination and instruction as to how he was to behave and conduct himself in the monastery that he would be begging admittance into. It was in this way that Śaivite monastics continued the Lemurian cultural standards for the entire community surrounding each temple and monastery. And if the senior minority group felt that the darshan was not reaching or penetrating deeply enough into the villages surrounding us, more ceremony, more *pūjā*, more *tapas* was performed to draw forth a greater darshan to correct and uplift the situation.

Guarding The Psychic Force Field

274 ℭ In their living in the third eye, constant surveillance occurred. Occasionally they would see a disincarnate animal in the Second World enter the monastery, and, because of this surveillance, he was fought with through *pūjā* and dismissed from our force field easily before causing psychic harm to any of the beginning *sādhakas*. They would sit together, often without discussion, just to tightly hold this darshan as a collective group, as a *chakram*, for, by being together, the inner bones of their bodies became the *chakram* for the Deity and his *devas* to send great cosmic rays through.

A Chakram Of Divine Upliftment

275 ℭ They also knew that by just their being together the *devas* would be able to adjust the monastic flows and bring individual *sādhakas* and initiates into a greater knowledge by using the force they generated by sitting together. During these times, our Deity and *devas* would project great and colorful rays through the entirety of their nerve systems. These rays would flow out through the entire monastery, adjusting and correcting the most subtle of issues. They acted as the hub, motionless. The other activities occurred around them. And at certain times, our guru would sit with this group to adjust the force field during this changing era of our time.

Implementing Without Ramifying

276 ℭ It was for this reason that any change or alteration in the general flow of the monastery or the timing of an event, even if our guru instigated it, had to have a unanimous nod of approval from this senior group. If the discussion occurred more than a moment or so, the matter was referred to our guru for elucidation, for we are just a channel for the Deity, a

dispenser, a container, a holder of darshan. We endeavor not to lower His vibration into the intellect of words and discussion, other than to convey information of which our answers are found quickly within our *śāstras* and from our guru. The pattern is set, was set long ago, and to fulfill it is our function. It was in the Second World, with the *devas* and our guru at night, when we all slept on these inner planes, that discussion occurred, clarification was given. This is why when issues arose we informed the *devas* in writing through the sacred fire and met with them there, for our senior circle met in two worlds; and so, in the First World we always endeavored to sit and feel what had occurred the night before, and it was through feeling that the unanimous nod of approval or disapproval occurred.

If the discussion occurred more than a moment or so, the matter was referred to our guru for elucidation, for we are just a channel for the Deity, a dispenser, a container, a holder of darshan.

The OTM's Requisite Aloofness

277 ℭ On occasion when there was congestion within the monastery due to the diminishing force of the imposing Kali Yuga, we would hold ourself apart, even live separately within the monastery, to equalize the pressures. The senior core never mixed closely with *sādhakas* in white other than being friendly, courteous and kind. Nor did they mix closely with newcomers or guests, except for the Hanumān, who initially interviewed, hosted, got to know them and was then able to inform the senior core about them.

The Unfailing Power to Add Or Detract

278 ℭ It was the comings and goings of *sādhakas*, initiates and guests that changed the force field the most and, therefore, always greatly concerned the senior core of each monastery. For they knew how things should be, and their mission was to refine, constantly refine, the *śāstric* flows and structures. And, because of this constant upgrading of Śaivite living, it was the newcomer who would add or detract, depending upon the quality of his being, his ability to change and adjust. For all of our monasteries, though the same, are different because of the conglomerate of souls in the First, Second and Third Worlds working within them. Therefore, each monastic's great endeavor by the wall is to adjust himself to this similar but new and different vibration he encounters.

When the Darshan Was Strongest

279 ℭ The darshan at times would become so strong that each monastic could do nothing but sit, absorb it, disseminate it. It was during these times that the *devas* from several monasteries moved to a single one to cause a certain impact to equalize the force of the surrounding population, and at these times each monastic acted as he would if he were within the senior minority group, as a great *chakram* for the divine darshan. This would come unannounced, never lasting too long, and would leave quickly. It was in this way that the Second and Third World controlled the instinctive forces within the animal bodies of us in the First.

The members of the monastery's senior minority were very careful that each member of the monastery was well trained and that the guru had full and immediate cooperation from each monastic in making manifest his word. The senior group also supervised the artisans with their training of the apprentices and observed closely the results obtained. Correction was freely given, but the attitude that nothing was amiss always preceded all others. Obedience, intelligent cooperation, was the keynote. The senior group and the artisans took time with each young apprentice, especially in the first few years, knowing that with a well-trained intellect he would enhance the darshan flow for the remainder of his life. The foremost lesson was that disseminating and being a channel for the divine energies is each one's major chore. Aum.

Venerable monasteries and their surrounding communities lived smoothly together up to this time. But as they advanced deeper into the Kali Yuga, conditions changed as unrestrained mating, land division by impenetrable oceans and misunderstandings arose. Being on the wall was intricate to monastic culture, protecting those within from forces on the outside, often guided by dreams.

Gurudeva

280 ℭ At this time in our *yuga,* the dark cloud in the distance is easily seen, and it is more and more difficult to quell the avaricious forces of the animal nerve system and cleave to our culture. The population surrounding the monasteries begins to give way to mating out of their season, thus producing no offspring but simply tantalizing and strengthening the animal nerve system. A new culture is developing, and some of our wisest and most refined of gurus are separated from us by the great condensation of our atmosphere into impenetrable masses covering the land and separating us from them. Still others have been separated by this change on the surface of the Earth of condensed atmospheric liquid, and these are groups in which there are no gurus or Śaivite monastics, and we are sure that they may forget the culture and the systems as the Kali Yuga persists. It will be difficult then for our gurus to reach them, even through incarnating into their midst. They may not be recognized.

Monastic Dharma and Destiny

281 ℭ When one becomes a monastic, he has arrived at his destination for this life. His perspective, his place, his life's work and the pattern for performing it are all set. The bones of his body become the *chakram* through which the darshan passes. And if he looks at the world but for short periods of time through the animal pulsations of his outer nerve system, his darshan turns to fire and heat within his body. This is closely watched by the senior minority group. And if this was found to be happening, stern *tapas* persisted. For each had to be a pure tube through which this darshan could flow. This was the only way, our Deity informed us, that the vibration could exist on the planet through the Kali Yuga and be picked up again by others as the Sat Śiva Yuga becomes the dawn again.

Portending Through Dreams

282 ℭ A lot of dependence was placed upon dreams, remembered when awake, of a God or a guru, a *deva* or a genie, and these were sent to the senior minority group—by anyone in the monastery—to be reviewed. If the dream was valid in nature, someone within the senior minority group would have had the same or a similar dream. Occasionally, if this occurred, the monastic who had the dream would be invited to tell of it to the senior group. In this way some of the prophecies in future events of our changing times came about. If a dream was had and

confirmed by the senior minority group, predicting a new innovation, the guru was told, and his nod of approval would allow it to become part of the monastic flow. As we get closer and closer into the vibration of the Kali Yuga, we will have to depend more and more on this method, it is predicted.

Activities of Those Sitting By the Wall

283 ℂ While monastics seeking entrance into a new monastery sat by the gate or wall begging admittance from the *devonic* guards and other inner *devas*, they were given useful things to do—such as working on the lands, gathering fruits, herbs—and various other kinds of preparatory studies to make their life more productive once they had entered the monastery. And, of course, after they had received a philosophical examination and review of their personal monastic life and conduct, they would be well prepared to assume the duties that they had been adjusted to before entering.

The Varied Nature of Our Walls

284 ℂ Occasionally, under the guru's direction, monastics would be kept by the wall for long, lengthy periods of time and then be sent to another monastery to seek entrance there. This denial of entrance in each monastery they pilgrimaged to after performing *tapas* by the wall discharged instinctive-intellectual patterns that had accrued through the centuries. The walls of the different monasteries became known for certain specific functions. The *devas* that guarded them and the others who worked behind them to adjust new monastics learned to perform well, and monastics having specific kinds of needs were, therefore, sent to sit before the wall of the monastery that would adjust them best as they endeavored to adjust to the monastery.

Respect, Hospitality, Scrutiny

285 ℂ The senior group was delighted when a greater soul than themselves entered the monastery, one who was more philosophically astute, more precise in his monastic conduct in the fulfillment of the Śaivite *śāstras*. With him they rejoiced, as they felt that his presence was a reward of all of their efforts, as they knew through his example he would upgrade the entire monastery. Each day, a few of the monastics, other than those on the senior minority group, who always kept unattached and apart from the monastics sitting by the wall seeking entrance, would go and visit with them, feeling that one or another might be a great *deva,* a God or one of the Śaivite gurus. Those by the wall were treated extremely well, therefore, and told how their presence would enhance the monastery, what a lovely place it was to be in. They would tell the newcomer of the history of it and what it currently was doing. This function of hospitality and encouragement the two-thirds majority would perform while the one-third minority, the senior minority group, would assume the opposite point of view, holding themselves apart from guests and newcomers, with the exception of the Hanumān. And when the philosophical examination occurred, they would let the monastic begging entrance know how strict and precise this monastery was, and that a lot of effort and *sādhana* was expected from each monastic.

While monastics seeking entrance into a new monastery sat by the gate or wall begging admittance from the devonic guards and other inner *devas,* they were given useful things to do.

Young Sādhakas by The Wall

286 ℂ Surrounding each of our monasteries there are, of course, *sādhakas*—sent by family men who had trained them for entrance—begging admittance for the first time into the monastery. They were kept by the wall for long periods of time before being admitted. Each moon they were given a philosophical examination and a close look at their deportment and conduct and fulfilling of the *śāstras* in their own life. Occasionally some were sent back to the family who had trained them, for additional acquisition of accomplishments in certain areas. During this time, they were always encouraged and shown great love and kindness, for it was important that the monasteries gain new *sādhakas* in order for our culture to persist. But this effort to increase our population and begin new monasteries did not in any way lower our standards.

The Power of Philosophical Discussion

287 ℂ Each one of us is categorized in the minds of all by how well he knows the philosophy of the three worlds. This was our one great skill, for when we had the opportunity to speak with the elders of the community through the holes in our walls, it was this philosophy that sustained the population. Therefore, the philosophical points were hairsplitting in nature, intricate in concept, and we delved into areas such as "how much energy would it take to look at an animal or smell a flower." Philosophical discussions would not end till they evoked a darshan so strong that we could not speak.

Observing Deportment During Sleep

288 The senior minority group had another power bestowed to them by the Deity and *devas* when they performed this function. They were able to follow a monastic seeking entrance into the monastery on the inner planes of the Second World at night while he slept. The monastic would generally know this and watch closely during his sleep as to the nature of his destination, for once accepted into the monastery he was not expected to leave it at night during sleep and go scouting out to the community at large, participating in activities and enjoyments that he had renounced to be in the monastery. This would deteriorate the power of the entire monastery if allowed to occur. Rather, he was expected to pursue inner study in the spiritual areas of the Second World and the Third during sleep. So, therefore, prior to entrance, he was carefully watched by the senior minority group, and they shared among themselves, during their meeting, any dreams or visions they had of him. In exercising this power of following him during his sleep before they entered him into their midst, the unanimous nod of approval always persisted, indicating that even during sleep he would be an asset to the monastery.

Stringent Criteria for Acceptance

289 It was on occasion—when a newcomer seeking entrance did not readily become accepted because of his failure to be able to adjust to the deep inner flow, participate in it in the monastery he was begging to enter—that, after many interviews and philosophical examinations and review of personal conduct, the Umāgaṇeśa had no choice but to suggest to the guru he be asked to seek entrance into another monastery that perhaps wasn't quite as strict. This monastery was carefully chosen for him, and because of the training he had just received by the wall, he more than often was accepted within a short time and enhanced this new monastery by his presence. Our monasteries are located within a day's journey, one from another, and each one has a facility for a pilgrim traveling to a far-off monastery to spend the night. It was the family educators of young monastics who were always appreciative of high and difficult standards arrived at by individual monasteries, and they would tell young potential *sādhakas* studying with them in their homes of the difficulties in entering one or another of them and the reasons why. This became a part of their training and is a part of our culture. These high standards which set certain monasteries apart from others strengthen Śaivism on this planet.

The Tapas Of not Being Admitted

290 ℂ It was on occasion that a fine potential *sādhaka* was not admitted into any monastery for a number of years, but always left to keep trying. Part of his training occurred in this way. This persisted till his entire vibration was as a senior monastic and he was difficult then not to admit. The guru would tell each of the senior groups that this was occurring and, because of one reason or another, a particular disciple was to be kept outside the walls and not entered while in the vibration of a beginning soul, but only when he attained the vibration of a senior monastic. This particular *tapas*, given only to a few, each of our Śaivite gurus used. This kept the wall actively strong, a great psychic barrier to all kinds of intrusions. Also, in each Śaivite monastery there were always five or ten percent of the monastics who were in yellow, for our *śāstras* say yellow and white should always occur. White alone can persist alone until yellow is seen, and orange. Yellow, white and orange should occur, never orange and white alone, as this would form two groups too drastically different in their discipline. The senior minority group observed this closely, so some were always in the *tapas* of yellow.

Once accepted into the monastery he was not expected to leave it at night during sleep and go scouting out to the community at large, participating in activities and enjoyments that he had renounced to be in the monastery.

Visitors Not Seeking Admittance

291 ℂ Visitors occasionally come who are not seeking admittance. These are family men who teach, as well as monastics passing through. They occasionally are invited to sit with the senior minority group, or just the Umāgaṇeśa, Hanumān and Umādeva, to share their message. It was depending upon their particular mission that this would occur. After the interview, they were invited to stay a short time, and then they would go on. The senior minority group was not formal with visitors, nor did they hold themselves apart from them, for they were not seeking admittance by the wall.

Hanumān's Supervision Of the Wall

292 ℂ During my life as a Śaivite monastic, occasionally I have been the Hanumān and supervised the comings and goings outside the wall. If forty or fifty were meditating at our wall, they would be living there for long periods of time, just waiting to meet with someone from inside the monastery. This is part of our culture. Some of these monastics patiently waiting have possibly come from the senior minority group of another monastery. I would generally get to know the ones with the most light on their face and depth of humility first and recommend to the senior minority group that they be considered. To these few I would talk and suggest they begin in earnest acquainting themselves with monastic procedures that we adhere to. Secretly they would be separated from the others into small training groups, and assistance given them to enable them to blend into our community. As the senior minority group was chosen as the one-third most senior who had actually been admitted free access into the monastery—so to them there was no wall—the comings and goings outside the wall, the monastics seeking admittance and guests and passersby were left for me to observe. It was the Hanumān, therefore, and the young *brāhmins* who functioned together as a similar kind of senior group in the *devasthānam,* and we met to sit and hold the emotional and spiritual vibrations within the *devasthānam* and supervise the comings and goings of all who lived there.

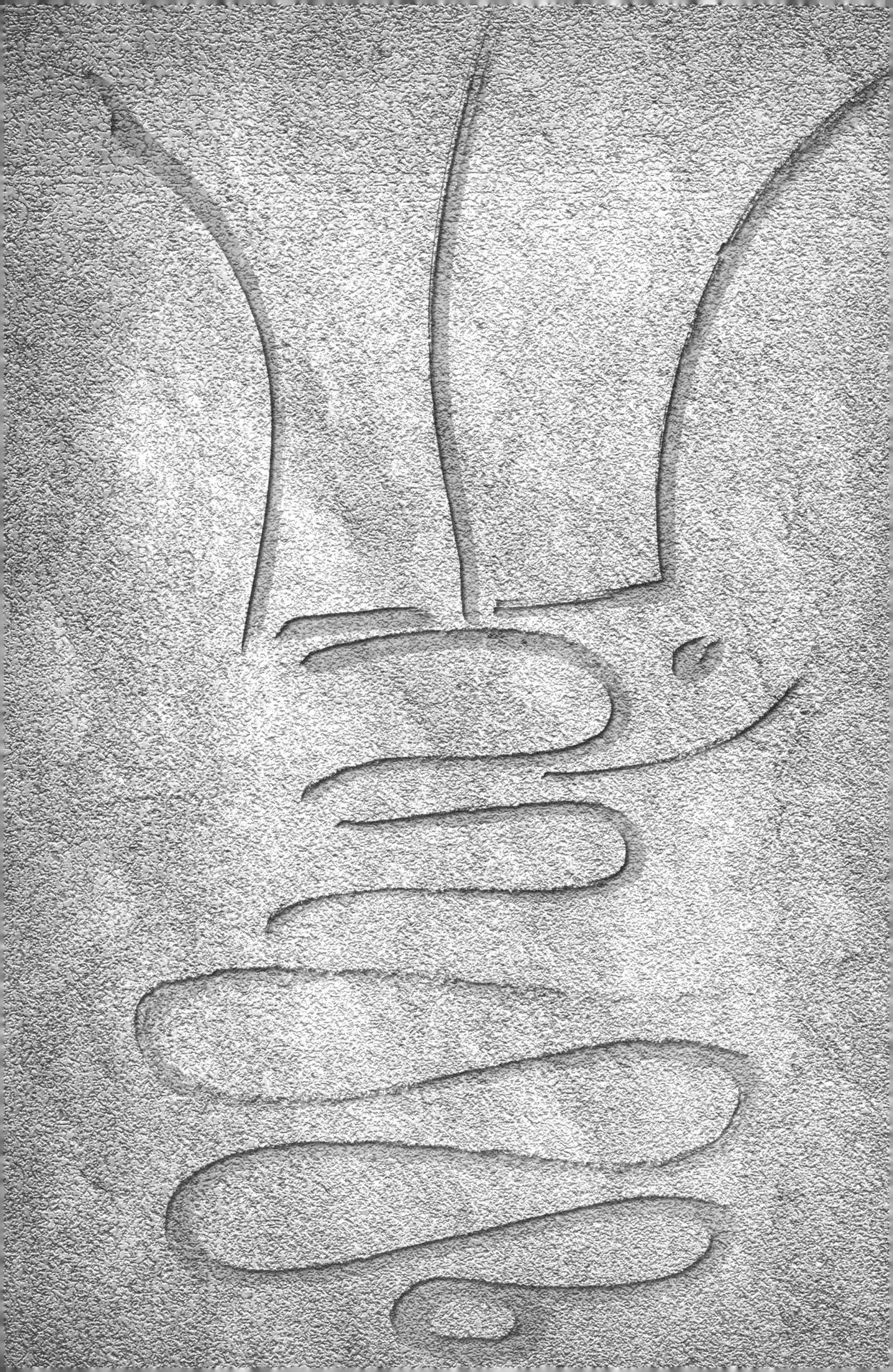

Apprentices of Dravidian times endeavored to relate to their artisan not merely as a physical person but a divine earthly channel who was always in direct communication with the devas of creation. The apprentices would serve the artisan in many ways to open themselves up to him and to the power of the inner worlds which caused the various skills to unfold within them. They brought flowers to each gathering, served refreshments and treated him with great respect bordering on reverence. Likewise, the artisans and executives felt themselves to be apprentices of the guru, as the guru felt himself to be an apprentice of the great Deities of the planet. Thus, this attitude of humble apprenticeship prevails on all levels and is a profound source of strength. Aum.

Working as a team, devoid of ego, is a spiritual imperative in a monastery. Visibility was always discouraged, and constant vigilance persisted to keep the devonic force constant, and rules evolved guiding the young and their training, assuring their success. The balance of young and old was monitored, as was the presence of a blood brother and the full renunciation of wealthy candidates.

Gurudeva

293 ℭA monastic who traveled between monasteries as a carrier of the force field was always considered a direct agent of our guru. The Śaivite gurus had many of these agents, whom they met with within an inner area of the Second World as one group to give instruction and directions and strength to fulfill their mission. Often these carriers of spiritual force never actually entered any of the monasteries they visited but lived by the wall, conferring secretly with the senior minority group the guru's wishes and purpose of their mission. Outwardly they were treated as any other monastic seeking admittance. One of the great purposes for this was to equalize the intensification simultaneously. This kept our standards high. If a monastic was performing certain kinds of *tapas* in which our Deity and the *devas* were working with him to untie entanglements, or causing new innovations in the service of his guru, or working directly with his guru, he was never considered to sit with the senior group. This is because of his inner involvement with the *devas* and his guru of a specific nature. Monastics in this category are carefully watched by the senior minority group and interviewed once a moon as to the nature of their *tapas* and as to how far they are progressing in fulfilling it, so that they will not drift apart from the monastery in their vibration and assume a personal life within it, thus inadvertently neglecting their *tapas*. This has unknowingly happened to some. That is why close supervision is given to maintain the high standards that we all seek for.

Residency Broken After Nine Days

294 ℭTo keep the monastery strong, if a monastic, once having been taken in, leaves for a span of more than nine complete suns, one phase, he loses his resident seniority, and upon returning must spend one full moon by our wall readjusting himself to our inner vibration. This, in itself, strengthens the entire monastery. Even though he enters on special invitation to perform his daily chores, he is given a private place to live within the *devasthānam*, as are all *sādhakas* once taken into the monastery, living privately and secludedly there, apart from the comings and goings of monastics and those seeking to become *sādhakas* in the major halls of the *devasthānam*.

Cleansing Streams of Darshan

295 ℭBeing a member of the senior minority group has no relationship to unfoldment or divine realization. We are all just channels for the divine darshan.

Our individual areas of concern are set aside by the *devas* as the darshan showers through us. Being in this group is unfoldment itself, like a stream of water falling upon our physical heads. The darshan stream, pouring through, cleanses the animal nerve system of its remembrances.

Realization And Selfless Service

296 ℂ It is not spiritual realization of the Self that we seek in our monasteries, though this is the eventual goal we attain—our purpose for being on this planet. We seek to serve our guru in his mission, fulfill the *śāstras,* our *sādhana,* do our *tapas* well when it comes, be precise in our philosophical involvements; and our destiny, Self, is assured. It is through the complete surrender, inner and outer, to the great darshan of our Lord that the past occurrences—and perceptive insights into future occurrences—which might disturb the external nerve system and strengthen it are caused to vanish. It is the realized beings, those who have realized Self, or God, that are the generators of certain kinds of darshan. The unrealized being is only the conductor. Therefore, if the senior minority group were made up of realized beings, the monastery would be strong, generating and conducting. However, if only conductors of the darshan were in this group, it would be a consumer monastery, disseminating the darshan. And the Deity and guru himself, the *devas,* too, would have to generate power for this monastery, as well as it would draw from other monasteries who generated new darshan.

Connectivity, Conductivity, Continuity

297 ℂ Pieces of gold placed together become very powerful conductors if unmoved. When moved to another place, much power is lost, for the inner plane beings lose track and connection with the conductor. Similarly, if members of a senior minority group would change often, it would decrease the power of the monastery, whereas if they remained part of that group in ever-increasing transparency and humility, the darshan flows in ever-increasing abundance, and the monastery stands as a fulfillment of its purpose. This is our philosophy.

Artisans' Resolving of Difficulties

298 ℂ It is our guru who is the absolute and only head of the monastery. The senior minority group is a balancing body. It is a coming together of the various matured forces within the monastery. Therefore, if a new monastic was not being trained properly by his artisan or executive, his forces began to pull on the senior group, for it was the senior group and *devas'* working with him that entered him into the monastery. To correct his training, they would send a message to or call his artisan or executive in to correct the situation, so that no outside duty the young monastic would perform would be too difficult for him, thus entering him into worldly confusion. This was closely watched as one thing that could deter the darshan flow quite rapidly.

We seek to serve our guru in his mission, fulfill the *śāstras,* our *sādhana,* do our *tapas* well when it comes, be precise in our philosophical involvements; and our destiny, Self, is assured.

Gods, Guru, Artisans, Senior Group

299 ℭ Each artisan and executive felt himself an apprentice of our guru and our Deity. So, basically everyone was an apprentice to the great Deities who guided the *yugas* and other universes. The Deities felt beholden to the Self God, as did each one of us in the monastery. This attitude of a humble apprentice, therefore, persists throughout and is our strength. Occasionally the Deity would appear on the pedestal and give definite instructions to artisans and executives alike, as did our guru. The artisans and executives then turned to the senior group to seek for the nod of approval as to the proper time these new innovations could be begun. The Umāgaṇeśa, in turn, asked the guru once again. A time was chosen, as no two activities ever occurred at once. Each monastery fulfills a certain function in our culture, carries the darshan in one specific way. All are the same but no two exactly alike.

Preparation Preceding Innovation

300 ℭ When a new innovation was started, the senior minority group and the artisan in charge, as well as some of his apprentices, spent long periods of time discussing each aspect of what was to occur so that the occurrence entered into direct manifestation, rather than causing confusion and a backup of the forces into the nerve system of the senior core. Because many of this group were artisans and executives, they took this training process of monastics to prepare them for new innovations very seriously and were tedious and precise in being sure each aspect of the innovation was well understood and the monastic was able to perform it. If any kind of resistance from a trainee-apprentice, artisan or executive was felt in the nerve system of the senior group, the project was halted, and an invocation to the Second and Third World was held within the temple to clear the inner barriers before it was commenced again.

Keeping Track of Residency

301 ℭ In order to determine the senior minority group, first find the length of time each one has been in the monastery, providing they are not living by the wall, and then fulfill the mathematical formula that succeeds this calculation. We do keep close track of the time that monastics live by the wall to assure ourselves that permanent residency there is not established.

White, Yellow, Orange

302 ℭ If the members of the senior group are mostly *sādhakas* in white, then we know it is a *sādhaka* monastery. If the majority are in yellow, on *tapas*, we know it is a *tapas* monastery. When *sādhakas* in white do appear in this group, this possibly shows that they have been too long in a particular monastery without intensification of *sādhana,* or that there are not enough monastics in orange to carry the darshan and the monastery balance; for, we must remember, a *sādhaka* is working through the *karma* and *dharma* and needs all of the darshan possible to help himself through it. Therefore, there are individual reasons why he is a *sādhaka* and not a monastic in yellow or orange. If an overabundance of monastics in yellow appears, this indicates, of course, that the monastery is losing its orange monastic seniority, and some adjustment in its population should be made to hold the darshan. To make an adjustment here, elderly senior monastics are generally sent by our guru who are dressed in orange to beg entrance into the monastery.

Astral Blueprints for Monasteries

303 ℭ The goal of a *sādhaka* monastery, therefore, would be to work to have the senior minority group dressed totally in orange as soon as possible, so that their monastery would be fulfilling itself by fully disseminating the darshan. There are *sādhaka* monastic groups in our land that travel together, remaining in one place not longer than three moons before they move on, settling down as a monastery only when an OTM in orange appears. Then from one place the darshan is disseminated. Our prophets tell us that these *sādhaka* monasteries will set the pattern for monastic living throughout the Kali Yuga, until these inner visionary texts are read again at the end of that time and some of the more subtle aspects of Śaivite monastic living are commenced again. We are even now placing vast books into the *ākāśa,* written about *sādhaka* monasteries, with suggestions as to how they are to be conducted through the Kali Yuga, some of which will be picked out of the *ākāśa* in the inner mind again by us who will be incarnating through that time. These will be our *śāstras*, our guidelines for conduct, and we are writing them now, taking into account the darkness of the mind that will be experienced during that time.

We are even now placing vast books into the *ākāśa*, written about *sādhaka* monasteries, with suggestions as to how they are to be conducted through the Kali Yuga, some of which will be picked out of the *ākāśa* in the inner mind again by us who will be incarnating through that time.

Regarding Brothers in the Monastery

304 ℂ Occasionally two brothers would be admitted into one of our monasteries. The younger of the two in physical years has to constantly demonstrate advanced fortitude, forbearance and seek the mercy of the Deity and *devas* to change the core of his nature, even unto himself. This is the *tapas* for the brother of lesser physical years. If he does not perform this *tapas* well, both he and his older brother (preferably the first born) could be held *status quo* in unfoldment, due to blood bonds, and this naturally would not be permitted to occur by the senior minority group after a respectful period of time. It is the first born that is allowed *tapas* in yellow and orange as a monastic. The second, third or fourth born may wear white. If the second, third or fourth born enters the monastery and no other brother does, we allow that he wear yellow and orange and perform the appropriate *tapas*, but would not admit to the monastery or *devasthānam* any brother older than he. A younger brother could, of course, come and wear white, perform *sādhana* and serve. It is through the blood ties of the older male that the younger is pulled into a comparable unfoldment, providing he works diligently to remain transparent, calling no attention to himself, and to change his nature through invoking *pūjā* at regularly prescribed intervals.

Renunciation Tapas for Sons Of Wealth

305 ℂ Upon occasion, the son of a wealthy family of great holdings begged entrance into the monastery and sought to dress in yellow and orange. For this he had to settle all affairs of possessions and kind and was allowed to give only that which was his to give for the betterment of all. This *tapas* of renunciation he worked with his family to perform after permission from the senior minority group had been obtained. The renunciation was allowed to be completed, and great rejoicing by himself and his family succeeded him as he entered the monastery to polarize the darshan as the fulfillment of his life.

Reverence Toward One's Artisan

306 ℭ The apprentice looked at the artisans and executives as the earthly channels to bring through that which was already finished on the inner planes, ones who have the direct communication with the *devas* of creation, ones who will open inner doors so that precise skill begins to come and unfold within them. Therefore, each of the apprentices approached his artisan or executive in a very humble and open way, being careful never to relate to him as a physical person or to seek special favors from him that the others did not receive. The artisans and executives were very careful also that they did not show any favoritism among their apprentices. This allowed each one to qualify himself only by his skills. Each artisan and executive, though of different natures, some in yellow or white and some in orange, distinguished themselves by their skills and abilities to pass them on in a transparent and humble way to others. For there was only one reward, that of excellence and precision in what they did produce, and all credit was given to the *devas* and the Gods.

The Tapas Of Perfect Transparency

307 ℭ It was the nameless one, the one in disguise, the one who changed the very core of his nature, that monkey that became the bird through deep *sādhana* and personal *tapas*, that was the one who held the force of creation within our monasteries. And if a brother were younger to his brother of blood and birth, he became unrecognizable even to the brother he was raised with from earlier years. This particular *tapas* all of us worked on and with to one extent or another, but it was and is particularly mandatory for artisans and executives and younger brothers who entered the monastery to make this total transformation of the core of the nature a reality in their experiences on the Śaivite path of enlightenment.

The Senior Group's Subtle Surveillance

308 ℭ In working within the Second World to change the very core of the nature, such as a younger brother, artisan or executive would do, daily prayers to the *devas* at a certain chosen time are performed, and the operation once commenced persists through the years. They each must be as transparent as possible and call no attention to themselves, so that no monastic resident is reminded in any way that an other than normal situation exists. Thus, this is the senior minority group's intricate

responsibility in our way of life through the years, as we view the comings and goings of monastics and guests and the fast-fading era of peace and forbearance into a dim, dark time separating one world from another, and the other from the other, as we sleep.

Each artisan and executive, though of different natures, some in yellow or white and some in orange, distinguished themselves by their skills and abilities to pass them on in a transparent and humble way to others.

n Dravidian times

the Deities were easily able to work through and contact monastics by using animals and plants as a vehicle. Lord Ganesha used fruits and vegetables that grew above the ground to transmit his darshan, providing wisdom and perfect timing, removing obstacles on the path. Lord Skanda worked through herbs and the milk of the goat to send His actinic rays of healing, psychic power and knowledge of interplanetary travel. Lord Siva used the cow to pour out the essence of Saivism and help clear conditions of the past. For these reasons, plants and animals were given the best of care, treated as the Deity Himself. This knowledge was carefully taught to newcomers. At milking time, mathavasis could be seen gathered around, brushing the cow, feeding her and chanting sacred mantras. Aum.

X is the magical, unknown quality of herbs and various kinds of fruits and foods which, consumed in appropriate and specific ways, change the consciousness, change the health, physically and astrally, of us on Earth. What has been predicted and what has been understood and what the future holds are summarized here, along with remedies of the birds, bees, goats, cows and other animals.

Gurudeva

309 We are told that at the end of the Tretā Yuga all life on this planet—humans, animals, trees, plants, flowers—was twice the size that they are now. It has changed so much, and it is predicted that by the end of the Kali Yuga all will be half again as small.

Seeds, Milk, Vegetables And Fruit

310 Seeds and their oils protect the body, for the life in the seed is condensed from the sun, so the seed itself must be ground and applied to the body or consumed. The immediate usage is the key to effective healing. Milk from the goat, provided it's taken alone at the same time it is taken from the animal, frees the spirit from attachments to external life by releasing actinicity within the cells upon the digestion of it. It is as a vegetable and should be taken with fruit, nuts and seeds in a ratio of one-third milk to two-thirds of the other for proper digestion and assimilation.

Qualities of Cow's and Goat's Milk

311 Milk that is taken one hour after being taken from the cow or goat produces a strong physical body, whereas intellectual nerve currents are strengthened with prepared butter, aged cheeses and the possession of possessions in the media of exchange. Seeds battery the sun's power and become self-producing sun, therefore, life the body. It is our custom to take care of milk-producing animals better than we take care of ourselves. These *devas* in the sky come to serve in this way. It is the energies within the milk that allow us to soar within ourselves, and if it is not taken with fruit, it should be taken alone, on an empty stomach, allowed to digest before other kinds of nourishment are entered into the body.

The Origins Of Cows, Goats Bees, Fruit

312 Our *śāstras* tell us that goat's milk is best for bodies with bones, and in ancient times, in the original body, they were soft and pliable, easily bendable; and for these bodies cow's milk was most suitable. In these more flexible bodies, that did not come out of the animal kingdom, the inhabitants could fly. The cow has been on this planet since before the Sat Yuga. We brought the goat with us, along with the bees, herbs and various kinds of fruit, when we arrived to begin our cycle of *yugas*. Therefore, we carefully nurture these species that are designed to give health and sustenance through the trying times of the Kali Yuga. To herd a group of goat *devas* clears instinctive patterns of the

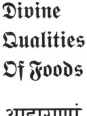

past and lays the foundation for avoidance of trouble and problems for the future. Thus, good *dharma* is accrued through the care of goat and bee, raising herbs and nurturing the tree that bears fruit. The cow, the sustainer of life on the planet for many *yugas*, was brought here another cycle of *yugas* ago, our *śāstras* tell us.

Milk as a Channel for Darshan

313 ℭ Our Deity puts His darshan through the goat, into its milk, to hasten its psychic power. Through His darshan, delivered in this way, He gives inner knowledge and stimulates extraterrestrial experiences. It has to be taken immediately to capture the darshan. Our Lord Skanda's darshan comes through the goat, and Lord Śiva's through the cow. Much milk from the goat will be used at the end of the Kali Yuga by the souls to make the transfer into the Sat Śiva Yuga in the same body. Through the Kali Yuga, we are told, the cow will be killed and eaten, but the goat will be left in peace, his nerve system not disturbed by brutal slaughter of his race, a perfect channel for Lord Skanda's darshan.

Our Attitude Toward these Divine Beings

314 ℭ Those *sādhakas* in white drink the milk of the cow, and monastics in yellow and orange the milk of the goat. In this way, the Deities reach each one directly through his chosen animal, conveying knowledge, psychic power and clearing conditions of past and future. In the families in our surrounding communities, it is Lord Gaṇeśa who sends His power through both goat and cow to bind tight the family, so that the reincarnation process can occur within the family, thus refining the bodies more like they were when we originally arrived. The families treat both goat and cow as they do our Deity. Within the goat a *devonic* soul is resting. The consciousness is partially asleep. His body in the Second World is dozing, resting. We are told to be kind and not disturb the goat, so that the *deva* who may have been tremendously upset in his nerve system before this birth can rest peacefully through it.

Gardens Of Herbs & Vegetables

315 ℭ In our gardens, Lord Umāgaṇeśa sends His power through fruits and vegetables, the ones that grow above the ground, to permeate our nerve system with wisdom, clearing obstacles in our path when eaten. The growers of them treat it like they would care for Gaṇeśa in His physical form. It is Lord Muruga that sends His darshan, with power, through the herb garden, which is always kept separate from Gaṇeśa's garden. Some of them should be taken alone for their efficacy to best persist and be allowed to pass through the entire physical system, and the radiation of that one particular darshan be placed into it, before anything else is eaten.

In our gardens, Lord Umāgaṇeśa sends His power through fruits and vegetables, the ones that grow above the ground, to permeate our nerve system with wisdom, clearing obstacles in our path when eaten.

Observing Nature's Responses

316 ℭ As the cow and goat, as well as the herb, the tree and the vegetation, can read the thoughts of us all, chanting and singing should occur while tending to their needs. This is carefully taught by the senior minority group to the *sādhakas* of the south wind and the *brāhmins* of the north wind so that the instinctive areas of the *sādhaka* do not dominate the *devas* working within these plants and animals, thus blocking and nullifying this efficiency through the uncontrolled thinking and emotionalism of the monastic tending to their needs. Our gurus always judged, they say, the abilities of Śaivite monastics according to the responses of the plants, animals and bees to them. They had but to ask the fruit tree and the bee, the cow or the goat and the herb as to whether they went out to or recoiled from a particular monastic. For there are two basic qualities of the instinctive mind: to recoil from or bloom to. These responses of animal and plant alike to a monastic were closely watched by the senior minority group so that no indwelling traits that would hurt a plant or an animal would grow and develop within the monastic and later hurt another monastic or inhibit the darshan flow.

Our Friend, The Regal Peacock

317 ℭ It is the peacock, our largest of birds, the most intelligent of all, that warns and protects our monasteries from all intrusion of the other developing species of animals that eat other animals. Through thought transference we speak to the peacock and understand his sounds and make sounds like his to him. At this time we have a happy balance between the animal world and the human world. But we are told that during the Kali Yuga these two worlds will pull far apart and be unable to communicate with or know each other, so great is the darkness of that time.

Partaking Of Specific Energies

318 ℭ One must always be careful to let an entire darshan flow pass entirely through the system before the next darshan is taken. Through this method our Deities can solve all problems. It is the darshan from cow's milk that will clear up subconscious conditions. Seeds should be ground and used immediately, for their oils are most effective if applied in this way. The oil from the seed, when applied to the external body and taken within simultaneously, will aid in connecting and strengthening inner bodies to the physical so that they can shine through. Otherwise, there is a tendency for them to hang in the Second World above it.

Physical, Spiritual Nourishment

319 ℂ It was the new *sādhakas* entering the monastery who were given special attention as to their intake of nourishment until they learned to intuit it for themselves. When visitors came to receive teaching and counsel, they were always given the appropriate milk, fruit or herb, impregnated with the darshan they needed to stimulate and to further the responsibilities they held beyond our walls. The core and essence of Śaivism poured out in this way, as the darshan penetrated the food. Upon occasion, a divine power to perform magical arts was given to some of us through the milk of the goat or the cow or hidden in a fruit on a tree.

Honey's Extraordinary Qualities

320 ℂ The bee that produces honey is of great value, for contained within the honey is the knowledge of planets whence we all came, and the health of all kinds of bodies that have ever existed on this planet. The bee gives us knowledge in the preservation of its culture, as to how the great *devas* work and serve in the Third World in developing and disseminating darshan, and keeps alive in our memory how we all lived in the vast caves on the great planets we came here from.

Powers Imparted by Nutrition

321 ℂ All knowledge of Śaivism can be imparted by our Lord Śiva when the milk of the cow is taken in the correct way. The knowledge of interplanetary travel through mental means is imparted by our Lord Skanda through goat's milk and honey, if taken according to the *śāstric* rules—when the body is empty, and allowed to pass completely through before something else is eaten. Similarly, vegetables, seeds and nuts grown according to the dictates of Lord Umāgaṇeśa, as well as fruit, give the physical power and perfect timing and abundance to our monasteries, along with the power to disseminate darshan and knowledge in a lasting way, removing obstacles effortlessly for others and having their worldly matters abundantly adjusted according to the highest measure of their *dharma.*

It is an art and an acquired ability of some of us to distinguish between different kinds of darshan and know the meaning, purpose and to whom they are directed through the different vehicles I have been describing by our Deities.

Discerning Varieties of Darshan

322 ℭ It is an art and an acquired ability of some of us to distinguish between different kinds of darshan and know the meaning, purpose and to whom they are directed through the different vehicles I have been describing by our Deities. The darshan flooding out from our temple from Lord Śiva Himself may at times be directed to a certain individual and not apply to others, who would simply feel blissful and uplifted because of it. This power comes to us from Lord Umāgaṇeśa. It is the ability to read the waves of darshan from inner planes of being.

Herbs Fortify The Inner Bodies

323 ℭ Herbs are the strengthening power of the fibers in the bodies that connect the physical to the body of the Second World. The consumer of herb potions can go through physical changes life after life without difficulty, for he carries the fiber developed by eating an herb with him in the body of the Second World from one physical body to another, thus refining that physical body to be punctual and alert to his bidding.

The Many Faces of Kuṇḍalinī

324 ℭ The fibrous bodies that we lived in when first arriving here were structured as a leaf is on a tree, and the liquid energy of the tree ran through its veins. The core of the body, which is, in these animal bodies, known as bones, was of the same or similar construction as branches on a tree. This kind of body, produced out of the central force of our being, *kuṇḍalinī*, and the intake of herbal essence, fruits and flowers, was able to fly in the atmosphere, as is still done now in the Second and Third World. At this time, in these animal constructed bodies, we are left with the *kuṇḍalinī* force, and that is all. When the *kuṇḍalinī* is well balanced in its ebb and flow, the entire nature becomes smooth and transformed. Through the night of the Kali Yuga, the *kuṇḍalinī* will no longer be the flying peacock, but will appear as a sleeping serpent in a cave, only lifting its head in a few, keeping some semblance of inner knowledge alive so that all is not forgotten in the great dream of the darkness.

Kali Yuga: Problems, Solutions

325 ℭ When most problems will arise in the nerve system of the animal instincts of man, at the end of the Kali Yuga, as the merger comes into the Sat Śiva Yuga, the *kuṇḍalinī* force awakens again in everyone simultaneously, some apparently sooner than others, depending on how lost they allowed themselves to become in their sleep and whether or not they applied certain kinds of discipline and formulas to awaken this primal force prematurely. As the Sat Śiva Yuga dawns, we are told, mankind will become friendly one to another again, because they will see more deeply into each other. Calm, creative, strong and full of love they will be, full of insight and understanding, as en masse they awaken out of the sleep of the Kali Yuga. Each one who awakens first will speak out the same message to all.

As the Kali Yuga Repeats

326 ℭ Toward the end of the Kali Yuga will be the same as it is now. Now at the time in the Dvāpara Yuga of entering the Kali Yuga it is a similar time, with the exception that in our time we see the dark clouds in the future, and sleep is imminent. But as this cycle repeats, at the same time, similar things will occur and be occurring as they are now when the Kali Yuga wanes—with one exception, the luminous sun is seen and awakening is imminent. But during the Kali Yuga, when the primal force sleeps, each one will be in his own dream and not be able to meet in harmony with another, so deep is his turmoil and confusion.

Kundalini, the primal force of man, is an extension of the force that comes from within the core of this planet deep within the Second and Third World. The kundalini of this planet is in two sections. One is an extension of the kundalini of other planets. The second is an extension of the Being of this planet. Where man situates his power within himself determines how he tunes into and is affected by this primal spiritual force. Only on those planets, called fire planets, that have great heat at their center can unfoldment proceed swiftly and naturally toward the ultimate destiny. During the Sat Siva Yuga, these rays, extending directly through the spine of man, will be intensified and alive, and humanity will awaken to the oneness of all and the Self within. During the Kali Yuga, these rays will be dormant in all but a few. Aum.

Yugas come and go in the great mind flow of these advanced beings, one leading to the next as night leads naturally to day, and memory is no barrier. As the kundalini lifts the planet, peoples move from slumber to awakening. All grow in mind powers and size, even plants and trees. Flower petals grow so large that children can romp and play on them. Timely teachers join us from other planets.

Gurudeva

327 ℂ The *kuṇḍalinī* force during the transition of the Kali Yuga to the Sat Śiva Yuga appears in the Second World as a great massive oil, slowly permeating body and mind, trees and foliage, in a great mass awakening, as did happen before on this planet when the Sat Yuga began. In the beginning of the Sat Siva Yuga the advancement will be rapid. As this begins to happen, the population will come to know the laws of life, transition and reincarnation and have mental facility to quickly adjust to the rapid changes, externally and internally, of one age fading into the other, giving new stability, peace, security and contentment.

Killing and Nonkilling Among Man

328 ℂ The sense of separateness will begin to fade as man is able to travel and communicate one with another once again. People will become more friendly one to another because they will see more deeply into one another. People will be calm, strong and full of love and understanding as a result of this mass awakening of the *kuṇḍalinī* force. No one culture or system will try to impose itself on another again. A common desire for peace among beings will persist, and man's wants will be few, for his fulfillment will come from the inside. It is predicted that the Kali Yuga will begin when the first human kills another and will actually end in its fullness when this process of killing one another ceases, as the power of the Sat Śiva Yuga is felt more eminently through the even distribution of *kuṇḍalinī* primal force pervading all beings. The veiling between the three worlds will fade. Transcendental beings will occasionally be seen, and then the turmoil that is beginning now in the Second World will cease. Those who first emerge, in groups small but strong, here and there around the planet, will be extremely careful in their dealings one with another, so that no traces of Kali Yuga habit patterns are allowed to persist among them. The first signs of this awakening will be a religious revival of the different religions. The religions will eventually merge into one, as the people will be one, due to the same existing awakening.

Global Kuṇḍalinī Awakening

329 ℂ There will be shocking new discoveries in science, as the scientists turn inward, that will give quiet security during this time to those who still slumber in the outer world. Each stratum of mind, represented by inhabitants of the planet, thus oiled, will not conflict one with another. The intel-

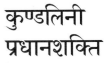

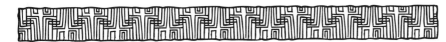

lectual will no longer conflict with the instinctive man, nor deny the existence of transcendental worlds. Each being will be free to serve and experience, without conflict, in his chosen strata of mind. Man will patiently make his planet a pleasant place in which to live as he moves into this new era. This new force awakening will give him light, insight and knowledge to handle each challenge in cleaning up and releasing old patterns from the Kali Yuga. This will not be so, however, through the Kali Yuga, when *kuṇḍalinī* sleeps and mind strata rub one upon the other as one branch does upon another on a tree when great gushes of air pass by. But when this primal force rises simultaneously in all beings, they will forget and forgive the past and work diligently in harmony, enjoying the present to solve the problems of the future, listening again to the advanced knowledge from the Deities governing this planet and our universe. It will be in this age that the leader who brought the people in the Sat Yuga will naturally be seen by the people of the world and be recognized when the *kuṇḍalinī* reaches a certain intensity. This primal force, when it reaches a certain level of intensity, would cause all beings on this planet again to realize the one major thing they will have forgotten by that time, that they are not of this planet but have come to this planet, and they will begin to think and see alike on every inner issue. No mystery will persist when the Sat Śiva Yuga is in full power. The Second World will fade in the glory of it all. A one darshan will permeate the entire planet and everything will double and triple its size, as it used to be, our old books tell us. The same darshan will permeate temples of all religions, because all of the people's *kuṇḍalinī* will be awakened and they will draw on the one darshan that existed in the last Sat Yuga. Finally that one darshan or feel will permeate the entire planet. The plants will grow better, and the animals will begin to talk. They will fly again as individuals and collective groups and travel from one planet to the next with ease even more actively than in the last Sat Yuga. The use of electronics and communication devices will be advanced to a very high degree as we go further into the *yuga*. The fire planet is cooling and there is a *kuṇḍalinī* force that comes from the inner part of it, deep within its Second and Third World—a very refined, primal force of which man's primal force on this planet is an extension. This force is what makes gravity. During the Kali Yuga, the primal force of the planet, as well as man, rests, withdrawn into itself, and regenerates as this Sat Śiva Yuga arrives. A systematic awakening, first of the planet and other planets and man, will come.

During the Kali Yuga, the primal force of the planet, as well as man, rests, withdrawn into itself, and regenerates as this Sat Śiva Yuga arrives.

Kuṇḍalinī's Sections and Intersections

330 ℂ The *kuṇḍalinī* of this planet is in two sections. One is an extension of the *kuṇḍalinī* of other planets, and the second lower section is an extension of the being of this planet. This creates gravity or anti-gravity, depending on where the pull is coming from. Depending upon where man situates his power within himself is how he tunes into and is affected by either one section or another of this planet's primal spiritual force. And in this way he will learn to fly once again. There are other kinds of rays from other planets that, when intersecting each other, form a planet such as this one. This is what occurs in the inner working of this universe.

Competition, Inspiration, Creativity

331 ℂ Through the Kali Yuga, great competition between individuals, groups and masses will occur to make it possible to live through the darkness. The excitement of fear will persist. But as it wanes, inspiration, creativity and divine energy will dislodge the spirit of competition; and the sense of one rising above another, because of his ability to do this, will also fade. Each one will be noted according to the age of his deepest inner body. Even now, we find among the people a sense of wanting to be better than another, and this is strictly handled within our Śaivite monasteries by the self-effacement of *tapas,* so that our original nature can shine forth in our awakened state. Each *tapas* given is clearly outlined. Sometimes it will take a monastic two or three days to prepare for it, clearly understanding each aspect of what was expected of him as he performed his *tapas.* The goals are clearly outlined.

Transition Into the Sat Śiva Yuga

332 ℂ Even now, we find that only certain ones have use of the third eye, and the two eyes in some are becoming dimmed. Through the Kali Yuga, they say that some will not see, hear or be able to speak, so deep will be their slumber. But as the Sat Śiva Yuga's great inner power and *kuṇḍalinī* force again equalizes all memories of the fading dream, seasonal mating will be inclined to occur, and the generations will adjust themselves into being born under certain kinds of astrological signs. There will be a new influx of visitors from certain neighboring planets, and the Deities will appoint carriers of their darshan to sustain it and disseminate it into places and to beings that it would not normally penetrate to spark them into the awakening, thus enlivening the *kuṇḍalinī* force in others through monastics of orders such as ours that will begin to appear. Some will enliven this force through the power of sight and sound; others will, inwardly, by being channels of an unseen force. The pattern will be the same as it is now. For we send carriers of the darshan forth from this monastery in which I write.

Rays through Earth and the Spine of Man

333 ℂ The *kuṇḍalinī* force comes as a ray directly through the Earth. And as these rays intersect, a tremendous fire and light is created within the center of the Earth. The ray goes directly through the spine of man. These rays, in the Sat Śiva Yuga, will be intensified and alive. In the Kali Yuga, they are dormant and sleep. Some of them are beginning to sleep now. And as a result, different sections of our population begin to lose the fullness of some of their faculties. These are unseen rays to the physical eye, but are similar to those that are felt from the Sun of our solar system that penetrate the nerve system and pass through the body.

Yoga Practices To Align the Kuṇḍalinī

334 ℂ Through the Kali Yuga, there will be certain kinds of practices to keep certain advanced souls on the planet aligned with the *kuṇḍalinī* ray. These practices will not be necessary during the Sat Śiva Yuga. The wise being will meditate on this *kuṇḍalinī* ray as an extension of his spine which penetrates totally through the Earth and on infinitely to the star or planet of its origin. Man is as a little knot in the ray or a bead on a single string, moving on the surface of this Earth. Wherever he goes, the ray goes with him. Meditating on the *kuṇḍalinī* in this way will bring infinite knowledge as to the nature of this universe and the next, our *śāstras* tell us. And they further say that the *kuṇḍalinī* ray is fibrous in nature, and as man awakens in the Sat Śiva Yuga he goes deep into the ray, or various depths of the ray penetrate out through the chakras.

Our Original Bodies

335 ℂ It was in the Sat Yuga that the physical body was made out of this ray and did not have many of the animal organs that we have acquired, though it looked similar to the ones that we have now, for our memory patterns have molded the animal bodies into looking like our original body. The original body had the chakras, the nerve ganglia and a few of the basic organs, such as the stomach, through which everything was absorbed into the body such as plants absorbed their nutrition.

Fibers of Kuṇḍalinī Force

336 ℂ Originally this body was twice the size that we are now, with a large forehead and eyes. During times of deep meditation, it took on a transparency, so the chakras could be seen through it, especially the one that was most highly activated. This body, made out of the *kuṇḍalinī* force, was fibrous in nature and very durable, created by flowing awareness through the fibers of the *kuṇḍalinī* when they were in their deep inner body, slowly spinning these fibers round and through that inner body, while simultaneously absorbing the essences of nutritious substances of this planet. However, deep in the Kali Yuga the vehicles that we will live in will be ninety percent more frail, brittle and less durable. But when the Sat Śiva Yuga equalizes the forces again, we will be able to weave a new body in the way we once did, for living here and interplanetary travel. This knowledge will come quite naturally to the older souls first and then be known by the others.

Originally this body was twice the size that we are now, with a large forehead and eyes. During times of deep meditation, it took on a transparency, so the chakras could be seen through it, especially the one that was most highly activated.

Signs of The Sat Yuga's Dawn

337 ℂ As the Sat Śiva Yuga comes into power, all of the many trillion rays which, when meeting, penetrate and actually make up the Earth become stronger and stronger. Every form again, on the planet, will become proportionately larger, and when light is seen at night, produced as a creation of man himself, and he flies and communicates into all areas of the planet, it is the dawn of the Sat Śiva Yuga. The new *yuga* will be heralded by people that think big, feel big and do big things.

Violence at The Initial Awakening

338 ℂ It is when this primal *kuṇḍalinī* force of this planet first awakens, at this time, that much of the population will become wild as animals, with high sex intensities, bursting anger and violence upon one another, and tremendous energies will be employed in doing things of no consequence. Startled by this first awakening, later on they will come

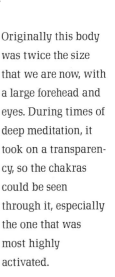

into the mind power of great universal laws and live peacefully together and discover interplanetary travel with ease, and many wonderful things will be done. At this time things will begin to grow large again. Our *śāstras* do not give any time when this is going to occur, but they say it is in layers. One group of people will be in violence, another in the next stage, and the next stage and finally all will be in the same stage like waves.

Teachers Will Help in the Transition

339 ☾Great teachers from other planets will come to Earth to help in this transition, inhabiting large population centers equally spaced on the planet. These souls will be from the same planet we came from long ago and they will begin to arrive at the time of electricity. The only way they will be recognized is through their extreme clarity of mind. They will never get confused. Physically one would tell by the clarity of their eyes, because these great souls move into an already developed body of any age or race three circles prior to the inhabitant's destined time to leave it, similar to taking a candle and placing it on top of a candle already lit and burned down. The transition takes three circles and is imperceptible. They will be found anywhere, in every walk of life. They would be the ones to settle disputes, the subtle leaders out of the darkness, and could be called "keepers of the clarity." They will be welded into every odic force group and known by their great adjustability, flexibility and lack of personal ego, and would not necessarily know who they are, because of the slow transition into physical elements of the meat-and-bone body, which will block out these memories and knowledge, unlike when souls lived in their fibrous bodies, having complete knowledge of themselves, present, past and future, and could converse about happenings that occurred millions of years ago like we speak of what occurred yesterday.

At forty-eight

physical years of age, the activity of kundalini force in humans takes on new patterns. These Lemurians intensified their meditations and physical exercise to hasten the change. The body was placed in quiet positions, one after another while taking deep and rhythmic breaths. Additional disciplines, called tapas, were often administered to control the fire of kundalini during times of adjustment, to help maintain perfect equanimity. When given the tapas of mauna, or silence, herbs were ingested to help strengthen the connection to inner bodies. Those who had mated prior to entering the monastery worked diligently during the six-year period prior to age fifty-four to redirect this powerful streamer of force. Kundalini is also the substance with which our inner connection with the guru is made. Aum.

Zenith awaited Saivite monastics, guided always by their shastras, which were more complete in those far-off days than now. They admonish us that tapas purified the inner mind, effecting changes in the astral body—tapas to incinerate the karmas tapas to harness the desires, tapas to test for strength and tapas to silence thought, all under the diligent direction of the satguru, whom they all venerated.

Gurudeva

340 ℭThe *kuṇḍalinī,* which permeates as a ray the physical body during the transition from the Kali Yuga to the Sat Śiva Yuga, determines the course of the individual life pattern of the soul until he has lived on the planet forty-seven years. It is at the age of forty-eight that a new course and intensification of physical exercise, breathing, meditation should be practiced, during this year, to hasten the change as the pattern of past *kuṇḍalinī* activity wanes and regenerative direction now forms new patterns.

Kuṇḍalinī's Redirection After Age 48

341 ℭThe *kuṇḍalinī* is the life of man. If it flows out to other physical plane beings, as it is beginning to at this time in our communities, with an effort to produce offspring, but for the pleasure of it and not producing offspring, with beings of an opposite sex, the force feeds out, for many years to come, its energies toward the being of the opposite sex the individual had intercourse with. This causes subconscious areas, within the individual mind of the person, and stratums of a conglomerate of mind energy. The redirection of this *kuṇḍalinī* force occurs at the age of forty-eight to the age of fifty-four, we have discovered, and if intensive exercise of the physical body occurs—in placing it into quiet positions, one after another, while breathing deeply and with regularity, as well as praying to the *devas* and Deities—this redirection can be accomplished in one circle. When the accomplishment has been made, it will manifest itself quite obviously, as attributes of the very core of the nature of the individual will change. And we have found that should a family man become a *sādhaka* at the age of forty-eight to fifty-four, this new direction of the *kuṇḍalinī* in its own natural phase of unfoldment would again be hastened.

The Tapas Of Midlife Transition

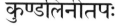

342 ℭIf a monastic in yellow or orange, at this time in his life, goes through this change, it will be imperceptible if his guru is in his physical body, for a great stability and natural darshan will be present to sustain him. Should his guru not be in his physical body at this time, additional *tapas* will have to occur to syphon this natural darshan though that automatically comes to one in yellow and in orange, when this change of the *kuṇḍalinī* flow has occurred. This will be so strong, it sometimes lifts the *tapas* of yellow and brings the monastic into orange. The monastic, however, through the time of this process of *kuṇḍalinī*

change, must never let this darshan turn to fire, and must maintain equanimity that he has been trained to cause to occur constantly within him. The gurus of our time occasionally used this fire to intensify the *tapas* some of us were going through. We were never allowed this privilege, however.

Governance Of Gurus in The Kali Yuga

343 ℭ The *tapas* controls the fire as the *kuṇḍalinī* makes its adjustments within us, as we serve in these great Śaivite monasteries preparing for the sleep of the Kali Yuga, when they will be no more than radiant vibrations permeating darshan, ready to spring up again when the time is right. Our gurus will go forth in the Kali Yuga, the ones that do not leave the planet, to return at the end of that time and become the adjustors, the lawmakers, and the intelligence governing vast communities. Lord Skanda will back them, empower them, direct them, nullify the *karma* of their errors and enhance their inherent success, of intelligence prevailing over ignorance and evil, through this time.

Umāgaṇeśa, Skanda and Lord Śiva

344 ℭ These Śaivite gurus of our time stand alone even now. Their innovations that we carry out come from Gaṇeśa, Skanda and Śiva, whom they counsel; and it is well known among us all that Lord Umāgaṇeśa overshadows, and Hanumān, too, the senior members on the senior minority group of each monastery. To them the guru appears as Lord Skanda with Śiva in his head. Śiva, stationary in the center of the universe; Lord Skanda travels among us all. Śiva moves from planet to planet above all, under all, in and through all. The two are one, yet appear as separate.

Tapas Quells The Fire Of Kuṇḍalinī

345 ℭ *Tapas* is given by gurus of our time to nullify the harmful effects of the *kuṇḍalinī* fire upon our inner bodies as we come closer and closer to Śiva. Our performing *tapas* also nullified the effect of our fire upon the external body of the guru. We each have a direct connection with our guru. This connection is most sacred and is to be cultivated and preserved at all times, else we cannot remain in these monasteries and would have to tread for a time in the consciousness of those that live surrounding them until a connection is renewed and we beg entrance again and are accepted. For through this connection with the guru—created through the exuding power of *kuṇḍalinī* force, to

work as a team—we fulfill our purpose for all of us on our planet.

Tapas is given by gurus of our time to nullify the harmful effects of the *kuṇḍalinī* fire upon our inner bodies as we come closer and closer to Śiva.

The Guru's Singular Channel

346 ℂ These gurus cannot be approached by any of us. They are unapproachable. They cannot be communicated with by any of us. They speak with our Deities, command the *devas* and genies who await their bidding. But they are bound to seek us out, for when we appear as Umāgaṇeśa in the senior minority group, our guru is there. He sought us out. He directs and advises and counsels and corrects.

Working Directly with The Guru

347 ℂ On occasion, a guru *tapas*, working with the guru himself, is given by him, who skillfully selects one who can fulfill the mission he has in store. When guru *tapas* is given, we are careful not to delve into his other areas of thought and activity, nor are we allowed to participate within the senior minority group. We wear yellow and take a more than humble position within any monastery we find ourselves. When traveling with him, our seniority is not lost in the monastery we started from, but guru *tapas* is never allowed to be concluded until we have stayed one moon within that monastery. Then we assume our natural position and duties there.

The Remedy For Pulling On the Guru

348 ℂ When a monastic is not handling his pattern of equanimity and humility well, due to his connection with his guru, he will pull upon the forces of his guru. This, our guru of this monastery tells us, is quite harmful to the members of all monasteries. Therefore, at times certain *tapas* is given by him through the senior minority group, with or without explanation, to allow the individual monastic pulling upon his guru to release, so that he, through the intensity of the *tapas*, can pull upon a new fibrous current of *kuṇḍalinī* force, thus strengthening his inner body in its connection with the outer, annihilating the ramifications of thought and renewing the destiny to be attained by throwing his forces back on himself. It is in this way, our guru tells us, that the Deities and himself can give great assistance of stability, and of giving a regulated force rather than being pulled upon and taken from by the indiscriminate monastic going through a trying time. This power, that our guru has been accumulating for many *yugas*, now is so subtle and refined that it is not noticed when we are one with him, but felt and missed when we are not. *Tapas*, turning *kuṇḍalinī* into fire of certain kinds of heat and intensity for certain specific purposes, is the method of cure of Śaivite gurus on this planet at this time. So, therefore, each Śaivite monastery is complete within itself, appreciating and even expecting our guru to visit, but always knowing he is near and in direct communication with the Umāgaṇeśa of our senior minority. For his existence is our existence and fulfillment.

Our Guru's Implacable Disposition

349 ℭ Our guru never discussed anything with us when we performed guru *tapas* with him or were in this seat of Umagāneśa within a senior minority. He listened to the information that we gave him and spoke out our answers and directions directly and precisely. We usually wrote it down for clarity to persist. He answered our questions and, when nothing of importance occurred, entertained us with his merriment and spoke of unusual things that he saw within the inner worlds that we could not see. Everything was perfect, is perfect, and will be perfect even through the darkness of the Kali Yuga, as far as he was concerned. This was difficult to totally encompass, though the philosophy is well founded, in these changing times, as the imposing darkness of the next *yuga* already casts certain shadows in the minds of some who surround our monasteries.

Mauna Tapas, The Remedy Of Quietude

350 ℭ *Mauna tapas*, that of silence, was given by our guru to those who concerned themselves with the community that surrounded our monasteries so thoroughly they could not forget it after they entered the monastery as *sādhakas*. They would travel past our walls at night, and the guards could not stop them; they would move so fast and with such desire. Though their desires are noble and motivations clearly beneficial, we'd rather they stay within the monastery and attend a lecture, the dissemination of great teaching from our guru, or one of the neighboring gurus, in the Second World. When speaking does not occur, thinking loses forcefulness; new channels of *kuṇḍalinī* are then activated and external concerns beyond monastery walls become only fleeting interests. This *tapas* was more than often employed for guidance of the *sādhakas* or monastics in yellow who could not remain here with us all at night, his only escape from us being the merger into the Central Sun, the Self beyond all the planets, universes and their complications which invoke our perceptive insight and understanding. During *tapas* of certain natures, such as *mauna tapas,* herbs should be taken to strengthen the connection to the inner bodies. Any kind of these herbs that do not have to be prepared by heating them, but picked and eaten occasionally, should be used.

Mauna tapas, that of silence, was given by our guru to those who concerned themselves with the community that surrounded our monasteries so thoroughly they could not forget it after they entered the monastery as *sādhakas.*

Seniority Staffs; Wands Of Power

351 ℂ As I look out from this place where I write, before committing this document to the inner ether to be read at another time, I see the youngest among us all here struggling with the choice of a new senior minority group. He has forgotten the formula, and one of the more mature monastics is helping him. He's holding a stick in his hand and asking the meaning of some of the notches he had not discovered before. Around the top of the stick, which is square with a rounded top—the mark of Śiva—is a group of notches on each corner, and then below them a line carved around, separating one group of notches from the other group of notches. On one corner there is one notch above the line carved around, indicating the physical age. On the next corner, two notches, as we turn the stick clockwise, indicating monastic age. All three of which are indicated by notches below, depicting a circle. On the fourth side are four notches indicating residency within the monastery, and these little notches, more close together than the others, indicate moons, with a larger notch, interspersed in-between, indicating a circle. The older the monastic became in one of these four areas, the longer the stick had to be, and the notches were placed together as are mountain ranges and their valleys; and so, even by the length of the stick, this monastic is telling the younger one, one can interpret the seniority of one monastic and another. These sticks in later years became wands of power, and energies could be transferred through them for a given end. They were kept most carefully, tucked neatly in the back of the waist, remaining always as a symbol of our Lord Skanda deep within our spine.

The Guru's Quizzing of Umāgaṇeśa

352 ℂ Once an Umāgaṇeśa was chosen by the little one, our guru would meet with him and test him as to his knowledge of the *śāstras* by asking him questions, as if he did not know the answers within the *śāstras,* for him to solve through his knowledge of them in solving current problems and situations. The solution was always there within the *śāstras.* The monastic consulted with Umāgaṇeśa Himself and sought the answer within his wisdom and our *śāstras.* When *śāstric* knowledge was memorized and juggled in wisdom, he became a perfect channel for Umāgaṇeśa to work through in keeping all of us in our proper categories in time and space.

Appreciation Of Śāstric Astuteness

353 ℂ If any of us had been in the monastery for any significant length of time, we studied the *śāstras* most faithfully and brought to the forefront of our knowledge much of which we took for granted in our culture; and though we knew and memorized it in our early training, we live it so well now that it has been forgotten. Our guru was always pleased when we were so astute that we would bring forth the solution, the answer, the direction, the *tapas* to be given that he in his own wisdom would have told us.

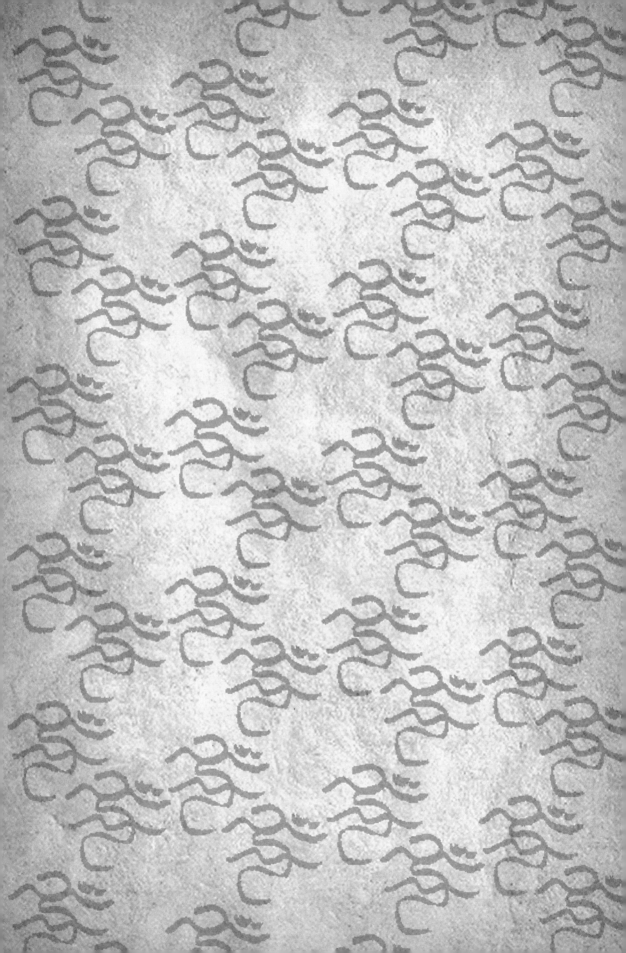

Prior to entering one of the Saivite monasteries, a sadhaka was expected to settle all worldly affairs, and after entering never look back. For it was found that the young monastic was psychically attached to his mother until twenty-four physical years of age, and if he allowed himself to brood over the past and mentally visit his family, it would strengthen the psychic bonds and cause confusion and unhappiness within the home. Likewise, the monastic who put full energy into his monastic life transferred to his family some of the darshan he was experiencing, creating a harmonious and happy home. Each young sadhaka made every effort to disconnect the psychic tubes that tied him to his relatives and weld them tightly to his guru, whom he deemed to be his new mother and new father. Aum.

ॐ marks time's continuum; the end is always a new beginning. Here are patterns of the past that forge cultures of the future for each monastic, a sustainable life born of love for God, Gods and guru, necessitating detachment from his birth family to enter his spiritual family. Keeper of the race is mother. Her importance will be felt in the Kali Yuga. Her neglect or unlimited caring will change humankind.

Gurudeva

354 ℂ Outside the walls, in the community, in some of the homes of enlightened family men, constant training of potential *sādhakas* goes on. It generally commences after the age of puberty, for then a young man automatically detaches from his mother. This is about twelve years of age. It takes another twelve years for the final detachment to occur, during which time he is primarily trained by the pattern his father sets for him, or he is taken by a guru from his family home and placed in the home of a *brahmachārī* family, a family that has no sexual intercourse, for training to enter the monastery. With special permission, a young soul might enter this family's household as early as nine or ten years of age, and the monastery as early as fourteen. If any attachment exists to mother or the rest of the family after the age of fourteen, it is only diminishing attachment, and if any attachment exists after the age of twenty-four, other than love, respect and honor to the mother on the part of the son, it is on the part of the son himself because of his not being sure of his way in the world and his seeking to reattach to his mother through psychic means.

Detachment From Family And Friends

355 ℂ Therefore, at any time after the age of fourteen, up to the age of twenty-four, he is accepted into one of our Śaivite monasteries, after proving himself, having settled his worldly affairs and obtained the good feeling of mother and father as the diminishing attachment fades away. If he enters the monastery after the age of eighteen, he should simply, courteously and lovingly beg leave of his mother, father and friends by informing them of his new position in *sādhaka* life that he hopes to attain by sitting by our wall. Then he should never look back, for that would strengthen the psychic bonds, that are in the process of diminishing from the age of eighteen to twenty-four, and cause congestion and confusion in the nerve system of the family.

Hanumān's Assurance to The Mother

356 ℂ It is the Hanumān of the senior minority group of each monastery who should make an effort to talk with his mother so that she feels secure and is assured that he will be well trained and cared for, even though she full well knows the nature of these monasteries. The mother needs this assurance for her son, that he be trained well and that some person within the monastery will continue to raise and love him, for she is still

psychically attached to him by a great tube of Second World matter, which though diminishing still exists. This tube is an extension of the umbilical cord that was with them both at birth. Once the Hanumān has made the mother feel as secure as possible that her son will be treated with due reverence and respect, and the entire senior minority group has satisfied itself that the entire family is not overtly objecting to his decision, but relatively pleased, his life as a *sādhaka* begins.

Directing the Sexual Forces After Puberty

357 ℭ Puberty begins when the awareness of the soul comes into the animal nerve system as a result of being in this particular kind of fleshy body. Before this time, the body is maturing and growing, and the nerve system of the soul's inner body governs it, much like it did when we had our original fibrous bodies. But when four cycles have passed, the external structure becomes firmed and strong, and the instincts for mating occur. Therefore, it is important that these forces be carefully directed so that the soul is not clouded by instinctive drives and still maintains its inner contact with the three worlds.

Stages of Heightened Divinity

358 ℭ When a soul is in a six-year-old physical body, he is in divine consciousness and in tune with the three worlds. At this time, the height of Divinity is manifest through him. He only comes again into this state after the age of fifty-four, which continues to the physical age of seventy-two, and then again enters this stage after the age of eighty-four, which continues on through the rest of his physical existence. From the age of seventy-two to the age of eighty-four, he is able to strongly express spiritual intellect. This is the time great manuscripts are written that are passed on through our walls to family *brahmachārī* men who train the youth to enter back through our walls. In writing this manuscript, I am in this age grouping and soon will be eighty-one.

The First Rites of Passage

359 ℭ This pure, childlike Divinity of the inner body of our soul is full of life, spontaneously joyous. It is always there within these bony bodies covered with flesh. It is only after the physical age of six years old that the awareness of the being comes into a slow understanding that he has a physical body. Therefore, in our temples, a ceremony is given at six years old as well as at birth, and the children are brought by their fathers after birth for the impact of the darshan. At six years old, the male child is brought to the temple, again at twelve, at eighteen and twenty-four. These ceremonies mark a total change, destined to occur, in his life and consciousness. So he is brought before our Deity at these auspicious times in his life to receive the special impact of the darshan to sustain him through the next six years.

This pure, childlike Divinity of the inner body of our soul is full of life, spontaneously joyous. It is always there within these bony bodies covered with flesh. It is only after the physical age of six years old that the awareness of the being comes into a slow understanding that he has a physical body.

Hair on the Head, Face and Body

360 ℭ At six years of age and before, the child lives in his head. His eye is open, undisturbed, and it takes great effort to keep the brow alive so that, as the time wears on and the physical body changes, the force does not become drained from it. Special ceremonies in our temple are always being held for the refinement of our bodies. The hair that appears on the face and body indicates to us the unfoldment of the instinctive nature of the animal forces of that nerve system. We seek through ceremony and *tapas* to deactivate and disengage that nerve system, thus minimizing the growth of these hairs on the face and torso of the body, whereas the hair on the head was part of the original fibrous body. The hair on other parts of it, though, are from a mutation out of the animal kingdom, and they should never be cut off but plucked out carefully and precisely while certain incantations are chanted. This aids in deactivating the instinctive drives of the animal nerve system so that the refined nerve system of the soul can replace and fully take over these bodies of bone and flesh.

Transferring Psychic Ties To the Guru

361 ℭ It is the guru that is the mother, the father, the close relative to the young *sādhaka,* and hence every effort is made to transfer the Second World psychic tubes connecting into his relatives, to weld them tightly with his guru. Sometimes they are given up willingly and joyously by the mother and father. Other times it is more difficult to pass them on, and they are left to fade away after the age of twenty-four. Then rapidly new psychic connections must be made with the guru, else there is a tendency for the young monastic to feel disconnected from the monastery itself and wander out beyond its walls. For it is not allowed to be connected fully with one's guru and parents at the same time.

Importance Of Mother's Blessings

362 ℭ It is in accordance with our law that at the point that the young disciple recognizes his guru and seeks entrance into one of our monasteries, it is the mother that must inwardly give blessing and assurance of harmony and forbearance. If she overtly objects by causing confusion or unhappy conditions, this signifies she holds tight to the psychic bonds and is not inwardly ready to release her offspring. If the guru were connected also to the young disciple, other than showering out a general love, her upset would be felt through his nerve system and the monastics working closely with him, even the entire senior minority group of the monastery he was seeking entrance into, so strong is the mother's attachment to her son in these fleshy bodies of ours.

Discerning The Mother's Disposition

363 ℂ If the condition of the mother at the time the son departs to sit before the monastery wall is relatively calm, and no argument or confusion occurs, this indicates her blessing and forbearance. Or if she cries, that is good and constitutes an inner dissolving of the psychic cords. Or if she sends a gift, large or small, with her son to the monastery, or before him or after him, this indicates her surrender to his destiny, even though she may have caused an unhappy condition of confusion and misunderstanding before. A silent gift speaks of the current inner state of her releasing him and is a confirmation of her blessing and good will. For until he passes age twenty-four, she does have the power to object and upset the nerve system of all concerned.

Families' Adjusting to Separation

364 ℂ It is considered that the blessing of the mother is like the darshan from the guru, an unspoken feeling. Our gurus cannot explain their darshan or even feel the effects of it, as a mother cannot explain her feelings. It is during this time on the planet that families are very close. Life in them is warm and beautiful, and the attachments are strong. In the years to come in the Kali Yuga this may not always be so. Therefore, it is with much difficulty a young man withdraws from his family and enters one of our monasteries. But more than usually, when he informed the family he was entering the monastery or their guru told them this, they adjusted quite readily.

Wisdom Bequeathed to The Future

365 ℂ I shall leave you now with this that I have written in assurance that it may be found in the *ākāśa* of the inner mind when needed most.

Timeline

कालचक्र

THERE ARE VARIOUS THEORIES REGARDING THE LENGTH OF THE *YUGAS,* OR ERAS, AND WHERE IN THE VAST SPAN OF TIME WE ARE TODAY. THE MOST WIDELY ACCEPTED VIEW IN THE HINDU TRADITION DATES THE BEGINNING of the Kali Yuga at 3102 BCE. Others believe we are beginning the Sat Yuga and some, such as Sri Yukteswar, have calculated we are in the Dvāpara Yuga. The *Scrolls* say that "Our Lemurian calculations of time will not be translatable into calendars of the Kali Yuga, so at that time there will be confusion about the length of time each *yuga* is supposed to contain. But it is discernable when another *yuga* is imminent by the changes that occur within the population." According to Hindu scriptures that speak of such matters (*Manu Saṁhitā, Surya Siddhānta* and the *Purāṇas*), the length of the Kali Yuga is 432,000 years. If we use the most widely accepted dating, we are just beginning the "great sleep," and Earth will not see the dawn of the Sat Yuga for roughly 427,000 years. Through the last twenty-five years, in reading *Lemurian Scrolls* within our monasteries, we came to accept the view given in this holy text that the Kali Yuga is now slowly coming to an end. So, we were content to live with the disparity between some Hindu views and the assertions in this text—that is until we decided to release *Lemurian Scrolls* to the world. It was then that I asked one of my *āchāryas* to study the matter in detail. This humble timeline is the result. It is not meant to be a definitive, final word on the matter by any means, but a tool for better understanding the times spoken of in the scrolls compiled for this book. It reflects the dating given in *Lemurian Scrolls,* drawing on the lengths of the major time periods of the Hindu system, and places that dating alongside key dates of modern scientific and archeological discoveries. ℭ We began our time quest by determining what *yuga* we are in now according to *Lemurian Scrolls.* Paragraph 163 states that the Sat Yuga will dawn "when the inhabitants of the Earth are able to light the night with their own devices...." This, history tells us, occurred in

1879 when Thomas Alva Edison invented the incandescent light bulb, and within three decades electric lighting was commonplace. So, from 1879 we worked backwards. Using the traditional length of the Kali Yuga as 432,000 years, we calculated that the Kali Yuga must have begun approximately 430,000 BCE. *Lemurian Scrolls* prophesied that the Kali Yuga would begin when man begins to kill one another. As indicated in this timeline, modern science verifies that man killed man as early as 450-350,000 BCE, as evidenced by skeletal remains found in Africa of a human who had been scalped by a stone knife. Continuing backwards in time through the *yugas* in this way, we discovered, to our astonishment, that science's dating corresponds with many of the major earth changes described and dated in *Lemurian Scrolls*. ℭ A note about terminology. It is important to understand that the word *yuga*, meaning an era, can refer to various periods of time. We found this useful information when studying out the *Scrolls'* various key references to *yugas*, because at first they seemed confusing, even contradictory. After some deep meditation and prayers sent to the holy *devas* through the sacred fire at Kadavul Temple, the answer to several apparent conundrums came to light. The key was in the phrase "cycle of *yugas*," which all these years we took to mean the duration of the four repeating eras, Sat, Tretā, Dvāpara and Kali Yuga, which in the cosmology of Sanātana Dharma last a total of 4,320,000 years. This is also called a *mahā-yuga* ("great age") or *chaturyuga* ("four-fold era"). In fact, in many cases, this we understand now to be the correct meaning, such as in paragraph eight: "When the next Sat Yuga arrives, those who have lived through the cycle of *yugas* will all finish their evolutionary processes and leave. More divine souls will come during that time as the cycle repeats." But in studying *Lemurian Scrolls* alongside science's knowledge of Earth's development and the assertions of various other schools of thought, it was evident that in certain key places "cycle of *yugas*" was referring to a far vaster period of time. So, we looked to the next larger increment in the remarkable system of Hindu dating—called the *manvantara*. It is an enormous period lasting, yes, 308,478,000 years. Each *manvantara* consists of 71 *chaturyugas*. For example, paragraph 26 of *Lemurian Scrolls* states, "During the second cycle of *yugas*, celestial beings arrived from other planets, bringing with them vegetation...." Here, by interpreting "cycle of *yugas*" as *manvantara*, the statement concurs with the discoveries of modern archeology. Science states that the first plant and animal life appeared on Earth during this second *manvantara*, which began approximately 61 million years ago. A *manvantara*, from the Sanskṛit *Manu* and *antara*, meaning, "an age of a *Manu* (or man)," roughly corresponds to the length of time it takes our solar system to make a complete revolution around the Central Sun, or galactic center. According to current scientific estimates, it takes 260 million years for our sun to make one revolution around the center of our galaxy—which is not far afield from Hindu scriptural dating of 306,720,000 plus the *sandhyā* (twilight) of 1,728,000 years for a *manvantara* cycle. We must keep in mind that a "year" is a period that can also vary in these vast time frames, as the Earth's orbit around the sun has been constantly changing since the Earth came into being. As we proceeded through our time study, carefully interpreting each "cycle of *yuga*" reference, the following timeline unfolded. ℂ Herein are cited significant events throughout Earth's history as told or predicted in *Lemurian Scrolls*, side-by-side with the findings of modern science, along with research by Hindu astrologers Pundit G.S. Sampath Iyengar and Vamadeva Shastri (Dr. David Frawley). One final note regarding the beginning of the Kali Yuga. There is a slow transition between one *yuga* and the next, called *sandhyā*, a word used to denote the twilight transition while one era is subsiding and the next has yet to fully dawn. Part of the population lives in the next while the rest is imbedded in finishing out the last *yuga*. There are always forerunners of the race, the inventors and implementors of positive changes. Our last Kali Yuga began to end as the Sat Śiva Yuga began to show the dim light of dawn when lighting the night was achieved. But the Kali Yuga will have truly ended for all when the sun is seen to peek the horizon of a peaceful ocean—when the last person is killed by another. When killing among people ends forever, true *ahiṁsā* reigns. This is the hallmark, the benchmark, the prophets say, of the true sunrise of the Sat Yuga. We are admonished to be patient, awaiting this most eventful day. It will come. It will come. To be sure, it will inevitably come.

FIRST CYCLE

-925,342,121 SCROLLS: The first time period *(manvantara)* referenced in *Lemurian Scrolls* begins [determined by calculating backwards from 1879, when man first learned to "light the night by his own devices"]. This is understood to be the first "cycle of *yugas*" in which there is a relationship between Earth and souls from several major planets in the galaxy. (In the Hindu time perspective, chanted today by priests at the start of *pūjā,* the universe was, at this point, in the fourth *manvantara* of the 51st year of Brahmā.)
SCIENCE: Earth becomes a recognizable but not yet habitable planet. Land masses are still forming, with many volcanic eruptions. The Earth has undergone more than 2.5 billion years of development, and the universe is more than 15 billion years old.

SECOND CYCLE

-616,994,121 SCROLLS: Second *manvantara* begins.
SCIENCE: Earth becomes habitable; water evaporates, forming air.
SCROLLS: Earth is seeded for future populations. "During the second cycle of *yugas,* celestial beings arrived from other planets bringing with them vegetation. Their spaceships passing over the Earth's surface dropped seeds and foliage...." ℂ.26

-435,000,000 SCIENCE: First evidence of plant life.
SCROLLS: Souls come to Earth and incarnate as animals. "Celestial beings came en masse and hovered over the Earth in their etheric bodies. Some became the birds and small and large animals...." ℂ.26

-410,000,000 SCIENCE: First land animals appear.

THIRD CYCLE

-308,446,121 SCROLLS: Third *manvantara* begins.

-300,000,000 SCIENCE: Evidence of dinosaurs.

-120,000,000 SCIENCE: Evidence of earliest warm blooded mammals.

-65,000,000 SCIENCE: Last of the dinosaurs disappear.

SAT YUGA

-4,318,121 SCROLLS: Seventy *chaturyugas* have passed in the third *manvantara*, and Earth enters the Sat Yuga (prior to the one we are in now), beginning the 71st and final *chaturyuga* of the third *manvantara*.

SCIENCE: "Human" life appears.

SCROLLS: Celestial beings manifest Earth bodies around their subtle form. "In the Sat Yuga, the air was thick and the Earth lush and tropical. The thick clouds of gases and healthful substances floating in the air were the materials the divine souls that came to the fire planet, as they referred to it, would use to materialize a physical body around the etheric body of the soul to express through while living on Earth.... They acquired a full physical form and could eat normally, as the animals did on Earth at that time." ℭ3

SCROLLS: First temples are built to bring through more souls. "In order to bring these divine souls through into physical form during the Sat Yuga, great temples to each of these planets began to form... The celestial beings would stand on the pedestal and absorb the Earth's pungent substances and with it materialize strong physical bodies.... But through the thousands of years that passed, it became a very rapid process, and the entire Earth became populated with celestial beings from several of the major planets in the galaxy...." ℭ5

-3,500,000 SCIENCE: Evidence of Hominids, first walking upright "terrestrial animals," East Africa.

SCROLLS: "As the Sat Yuga ended with the advent of the Tretā Yuga, the ratio of divine beings to those entering the animal kingdom was something like three to one...." ℭ20

TRETA YUGA

-2,590,121 SCROLLS: Tretā Yuga begins. The first human body originating in the animal kingdom develops as a result of the original body being eaten by animals. "Many of these divine, Earthly bodies, constructed from fruit ambrosia, herbal essences and the pungent air, could no longer fly and have been eaten by the carnivorous beings of the animal kingdom.... These souls got caught within the evolutionary cycle of the particular species that had eaten their original body.... They finally cultivated a body similar to the first Earth body devoured long ago. This human body had animal instincts and was difficult to live in...." ℂ12

SCROLLS: Many of the souls who came during the second *manvantara* begin to evolve human bodies. "Even during this *yuga,* the small animals from the second cycle of *yugas* are coming into human form...." ℂ26

-2,000,000 SCIENCE: *Homo habilis* appears. Known as "handy man," stone tools made by this species found in South Africa.

-2,000,000 SCIENCE: *Australopithecus robustus,* a vegetarian species, thrives in East Africa over next million years.

-1,900,000 SCIENCE: Evidence of first stone building in East Africa.

SCROLLS: Human flesh bodies are perfected. "The Tretā Yuga is a wonderful period in which intense cosmic rays still penetrate Earth. This makes such evolution possible as creating a flesh body that appears to be like the original one for these celestial beings caught in animal reincarnation cycles to inhabit. These flesh-and-bone bodies will last through the Dvāpara and Kali Yugas..." ℂ13

-1,500,000 SCIENCE: *Homo erectus,* considered the first humans, appear. Remains of a six-foot-tall, twelve-year old found in Kenya.

SCROLLS: Half are still in their original bodies. "One half to one half was the ratio during the Tretā Yuga." "Toward [the Tretā Yuga's] end, the ratio is one in the original body to three in the others." ℂ20

SCROLLS: Souls avoid being caught in the animal kingdom. "The few left who have original bodies will live in caves high in the mountains during the end of the Tretā Yuga to avoid being caught in the fleshy, hot body of the animal...." ℂ15 "It has been observed, now that we are approaching the end of the Tretā Yuga, that a sense of fear is being experienced for the first time as a result of eating wrong kinds of foods, along with losing some of the personal abilities to fly." ℂ13

DVAPARA YUGA

-1,294,121 SCROLLS: Cataclysms begin the Dvāpara Yuga, and the race of celestial beings, having lost their original bodies, become grounded. "The sign of our losing our ability to fly is the official beginning of the Dvāpara Yuga's advent in space and time. Then vast substances will form and divide the land." ℂ21 "Our prophecies read out that during the Dvāpara and Kali Yugas every celestial soul will either be in an animal body or in a human body made of its flesh, fire and bones...." ℂ20

SCROLLS: Early Dravidians perpetuate Lemurian culture. "The Lemurians that became divided from the others through the formation of vast bodies of water, so great they were unable to go around them through the thousands of circles, took on other ways of living. The Dravidians, formerly Lemurians, formerly the first priestly inhabitants, the leaders, the guardians of the primal race, have never had a break in continuity...." ℂ164

-900,000 SCIENCE: *Homo erectus* migrates through Egypt, India and Java to China.

-450-360,000 SCIENCE: Early cave-dwelling *Homo sapiens* master the use of fire in China and later migrate to Britain.

SCROLLS: Earth's gravity is becoming stronger. "Toward the end of the Dvāpara Yuga, new magnetic forces will begin to develop so very strongly on the planet, as the gravity on the Earth gets stronger and stronger and nothing floats in the air anymore...." ℂ43

SCROLLS: As cataclysms began the Dvāpara Yuga, so do they bring it to an end, as the darkness of the Kali Yuga looms. "In the end of the Dvāpara Yuga is seen the destruction of everything that had been built in the Tretā Yuga in the dark area of the world. The races of light and the races of darkness become divided by water. The air becomes thinner....Everyone will try to influence everyone else through the powers of his mind. People try to convert other people to their religion and philosophy. No one is left on his own. Thought becomes very important to everyone. Everyone tries to program everyone else's thoughts. The destruction of this civilization will begin the Kali Yuga...." ℂ22

KALI YUGA

-430,121 SCROLLS: Man kills man. The Kali Yuga begins. "These books prophesied that when one of the first inhabitants of the fire planet is so antagonized by the building of these forces in the Second World that he destroys the body of another inhabitant, that will mark the point in time and space when the Kali Yuga will begin;..." ℂ163

-450-350,000 SCIENCE: *Homo sapiens* found scalped by a stone knife in Ethiopia.

SCROLLS: War and turmoil prevails. "It will be during the Kali Yuga that a human kingdom will eventually fully come out of the different species of animals and form different groups on Earth, some of whom will be the predators of others,..." ℂ16

-150,000 SCIENCE: Ice age. Cave dwellers are known to have inhabited Europe.

SCROLLS: Climate changes. "The atmosphere will change again in the Dvāpara Yuga and Kali Yuga,..." ℂ30 "Most all of Lemuria will be under vast bodies of liquid during the Kali Yuga,..." ℂ27

-128,000 SCIENCE: Climate warms and the great glaciers of the ice age melt, causing seas to rise.

-120,000 SCIENCE: Neanderthals, a species with larger brains than *Homo sapiens*, appear.

-100,000 SCIENCE: In South and East Africa, *Homo sapiens sapiens* are known to have had the same brain size as they do today.

-70,000 SCIENCE: Earth grows colder over the next 40,000 years.

-30,000 SCIENCE: Ice age begins. (During the last two million years at least ten ice ages have occurred.)

-30,000 SCIENCE: Neanderthals vanish.

SCIENCE: Native Americans spread throughout the Americas.

SCIENCE: Dravidians, the Caucasian equator people, exist.

-10,000 SCIENCE: Ice melts, seas again rise.

LITERATURE: Plato states that the legendary Atlantis sinks because of a cataclysm at the end of the last ice age.

-8576 ASTROLOGY: Beginning of Saptaṛishi era calendar.

-7000 SCIENCE: Farming begins in Indus Valley.

-6500 ASTROLOGY: *Ṛig Veda* verses (e.g., 1.117.22, 1.116.12, 1.84.13.5) say winter solstice begins in Aries, indicating the antiquity of this section of the *Vedas*.

-5000 SCIENCE: Early Harappa Valley civilization thrives.

-3139 SCIENCE/ASTROLOGY: *Mahābharata* war between the Kauravas and the Paṇḍavas.

-3114 ASTROLOGY: Beginning of Mayan era calendar.

-3102 ASTROLOGY: Beginning of Kali era calendar according to contemporary Hindu scriptural calculations.

FOURTH CYCLE

1879 CE SCROLLS: Fourth time period *(manvantara)* referenced in *Lemurian Scrolls* begins.

SAT YUGA

1879 CE MODERN HISTORY: Thomas Edison invents the incandescent bulb, and man learns to light the night.

SCROLLS: The fourth *manvantara* and current Sat Yuga begin. "When the inhabitants of the Earth are able to light the night with their own devices…the Sat Śiva Yuga will begin through this one advent in time and space…." ℂ.163

1945 MODERN HISTORY: As chronicled in *Lemurian Scrolls,* revolutionary advancements are seen in technology and communication, and a blending of the races begins.

Let it be hereby known that the original dictations, notes, individual summaries, essays, teletype and computer files of Lemurian Scrolls have by my own hand been destroyed on February 26, 1998, at 7:30 AM, the time of a lunar eclipse, in a large fire in the fireplace of the Kadavul Hindu Temple. This book you now hold in your hands is the final rendering of the revelations, carefully selected and edited by me, Satguru Sivaya Subramuniyaswami. Anytime in future years that comments or what are said to be writings of the original texts or other interpretations of this work arise, they must be considered fraudulent and disregarded as such. I make this statement in wisdom to avoid misunderstanding that may come up in the future, as it often does. We can consider that what has happened in the past may, and most likely will, happen in the future. Below are the signatures of all who have witnessed the cremation of the earlier edition, original dictations, analyses and musings. They together attest that the copy of Lemurian Scrolls you now hold in your hands is the final of finals and only authentic text. Let it be hereby known that the original dictations, notes, individual summaries, essays,

LET IT BE HEREBY KNOWN THAT THE ORIGINAL DICTATIONS, NOTES, INDIVIDUAL SUMMARIES, ESSAYS, teletype and computer files of *Lemurian Scrolls* have by my own hand been destroyed on February 26, 1998, at 7:30 AM, the time of a lunar eclipse, in a large fire in the fireplace of the Kadavul Hindu Temple. This book you now hold in your hands is the final rendering of the revelations, carefully selected and edited by me, Satguru Sivaya Subramuniyaswami. Anytime in future years that comments or what are said to be writings of the original texts or other interpretations of this work arise, they must be considered fraudulent and disregarded as such. I make this statement in wisdom to avoid misunderstanding that may come up in the future, as it often does. We can consider that what has happened in the past may, and most likely will, happen in the future. Below are the signatures of all who have witnessed the cremation of the earlier edition, original dictations, analyses and musings. They together attest that the copy of *Lemurian Scrolls* you now hold in your hands is the final of finals and only authentic text.

Sivaya Subramuniyaswami

Paramacharya Bodhinatha

Acharya Palaniswami Saravananathaswami

Acharya Ceyonswami Sadhaka Jothinatha

Acharya Kumarswami Sadhaka Tyaganatha

Sannyasi [illegible] Yogi Tapodhanar

Yogi Vairaganatha Yogi [illegible]

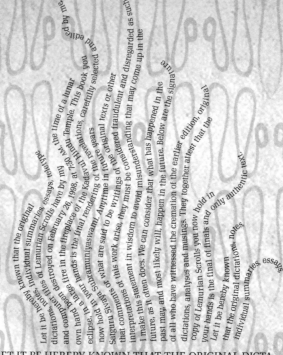

Conclusion

निर्वहणम्

HONORABLY, WE LET THIS BOOK LIE ON THE SHELF FOR TWENTY-FOUR YEARS, WAITING TO SEE IF IT WOULD BE USEFUL AND APPROPRIATE TO EACH AND ALL WHO ARE MYSTICALLY INCLINED. NOW, WE CAN, WITH GOOD conscience, decree this a most excellent and mature revelation that has stood the test of time. Over the years these *śāstras* have matured my monastic order and close devotees who molded their lives according to the culture of the very ancient times described herein. These scrolls eventually became the legend of human origin in our own *Holy Orders of Sannyāsa* and *Śaiva Dharma Śāstras,* as do the Mayans have their stories of man's origins, as do so many other religions. The basic teaching in this remarkable tome, that man came to Earth from other planets over four million years ago, seemed revolutionary when we first received it.

Gracing the Release of These Scrolls

In early days, there were many discussions among the *āchāryas,* swāmīs, *yogīs* and *sādhakas* of my order as to how, or even if, we should release these revelations. To settle their mind, they were instructed to research other cultures, religions and modern faiths as to their perceptions of the origins of man. They did, and that, too, was a revelation. They found that in recent times there has emerged a whole school of thought in modern science that understands and promotes the view of life's coming from other planets, in juxtaposition to the Darwinian theory that life began as a microorganism and slowly evolved to what we now know as modern humans. In 1997, scientists examined meteorites, collected in Alaska two decades earlier, containing apparent fossilized evidence of simple life from Mars. During the months this book was being prepared for press, the world was viewing the Red Planet up close on TV, following the adventures of the first robot explorer as it studied the rock-strewn, rugged landscape and examined the composition of a small boulder called Yogi. Even more compellingly, as documented in our preface, man's extraterrestrial origins echo through the great creation myths of several of Earth's ancient cultures. According to a legend of Tibet's pre-Buddhist Bon religion, the first Tibetans descended from the sky to the mountaintops on ladders of rainbow light. Hindu creation accounts, as in the millennia-old *Vedas,* speak of the creation of humanity as a sacrifice, a *yajña,* a mystic rite through which the Divine Being is divided to create man. The Australian Aborigines, among Earth's oldest continuous cultures, preserve a perspective that it was the Gods in our ancient past who established life on Earth. Legends of North America's Omaha tribe describe an early period in which souls, or spirits, sought a planet on which they could take physical form, a view exactly paralleling that of *Lemurian Scrolls.* "The hosts of the spirits descended and became flesh and blood. They fed on the seeds of the grasses and the fruits of the trees, and the land vibrated with their expressions of joy and gratitude to Wakonda, the maker of all things." Theosophists also speak of Earth's early non-physical inhabitants, and of the first group's traveling here from the moon. Their third root race, the first to take physical form, were called the Lemurians.

A Vision of Earth's Early Inhabitants

Indeed, this early time in Earth's history was revealed to me in 1973 when I inwardly saw great intelligences that were totally one with space, who moved through space as a jellyfish moves through water, but much more refined than that comparison. These beings, it was conveyed to me psychically, were the first original-bodied people spoken of in the text, and they indicated they will become an essence of intelligence. I, like you who have now read this, had no knowledge of such happenings before the inner-world beings brought these texts before my astral vision. It was as revealed to me then as it is now to you. Yes, considering the insights of Earth's ancient cultures, the findings of modern science and the revelations of these *śāstras* themselves, the idea of life from beyond the Earth has, as the millennium draws near, emerged as a very real, some say highly probable, possibility. Prior to this date, the *Lemurian Scrolls* were only allowed to be studied or read to others by lifetime renunciates at auspicious times. In late 1997 it was planned to release them to a select group of long-time initiates. Then, surprisingly, in the midst of final preparations for publication of what would have been only a few hundred copies of this vast wisdom, the divine thrust came to release them freely to the world at large.

Karttikeya, Lord of the Pleiades

It was our great Pleiadian God Muruga—known around the globe as Kārttikeya, Subramaniam, Sanatkumār, Skanda and Ku—who opened His most private library to us revealing these scrolls and personally helped through the years until now, the right time before His Tamil peoples experience the year 5100 of their Hindu calendar, which happened April, 13, 1998. This definitely marked a turning point in the destiny of this 60-million-strong Dravidian community. He is the multi-faced God of a variety of levels of intelligence. With his six faces, He sees all. No devotee who comes to His over 100,000 temples, which remain alive and vibrant in His worship today, is neglected. All who come feel a personal relationship with Him, as He channels the divine energies from the Pleiades into the depths of their souls. With His twelve arms, He embraces everyone and tends to the minutia and the magnified with equal eagerness. Such is this Pleiadian master, whose knowledge is broad, whose intelligence is penetrating and wisdom is as sharp and timely as His mighty *vel.* The research done by the *maṭhavāsis* into the views of Earth's cultures on man's origins and links with other planets showed a deep connection with the Pleiades. I thought you might enjoy a few of our findings. The Pleiades constellation is a star cluster, also known as M45, located in the zodiacal constellation Taurus, approximately 400 light years from our solar system, of which six or seven stars can be seen by the unaided eye. The Pleiades are central to stories from religions and cultures the world over. My dear friend, Manly P. Hall (1901–1990), the famous occultist, wrote in *The Secret Teachings of All Ages,* "The sacred Pleiades were famous to Freemasonry as the Seven Stars at the upper end of The Sacred Ladder." An ancient Peruvian legend identifies them as the "arbiters of human destiny." The Toraja people of Celebes, Indonesia, identify the Pleiades as the source of their ancestral heritage. They ceremoniously prepare their dead for the voyage back to the home of their predecessors in the not-too-distant stars and continue to this day to build their houses in the likeness of the starships that brought them here long ago. The *Holy Koran* of Islam states that the spirit who spoke to the Prophet Mohammed came from the Najm, the

Pleiades. Numerous Egyptian cuneiform tablets were addressed to the Pleiades, as if thoughts to one's mentors. Numerous ancient landmark edifices are said to orient toward this constellation, including the Egyptian pyramid of Cheops, several Greek temples and the Great Pyramid of the Sun in Mexico. Many old calendars are based on the cycle of Pleiades, such as that of the Mayans and the Native American Hopis. Thus, we could say, our beloved six-faced Lord of the Pleiades, Kārttikeya, Skanda, Subramaniam, Saravaṇabhava, looks in all directions, simultaneously helping all, inspiring all, guiding all.

The Way of Consensual Government

In the twenty-five years that have followed these revelations, we as a monastic order have continued to mature in our adjustment to and implementation of the flows and procedures elucidated in *Lemurian Scrolls,* implied, stated between the lines, so subtle, so unimposing. In choosing to follow many of the cultured patterns of those earliest humans, we came into a marvelous system of transparent government by which we now joyously manage our several cloistered monasteries and numerous extended families individually and in mission groups in more than eight countries. The dire need for such a system was, after all, the impetus that caused me to go so deeply into meditation and prayer that the inner worlds burst forth in response and the doors of the inner plane library opened to my inner eye. It is a system of subtle guidance and mature training rather than overt correction, of seeing God in everyone rather than liking one person more than another, a selfless life in which all are dedicated to realization of a greater reality and therefore relinquish selfishness, cultivate generosity, appreciation, and bond together to create an environment in which a selfless, nonobtrusive government can preside.

Various Forms of Management

There are many forms of government and management of people that have evolved over the centuries in social and religious groups, businesses and institutions of every kind. History tells a story of evolution from autocracy, where one man or overpowering council of men rules, then to the familial control of the oligarchy, then to socialism's state-centered style, and finally to democracy. There is another force that rules, which I call corporacracy, government by monetary might. The world has seen the impact of multi-national corporations, banks and more-than-wealthy individuals who use their corporate muscle to take over countries, intimidate and control their leaders and thus influence their citizens, all through the power of money, media, knowledge and privilege. Corporacracy is the contemporary power of money at work. Its organized materialism crosses all boundaries of all other forms of government. *Lemurian Scrolls* describe a higher form of government that we might call consensual governance. This is a style of rule that has neither a single person nor a majority as the controlling force, but which embraces all its peoples, needs and constituents in a special way at every meeting. Ironically, such a system could not evolve on its own, but only under the special circumstances of a spiritual leadership, provided by great beings of all three worlds, as described in these scrolls. Under this system, there is deference to seniority and special care and nurturing of the youngest. Under this system, there is no voting, no rule of the majority and thus submission of the unenfranchised or the out-numbered. All have a voice; all have an urge to sacrifice their needs to the greater good of all others. In this system, major decisions are ratified not by vote but by a consensual process that brings all parties together to find a unified agreement as to the best course of action for the highest good of all. Its process may be slow, even tedious when new members are involved who do not understand its subtle ways, yet in the long run it accrues a great power, the power of 100 percent heartfelt support of all members for all decisions. Inspiration flourishes. Consensual governance is a difficult form of governance, but worth the effort to achieve. Thus, we have government by chaos (anarchy), government that gives permission for guerrilla force (terrocracy). This is government that incites deadly acts of terrorism to gain its ends. Then we have government by one ruler's force (autocracy), government by military force (dictatorship), government by social and financial force (oligarchy), government by statist force (socialism), government by numerical and emotional force (democracy), government by kings and queens (monarchy), government by religious leaders supported by the inner worlds (theocracy), and government by shared soul force (consensualocracy). This is a form of government based on Sanātana Dharma. It is a rule that values intelligent cooperation and is *prāṇically* binding on all concerned. It is the exact same way that divine souls in the Second World and highly evolved beings in the Third World get things done, by managing to keep the actinic *prāṇas* flowing in the right direction, first with impulse, the birth of an idea, then pulse, the development of a plan, and creation, the totality of the group vision and effort, leading to its manifestation into astral or physical reality. Thus, consensualocracy is what the *Vedas* record. It is how the great cultures existed. It is the method of government that large, joint and extended families and tribes have perpetuated for generations and use to this very day. Consensualocracy is indeed the method of government of a new age of peace, productivity and the perpetuation of intellectual cooperation in small and large groups and provincial governments. All involved are agreeably involved, all high minded, all unified, all of one mind, with no dissension, all working toward a common goal. Other forms of government provide for dissension and, therefore, open the door to disharmony, anarchy and potential dissolution. This is the vision of the future and, as we know, the future is now. Consensualocracy, begun within each home, will radiate out into the community as the sun rises and brightens, as it always does. High noon is the great day of the *yuga* we are now in, as these mystical scrolls predict. Consensualocracy is a most compassionate form of governance, well suited for spiritually dedicated groups, highly ethical and dedicated communities with a singular vision and purpose. In it, all concur as to the goals, the methods to be employed to achieve those goals and the day-to-day activities that implement those methods. It is, simply put, management by intelligent cooperation.

May This Text Enhance Your Life

We have taken great pleasure in offering *Lemurian Scrolls* to you to use in your wisdom. These scrolls and the knowledge contained within them are yours to pass on to the next generation, the next and the next. Proceed with confidence and learn of your divine origins, of the far-off home of your farther-most ancestors, of your own scintillating soul body of light and how it descended into a substratum of astral, *prāṇic* and physical encasements to catalyze your evolution under the guidance of the laws of *āṇava,* karma and *māyā* toward your ultimate attainment of Self Realization, through *charyā, kriyā,* yoga and *jñāna,* leading first to the release from the need to return to Earth, called *mok-*

sha, and finally to merger in Śiva, called *viśvagrāsa*. We are pleased that you have perused these *Lemurian Scrolls* and do hope beyond hope that they have invested you with a new vision or outlook on life. It is the future that must be lived in its totality—the past is an overlay into it—being guided by the elders, seen or unseen, the wisdom is obvious. Take these scrolls in their totality and refrain from laboring over a sentence or paragraph. They were revealed to be a springboard into a broader view of life, a revelation that has built within it a vision that is truly livable, truly relevant in your life as it has been to ours. So, proceed with confidence and make the *Lemurian Scrolls* a living, vital reality in your life.

An image to leave you now with. Late in 1997, during the time of preparing this text for publication, analyzing the many nuances of these akashic readings, I had a vision of the universal Cosmic Sun of all the galaxies. I saw all known and unknown galaxies converge or intersect, then burst out into a Cosmic Sun which connected each of their Central Suns. This then emanates out through each fire planet, earths, such as ours. This then emanates out through all beings, such as you and me. And in that vision—of the emanation of the Cosmic Sun of the universe through the Central Suns of all the galaxies and the connection of the entire inner universe and inner galaxies on the astral plane of nonphysical existence—I saw the inner, not the outer, not the physical but the subtle, as an interrelated one.

Glossary

सब्दकोश

Aadheenam: ஆதீனம் "Ownership, possession, dependence; institution, premises; Śaiva monastery." A Śaivite Hindu monastery-temple complex in the South Indian, Śaiva Siddhānta tradition. The *aadheenam* head, or pontiff, is called the *guru mahāsannidhānam* or *aadheenakartar,* who traditionally empowers the scepter of the *mahārāja* through sacred ceremony. See: *Hinduism, Śaiva Siddhānta, sannidhānam.*

Abrahamic religions: The three religions: Judaism, Christianity and Islam, which descend from the lineage of Abraham, originating in the Middle East. They are all based in the Biblical tradition, which holds that God and man are eternally separate.

acquiesce: To agree or consent quietly without protest.

actinic: Spiritual, creating light. From the Greek *aktis,* meaning "ray." Of or pertaining to consciousness in its pure, unadulterated state.

adroitly: Skillfully doing something in a physical or mental way; cleverly; expertly.

advent: A coming or arrival.

African Dogon: The native people of Mali. Their metaphysical system is more abstract than that of most other African religions. The high point of their religious life is in a ceremony called *sigui,* which occurs every sixty years. The ceremony is based on the belief that 3,000 years ago, amphibious beings visited the Dogons from other planets.

Āgama: आगम "That which has come down." An enormous collection of Sanskṛit scriptures which, along with the *Vedas,* are revered as *śruti* (revealed scripture). Dating is uncertain. They were part of an oral tradition of unknown antiquity which some experts consider as ancient as the earliest *Vedas,* 5000 to 6000 BCE. The *Āgamas* are the primary source and authority for ritual, yoga and temple construction. Each of the major denominations—Śaivism, Vaishṇavism and Śāktism—has its unique *Āgama* texts. Smārtas recognize the *Āgamas,* but don't necessarily adhere to them and rely mainly on the *smṛiti* texts.

ājñā chakra: आज्ञाचक्र "Command wheel." The third-eye center. See: *chakra, inner eye.*

ākāśa: आकाश "Space." The sky. Free, open space. Ether, the fifth and most subtle of the five elements—earth, air, fire, water and ether. Empirically, the rarified space or ethereal fluid plasma that pervades the universes, inner and outer. Esoterically, mind, the superconscious strata holding all that exists and all that potentially exists, wherein all happenings are recorded and can be read by clairvoyants. It is through psychic entry into this transcendental *ākāśa* that cosmic knowledge is gathered, and the entire circle of time—past, present and future—can be known. See: *mind.*

***ākāśic* records:** Inner etheric area within the Second and Third Worlds where all events, thoughts and impressions are indelibly recorded. Seers in the First World can read the *ākāśic* records as one reads from a library. It was in this manner that Satguru Sivaya Subramuniyaswami read the *Lemurian Scrolls* and supplementary texts and dictated them to a scribe. See: *Lemurian and Dravidian Śāstras.*

***ākāśic* wind:** Generally, the force or vibration of the guru in the monastery—a sublime yet all-powerful energy which permeates and harmonizes all the other winds. Also names the condition within the monastery force field after the guru has been in residence for thirty-nine days without a break of more than nine days. His vibration then becomes so dominant that, following the rules within this text, he assumes many of the functions of the Senior Minority Group and personally begins to oversee the overall running of the monastery in a dynamic way. See: *winds*

aloofness: Condition of being distant physically or emotionally; reserved and remote.

ambrosia: The food of the Gods. Anything that tastes or smells good.

anarchy: Without leadership. The absence of government; chaos, disorder.

āṇava mala: आणवमल "Impurity of smallness; finitizing principle." The individualizing veil of duality that enshrouds the soul. It is the source of finitude and ignorance, the most basic of the three bonds *(āṇava,* karma, *māyā)* which temporarily limit the soul. The presence of *āṇava mala* is what causes the misapprehension about the nature of God, soul and world, the notion of being separate and distinct from God and the universe. *Āṇava* obscures the natural wisdom, light, unity and humility of the soul and allows spiritual ignorance, darkness, egoity and pride to manifest. See: *mala, pāśa.*

androgynous: Being neither masculine nor feminine, or having both female and male characteristics.

animal sacrifice: The ceremonial process of killing an animal for religious purposes. Used in Dravidian times to release souls from animal bodies into human reincarnation cycles.

Antarloka: अन्तर्लोक "Inner or in-between world." The astral plane. The Second World where souls live in their astral body during sleep and between births. The Antarloka includes: 1) the higher astral plane, Mahārloka, "plane of balance;" 2) mid-astral plane, Svarloka, "celestial plane;" 3) lower astral plane, Bhuvarloka, "plane of atmosphere," a counterpart or subtle duplicate of the physical plane (consisting of the Pitṛiloka and Pretaloka); and 4) the sub-astral plane, Naraka, consisting of seven hellish realms corresponding to the seven chakras below the base of the spine. See: *Antarloka, three worlds.*

artisan: A highly skilled, trained leader or teacher of apprentices. See: *south wind.*

artisan-apprentice system: The system of training and organization employed in the south wind groups of the monastery. Each group has one artisan, who works closely with the guru and oversees the work of those in training under him. See: *winds*

Aryan: A member of the people who spoke the parent language of the Indo-European languages.

āśrama sādhana: आश्रम साधन The discipline of cleaning the monastery, in order to maintain purity. It also has the effect of cleansing the subconscious mind.

āśrama: आश्रम "Place of striving." From *śram,* "to exert energy." Hermitage; order of the life. Holy sanctuary; the residence and teaching center of a *sādhu,* saint, swāmī, ascetic or guru; often includes lodging for students. An *āśrama* is a meeting place where devotees gather with their guru to learn and practice spiritual disciplines, including the many yogas. Today there are two primary types of *āśramas,* the coed *āśrama,* more properly labeled a commune, where the permanent resident facilities provide for both men and women, and the more traditional *āśrama,* where permanent residents are either strictly men or strictly women. For centuries, Asian tradition has said there is wisdom for unmarried men and women to live separately, and even when the two genders gather to eat, sit and meditate they do so in distinct groups. Women sit on the left when facing their guru and men on the right. A traditional *āśrama* differs from a coed *āśrama,* in that the two genders do not freely intermingle. *Āśrama* also names life's four stages: student, householder, elder advisor and religious solitaire. See: *commune, cult, monastery, monk.*

assimilation: The absorption of nutrients from food into the body.

ashṭāṅga yoga: अष्टाङ्गयोग See: *rāja yoga.*

astral body: The subtle, nonphysical body *(sūkshma śarīra)* in which the soul functions in the astral plane, the inner world also called Antarloka. The astral body includes the *prāṇic* sheath *(prāṇamaya kośa),* the instinctive-intellectual sheath *(manomaya kośa)* and the cognitive sheath *(vijñānamaya kośa)*—with the *prāṇic* sheath dropping off at the death of the physical body. See: *soul.*

astral plane: The subtle world, or Antarloka, spanning the spectrum of consciousness from the *viśuddha* chakra in the throat to the *pātāla* chakra in the soles of the feet. In the astral plane, the soul is enshrouded in the astral body, called *sūkshma śarīra.* See: *astral body, Antarloka, Devaloka, Second World, three worlds.*

astral: Of the subtle, nonphysical sphere (astral plane) which exists between the physical and causal planes.

astrology: Science of celestial influences. See: *jyotisha.*

asura: असुर "Evil spirit; demon." (Opposite of *sura:* "deva; God.") A being of the lower astral plane, Naraka. *Asuras* can and do interact with the physical plane, causing major and minor problems in people's lives. *Asuras* do evolve and are not permanently in this state. See: *astral plane.*

attachments: That which one holds onto or clings to with the energy of possessiveness (odic force), which is a natural function of the inner and outer ego of an individual. As one unfolds through the chakras, the force of attachment naturally diminishes through *sādhana, tapas* and the grace of the guru.

attunement: The act of coming into harmony with something.

aura: The luminous colorful field of subtle energy radiating within and around the human body, extending out from three to seven feet. The colors of the aura change constantly according to the ebb and flow of one's state of consciousness, thoughts, moods and emotions. Higher, benevolent feelings create bright pastels; base, negative feelings are darker in color. In Sanskṛit, the aura is called *prabhāmaṇḍala,* "luminous circle," or *dīptachakra,* "wheel of light." See: *mind.*

auspicious: Favorable, of good omen, foreboding well. *Maṅgala.* One of the central concepts in Hindu life. Astrology defines a method for determining times that are favorable for various human endeavors.

austerity: The quality or condition of showing strict self-discipline and self-denial; an austere habit or practice.

Australian Aborigine: The indigenous people of Australia and Tasmania. In the 18th century, at the time of European invasion, their population was believed to be 300,000 divided into 500 tribes. They believe in reincarnation and spirits.

autocracy: Absolute authority. Government by one ruler's force.

avail: To be of use or advantage in completing an end.

avaricious: Greedy for riches; overly desirous of material things.

āyurveda: आयुर्वेद "Science of life." A holistic system of medicine and health native to ancient India. The aims of *āyurveda* are *āyus,* "long life," and *ārogya,* "diseaselessness," which facilitate progress toward ultimate spiritual goals. Health is achieved by balancing energies (especially the *doshas,* bodily humors) at all levels of being.

Babylonian: Of or relating to Babylonia or Babylon or their people, culture or language. Characterized by a luxurious, pleasure-seeking and often immoral way of life.

Bala Muruga: பால முருகன் "Young Muruga." The form of Muruga as a child.

***Bantu* peoples:** Speakers of the Bantu subgroup of the Niger-Congo family of languages who occupy nearly all of the southern portion of the African continent. This linguistic classification covers approximately 60,000,000 people with extremely diverse cultural, religious, economic, social and political patterns.

bce: Abbreviation (equivalent to BC) for "before common era," referring to dating prior to the year zero in the Western, or Gregorian calendar, system.

bedeck: To cover with decorations; adorn.

beholden: Obliged to feel grateful; owing thanks; indebted.

bhakti yoga: भक्तियोग "Union through devotion." *Bhakti* yoga is the practice of devotional disciplines, worship, prayer, chanting and singing with the aim of awakening love in the heart and opening oneself to God's grace. From the beginning practice of *bhakti* to advanced devotion, called *prapatti,* self-effacement is an intricate part of Hindu, even all Indian, culture.

Bhūloka: भूलोक "Earth world." The physical plane. See: *First World, three worlds.*

Bon: Indigenous religion of Tibet which, when absorbed in the 8th century by the Buddhist traditions introduced from India, gave Tibetan Buddhism much of its distinctive character. (Pronounced *Pern.)*

Brahmā: ब्रह्मा The name of God in His aspect of Creator. Śaivites consider Brahmā, Vishṇu and Rudra to be three of five aspects of Śiva. Smārtas group Brahmā, Vishṇu and Śiva as a holy trinity in which Śiva is the destroyer. Brahmā the Creator is not to be confused with 1) Brahman, the Transcendent Supreme of the *Upanishads;* 2) *Brāhmaṇa, Vedic* texts; 3) *brāhmaṇa,* the Hindu priest caste (also spelled *brāhmin).* See: *Hinduism.*

brahmacharya: ब्रह्मचर्य Sexual purity—restraint of lust and the instinctive nature. The practice of celibacy accompanied by the performance of *sādhana* and adherence to dharma. The process of unfoldment through the chakras which is sustained through regulated living in a monastery under the guidance of the guru.

brahmachārī: ब्रह्मचारी An unmarried male spiritual aspirant who practices continence, observes religious disciplines, including *sādhana,* devotion and service and who may be under simple vows. Often used in this text to designate those monastics who are not *naishṭika.*

brāhmin (brāhmaṇa): ब्राह्मण "Mature or evolved soul." The class of pious souls of exceptional learning. From *Brāhman,* "growth, expansion, evolution, development, swelling of the spirit or soul." The mature soul is the exemplar of wisdom, tolerance, forbearance and humility.

brāhmin: ब्राह्मण In *Lemurian Scrolls,* refers to monastics who have never mated, virgins. See: *naishṭika.*

Buddha: बुद्ध "The enlightened." Usually refers to Siddhārtha Gautama (CA 624–544 BCE), a prince born of the Śākya clan—a Śaivite Hindu tribe that lived in eastern India on the Nepalese border. He renounced the world and became a monk. After his enlightenment he preached the doctrines upon which followers later founded Buddhism.

Buddhism: The religion based on the teachings of Siddhārtha Gautama, known as the Buddha (CA 624–544 BCE). He refuted the idea of man's having an immortal soul and did not preach of any Supreme Deity. Instead he taught that man should seek to overcome greed, hatred and delusion and attain enlightenment through realizing the Four Noble Truths and following the Eightfold Path. Prominent among its holy books is the *Dhammapada*. Buddhism arose out of Hinduism as an inspired reform movement which rejected the caste system and the sanctity of the *Vedas*. It is thus classed as *nāstika*, "unbeliever," and is not part of Hinduism. Buddhism eventually migrated out of India, the country of its origin, and now enjoys a following of over 350 million, mostly in Asia. See: *Hinduism*.

Carbonaceous chondrite: A stony meteorite containing material associated with life, possible microfossils, amino acids, etc. Some researchers believe this to be evidence of extraterrestrial biological origin.

ce: Abbreviation for "common era." Equivalent to the abbreviation AD. Following a date, it indicates that the year comes after the year zero in the Western, or Gregorian calendar, system.

celestial: "Of the sky or heavens." Of or relating to the heavenly regions or beings. Highly refined, divine.

Central Sun: The center that each galaxy revolves around which emits life-giving rays and contains an opposite force to each sun within each solar system. Scientific evidence indicates that at our galactic center is a massive black hole, an "object" that sucks matter into it and has a mass two to four million times greater than our sun. Because of the center's strong gravitational pull, all matter in the galaxy is caused to move in a circular orbit around it. At the same time, science has discovered, the galactic nucleus is emitting a bright radio source, infrared radiation and x-rays, which Vedic knowledge tells us are indications of the energy rays that sustain and nurture all life and intelligence. Around the nucleus is a large "bulge" of intense light, caused by a dense cluster of stars held in a spherical shape near this black hole, giving the dark galactic center the appearance which is likened to a brilliant sun. The Central Sun is presently obscured from optical wavelengths by a thick screen of intervening dust composed of more than 50 different molecules, including carbon monoxide and formaldehyde. *Lemurian Scrolls* explain that the obscuration or release of the life-giving rays emitted from the Central Sun, as our Milky Way Galaxy moves around its center, causes the four *yugas* to be experienced by our solar system. Our galaxy is estimated by scientists to span a diameter of 75,000 light years, containing 400 billion suns. An estimated 1.3 billion of these suns are thought to have planets revolving around them, comprising solar systems. From our solar system, the Central Sun is approximately 30,000 light years away, in the direction of the constellation Sagittarius. See: *Cosmic Sun*.

cessation: A stopping for some time.

chakra: चक्र "Wheel." Any of the nerve plexes or centers of force and consciousness located within the *inner bodies* of man. In the physical body there are corresponding nerve plexuses, ganglia and glands. The seven principal chakras can be seen psychically as colorful, multi-petaled wheels or lotuses. They are situated along the spinal cord from the base to the cranial chamber. Additionally, seven chakras, barely visible, exist below the spine. They are seats of instinctive consciousness, the origin of jealousy, hatred, envy, guilt, sorrow, etc. They constitute the lower or hellish world, called Naraka or *pātala*. Thus, there are 14 major chakras in all. The seven upper chakras, from lowest to highest, are: 1) ***mūlādhāra*** (base of spine): memory, time and space; 2) ***svādhishṭhāna*** (below navel): reason; 3) ***maṇipūra*** (solar plexus): willpower; 4) ***anāhata*** (heart center): direct cognition; 5) ***viśuddha*** (throat): divine love; 6) ***ājñā*** (third eye): divine sight; 7) ***sahasrāra*** (crown of head): illumination, Godliness. The seven lower chakras, from highest to lowest, are 1) ***atala*** (hips): fear and lust; 2) ***vitala*** (thighs): raging anger; 3) ***sutala*** (knees): retaliatory jealousy; 4) ***talātala*** (calves): prolonged mental confusion; 5) ***rasātala*** (ankles): selfishness; 6) ***mahātala*** (feet): absence of conscience; 7) ***pātala*** (located in the soles of the feet): murder and malice.

chakram: A magnetic center or source of spiritual power. In this text, a group of people working together and concentrating on the darshan so persistently that their bones became a channel for the Deity and His *devas* to send forth cosmic energy. See: *cosmic energy, darshan.*

charyā pāda: चर्यापाद् "Conduct stage." Stage of service and character building. See: *pāda, Śaiva Siddhānta, Śaivism.*

chaturyuga: Cycle of the four *yugas:* Sat, Tretā, Dvāpara and Kali, making a total of 4.32 million years. See: *cosmic cycle, yuga.*

circle: One year, the circle of the Earth around the sun.

citation: A quoted passage.

clairaudience: "Clear-hearing." Psychic or divine hearing, *divyaśravana.* The ability to hear the inner currents of the nervous system, the *Aum* and other mystic tones. Hearing in one's mind the words of inner-plane beings or earthly beings not physically present. See: *psychic.*

clairvoyance: "Clear-seeing." Psychic or divine seeing; the ability to have visions. Seeing inner-plane beings, or earthly beings not physically present. See: *psychic.*

clamor: A loud outcry usually expressing discontent or protest.

clan: A group of people with common interests; family.

cleave: To split; separate. As used in this text, to separate from the whole.

cohabitation: Living together and having sexual relations outside of wedlock, often known as commonlaw marriage.

commune: To communicate closely, sharing thoughts, feelings or prayers in an intimate way. To be in close rapport. Also a community of people living together and sharing in work, earning, etc. In modern-day practice, communes, which are often called *āśramas,* have become places where seekers strive to balance the male and female energies by mingling together, residing in the same or adjoining rooms. Unlike *āśrama* residents, commune inmates sit at random while learning, singing and eating. Members are not necessarily celibate, and may form temporary or long term relationships with other members. Marriages are often open to freedom in intimate relationship with others. Residents are generally of various faiths and religious backgrounds, whereas a traditional *āśrama* is Hindu based. See: *āśrama, cult, monastery, monk.*

comprehensive: Including a large scope of things; showing extensive understanding.

conclave: A secret or confidential meeting.

conglomerate: A group of things.

conscious mind: The external, everyday state of consciousness. See: *mind.*

consciousness: *Chitta* or *chaitanya.* 1) A synonym for mind-stuff, *chitta;* or 2) the condition or power of perception, awareness, apprehension. There are myriad gradations of consciousness, from the simple sentience of inanimate matter to the consciousness of basic life forms, to the higher consciousness of human embodiment, to omniscient states of superconsciousness, leading to immersion in the One universal consciousness, Parāśakti. See: *mind.*

consensualocracy: Government by intelligent cooperation, based on a shared vision and adherence to dharma. *Ahiṁsā,* nonhurtfulness—spiritually, physically, emotionally and mentally—is the keynote of this tribal/family system of rule.

continuum: A continuous whole, quantity, or series; thing whose parts cannot be separated or separately discerned.

corporocracy: Modern corporate government wherein multi-national conglomerates influence governments by the power of business, legal and monetary might.

cosmic cycle: One of the infinitely recurring periods of the universe. These cycles are measured in periods of progressive ages. The smaller cycles, called *yugas,* are known as the Sat (also Satya or Kṛita), Tretā, Dvāpara and Kali, which repeat themselves in that order, with the Sat Yuga being the longest and the Kali Yuga the shortest. The comparison is often made of these ages with the cycles of the day: Sat Yuga being morning until noon, the period of greatest light or enlightenment, Tretā Yuga afternoon, Dvāpara evening, and Kali Yuga the darkest part of the night. Four *yugas* equal one *chaturyuga.* Theories vary, but by traditional astronomical calculation, a *chaturyuga* equals 4,320,000 solar years (or 12,000 "divine years;" one divine year is 360 solar years)—with the Sat Yuga lasting 1,728,000 years, Tretā Yuga 1,296,000 years, Dvāpara Yuga 864,000 years, and Kali Yuga 432,000 years. By current, traditional dating, mankind is now experiencing the Kali Yuga, which began at midnight, February 18, 3102 BCE (year one on the Hindu calendar) and will end in approximately 427,000 years. According to *Lemurian Scrolls,* we are actually in the Sat Yuga, which began when man learned to light the night by his own devices, marked by the inventions of Thomas Edison in 1879. A partial dissolution, called *laya,* occurs at the end of each *manvantara,* when the physical world is destroyed by flood and fire. Each destructive period is followed by the succession of creation *(sṛishṭi),* evolution or preservation *(sthiti)* and dissolution *(laya).* A summary of the periods in the cosmic cycles: one *chaturyuga* = 4,320,000 years (four *yugas);* 71 *chaturyugas* = one *manvantara* or *manu;* 14 *manvantaras* = one *kalpa* or day of Brahmā; two *kalpas* = one *ahoratra* or day and night of Brahmā; 360 *ahoratras* = one year of Brahmā; 100 Brahmā years = 309,173,760,000,000 years (one "lifetime" of Brahmā, or the universe). By traditional Hindu reckoning, chanted by priests daily the world over at the start of any *pūjā,* we are in the 28th chatur-yuga of the seventh *manvantara* of the 51st year of Brahmā. *Lemurian Scrolls,* by our study as detailed in the Timeline, numbers time's cycles back only to mankind's arrival on Earth, indicating that we have just entered the first Sat Yuga of the fourth *manvantara.* There are smaller cycles of *yugas* spoken of by Sri Yukteswar, the guru of Swami Paramahansa Yogananda. In the introduction to his *sūtras* in *The Holy Science,* Sri Yukteswar explains a cycle of the four *yugas* that totals only 24,000 years, which puts us in a period of the early Dvāpara Yuga. This cycle, he says, is caused by our solar system's revolving around another "fixed star" as they both revolve around the galactic center, similar to the moon circling the Earth as it goes around the Sun. When our solar system is on the side of the star closest to the Central Sun, we experience the Sat Yuga. As we revolve to the farthest position from the Central Sun (which takes 12,000 years), we gradually descend into the Kali Yuga. Then we slowly revolve back again to the closest side of the orbit, experiencing the *yugas* in reverse (from Kali to Dvāpara, Tretā, Sat) for another 12,000 years. Sri Yukteswar mistakenly attributed this 24,000 year orbit as the cause of the precession of the equinoxes, which today science knows is caused by the earth's wobble on its axis and calculates to be a 25,900 year cycle. ℂ Hindu wisdom tells us that at the end of every *kalpa* or day of Brahmā, a greater dissolution, called *pralaya* (or *kalpanta,* "end of an eon"), occurs when both the physical and subtle worlds are absorbed into the causal world, where souls rest until the next *kalpa* begins. This state of withdrawal or "night of Brahmā," continues for the length of an entire *kalpa* until creation again issues forth. After 36,000 of these dissolutions and creations there is a total, universal annihilation, *mahāpralaya,* when all three worlds, all time, form and space, are withdrawn into God Śiva. After a period of total withdrawal a new universe or lifespan of Brahmā begins. This entire cycle repeats infinitely. This view of cosmic time is recorded in the *Purāṇas* and the *Dharma Śāstras.* See: *yuga, chaturyuga, manvantara.*

cosmic rays: Rays from the Central Sun.

Cosmic Sun: The Cosmic Sun is the ever-present, one spiritual Sun and source of life-giving rays that emanate out of each galactic Central Sun and which are also all-pervasive and within everything. The Cosmic Sun, also called the Universal Sun, exists at the most subtle level of creation at the core of existence, on the brink of the Absolute. The Cosmic Sun is also the timeless, causeless, spaceless, formless power, existence and nonexistence that sustains all form, is detached from it but because of its existence within everything—atom, molecule and quantum—is present everywhere at all points of time and space as the sustainer of the causes of the changing forms within it. This mystery has to be realized to be known—Absolute reality versus the relatively real. That is the mystery. See: *Central Sun.*

culminate: To reach the highest point; climax.

cult: From *cultus* meaning care, cultivation. A system of worship or ritual. A religious sect or group. The word *cult* is used freely within the broad base of Sanātana Dharma as the name of a sub-sect of one of its many denominations. The modern news media chose this word to describe certain communes that began to arise in the US in the early 1960s led by charismatic and often autocratic leaders. It has become a buzz word to degradate groups, claiming their leaders demand blind obedience and brainwash their followers, often against their will or better judgment. Certain of such cults are truly harmful. *Cult* has been humorously and more accurately defined as "a small religious group one doesn't like." The common definition of *cult* would apply equally to the Catholic Church, the Army, Navy, Marines and the Boy and Girl Scouts. This is directly opposed to the educated original meaning of *cult,* which implies a familial group whose leader requires intelligent cooperation and group acceptance as they move forward in their worship and service. See: *āśrama, monastery, maṭha, commune.*

cycle: In *Lemurian Scrolls,* three years, or three circles of the Earth around the sun.

Darshan (darśana): दर्शन "Vision, sight." Seeing the Divine. Beholding, with inner or outer vision, a temple image, Deity, holy person or place, with the desire to inwardly contact and receive the grace and blessings of the venerated being or beings. Also: "point of view," doctrine or philosophy. Darshan is also the feeling of the emotions of a holy person, the intellect, the spiritual qualities that he has attained, and most importantly the *śakti,* the power, that has changed him and is there constantly to change others. Darshan encompasses the entirety of the being of a person of spiritual attainment. Darshan is the emanating rays from the depth of an enlightened soul's being. These rays pervade the room in which he is, penetrating the aura of the devotees and enlivening the *kuṇḍalinī*, the white, fiery, vapor-like substance that is actually the heat of the physical body in its natural state. ℂ Hindus consider that when you are in the presence of the guru that his seeing of you and therefore knowing you and your karmas is another grace. So, darshan is a two-edged sword, a two-way street. It is a process of seeing and being seen. The devotee is seeing and in that instant drawing forth the blessings of the *satguru*, the swāmī or the *sadhu*. In turn, they are seeing the devotee and his divine place in the universe. The sense of separation is transcended, so there is a oneness between seer and seen. Darshan is physical, mental, emotional, spiritual perception. Hindus believe that the darshan from a guru who has realized the Self can clear the subconscious mind of a devotee in minutes, alleviating all reaction to past actions and alter his perspective from an outer to an inner one. Seeing is such a powerful dimension of life, and it affects us in so many ways, inside and out. Darshan, in the true meaning of this mystical, complex and most esoteric word, conveys all of this. See: *Disseminating the darshan, Hinduism.*

Darwin's theory: Theory of evolution developed by Charles Darwin (1809–1882) stating that plant and animal species develop or evolve from earlier forms due to hereditary transmission of variations that enhance the organism's adaptability and chances of survival. See: *evolution of the soul.*

deem: To have as an opinion; judge.

deified: To be made into a God.

Deity: "God." Can refer to the image or *mūrti* installed in a temple or to the Mahādeva the *mūrti* represents. See: *Māhadeva, mūrti.*

delectable: Pleasing to the taste; delicious.

delineate: To represent pictorially or in words or gestures; depict; describe.

delve: To investigate for information, usually with vigor.

demigod: Minor Deity; a Mahādeva or *deva.*

democracy: Government by the people. A system of majority rule with emphasis on equality of rights and opportunity.

deva: देव "Shining one." A Second World being living in the higher astral plane in a subtle, nonphysical body. See: *Mahādeva, astral plane, Devaloka, Second World.*

Devaloka: देवलोक "Plane of radiant beings." Devonic realms of the Second World or astral plane, where souls live in mental or astral bodies. See: *Antarloka.*

devasthānam: देवस्थानम् The place where the *sādhakas* and resident guests live within a monastery or near a temple, usually a separate building with a kitchen and a shrine.

devonic kingdom: Second World. See: *Antarloka, Devaloka.*

devonic: Angelic, heavenly, spiritual. Of the nature of the higher worlds, in tune with the refined energies of the higher chakras or centers of consciousness. Of or relating to the *devas*. Implies that something is divinely guided. See: *deva.*

dharma: धर्म From *dhṛi*, "to sustain; carry, hold." Hence dharma is "that which contains or upholds the cosmos." Dharma is a complex and all-inclusive term with many meanings, including: divine law, law of being, way of righteousness, religion, duty, responsibility, virtue, justice, goodness and truth. Essentially, dharma is the orderly fulfillment of an inherent nature or destiny. Relating to the soul, it is the mode of conduct most conducive to spiritual advancement, the right and righteous path.

dictate: A guiding principle or command; to command or give with authority.

dictatorship: Government by a ruler with

absolute authority, generally implemented with military force.

dīkshā: दीक्षा "Initiation." Action or process by which one is entered into a new realm of spiritual knowledge and practice by a teacher or preceptor through the transmission of blessings. Denotes initial or deepened connection with the teacher and his lineage and is usually accompanied by ceremony. Initiation, revered as a moment of awakening, may be bestowed by a touch, a word, a look or a thought. Most Hindu schools, and especially Śaivism, teach that only with initiation from a *satguru* is enlightenment attainable. Sought after by all Hindus is the *dīkshā* called *śaktipāta,* "descent of grace," which, often coming unbidden, stirs and arouses the mystic *kuṇḍalinī* force. See: *Hinduism.*

diminution: A lessening or reduction. The resulting reduction; decrease.

disbursement: The act or process of giving out.

discernable: Able to be recognized.

disincarnate: Not having a physical body; of the astral plane; astral beings. See: *astral body, astral plane.*

disseminate: To spread far and wide.

disseminating the *darshan:* Bestowing the blessings of the monastery and temple upon those of the world. Names the function of monks travelling outside the monastery in which they absorb as much darshan as they can before leaving the monastery to perform some type of work or service in the world. See: *Darshan.*

Dravidian: The term used in this text to name the monastic communities of the Dvāpara and Kali Yugas. In modern times it refers to the various Caucasoid peoples of southern India and northern Sri Lanka. From the Sanskṛit *Drāviḍa,* of which it is believed the original form was *Dramid* (or *Dramil),* which meant "sweet" or "good natured," and is the source of the word *Tamil,* naming the Dravidian people of South India and Sri Lanka and their language.

dual: Having or composed of two parts or kinds. **—duality:** A state or condition of being dual. **—realm of duality:** The phenomenal world, where each thing exists along with its opposite: joy and sorrow, etc.

Dvāpara Yuga: द्वापरयुग "The age of two" or era of duality; third of the four *yugas,* or eras, consisting of 864,000 years, during which the light of the Central Sun is reduced by one-half. The era of impending darkness prior to the Kali Yuga. It is compared to the afternoon and evening of a day. See: *yuga, cosmic cycle.*

dwindle: To become gradually less and less until little is left; decrease.

East wind: The group within a monastery who give forth the teachings as their primary duty. The particular vibration of this realm of human activity.

ego: The external personality or sense of "I" and "mine." Broadly, individual identity. The *tattva, ahaṁkāra,* "I-maker," which bestows the sense of I-ness, individuality and separateness from God.

emanate: To come forth, as from a source; send forth; emit.

embellishment: The act of decorating; a decoration.

eminence: A position of greatness.

en masse: In a group; all together.

engender: To bring into existence.

enlightenment: For Śaiva monists, Self Realization, *samādhi* without seed *(nirvikalpa samādhi);* the ultimate attainment, sometimes referred to as Paramātma *darśana,* or as *ātma darśana,* "Self vision" (a term which appears in Patañjali's *Yoga Sūtras*). Enlightenment is the experience-nonexperience resulting in the realization of one's transcendent Self—Paraśiva—which exists beyond time, form and space. Each tradition has its own understanding of enlightenment, often indicated by unique terms. See: *enstasy, kuṇḍalinī, nirvikalpa samādhi, Paraśiva, samādhi, Self Realization.*

enstasy: A term coined in 1969 by Mircea Eliade to contrast the Eastern view of bliss as "standing inside oneself" (enstasy) with the Western view as ecstasy, "standing outside oneself." A word chosen as the English equivalent of *samādhi*. See: *enlightenment, nirvikalpa samādhi, samādhi, Self Realization.*

entanglements: See: *psychic tubes.*

enthrone: To give the highest place to; exalt.

entourage: A group of accompanying attendants, associates or assistants.

eon: An indefinitely long period of time; an age. The longest division of geologic time, containing two or more eras. See: *era.*

equanimity: The quality of remaining calm and undisturbed. Evenness of mind; composure.

equilibrium: Evenly balanced. A quality of good spiritual leadership. "Having attained an equilibrium of *iḍā* and *piṅgalā,* he becomes a knower of the known."

era: A point that marks the beginning of a period of time characterized by particular circumstances, events or personages. A period of time. See: *eon.*

esoteric: Hard to understand; secret. Teaching intended for a chosen few, as an inner group of initiates. Abstruse or private.

ether: *Ākāśa.* Space, the most subtle of the five elements. See: *ākāśa.*

etheric: Having to do with ether or space.

etheric body: Soul body. The body in which mankind came to this planet. In Lemurian times, a fibrous physical body was formed around this etheric body from fruits and fragrances. See: *fibrous body, original body.*

evoke: To call forth; summon.

evolution: A process of change, development or unfoldment. See: *evolution of the soul, karma, Darwin's theory.*

evolution of the soul: *Adhyātma prasāra.* In monistic Śaiva Siddhānta, Advaita Īśvaravāda philosopy, the soul's evolution is a progressive unfoldment, growth and maturing toward its inherent, divine destiny, which is complete merger with Śiva *(viśvagrāsa).* In its essence, each soul is ever perfect. But as an individual soul body emanated by God Śiva, it is like a small seed yet to develop. As an acorn needs to be planted in the dark underground to grow into a mighty oak tree, so must the soul unfold out of the darkness of the *malas* to full maturity and realization of its innate oneness with God. The soul is not created at the moment of conception of a physical body. Rather, it is created in the Śivaloka. It evolves by taking on denser and denser sheaths—cognitive, instinctive-intellectual and *prāṇic*—until finally it takes birth in physical form in the Bhūloka. Then it experiences many lives, maturing through the reincarnation process. Thus, from birth to birth, souls learn and mature. See: *liberation, mala, reincarnation, Śaiva Siddhānta, soul, viśvagrāsa.*

externalized: Preoccupation; awareness temporarily cut off from superconsciousness. A condition monastics seek to avoid through their *sādhana* and *tapas*; allowing awareness to become involved in outer life to the exclusion of one's inner life and goals, spiritual unfoldment, purification, transmutation, obedience to the guru and worship of the Deities.

extraterrestrial: Existing, taking place, or coming from outside the limits of Earth.

exude: To discharge or emit gradually. To show in abundance.

Facilitate: To make easy or easier; help; guide.

faring: Condition or status, as in, "He fared well during the journey."

fibrous body: The first physical bodies that souls lived in after first arriving on Earth.

In these bodies, produced out of the *kuṇḍalinī* force and the intake of herbal essence, fruits and flowers, souls were able to fly in the atmosphere. These original bodies had a high oil content, were very pliable, neither male nor female. Nor did they sleep or experience heat, cold or fear. See: *etheric body, original body.*

First World: The physical universe, called Bhūloka, of gross or material substance in which phenomena are perceived by the five senses. See: *Bhūloka, three worlds.*

forbearance: Self-control; responding with patience and compassion, especially under provocation. Endurance; tolerance.

force field: The cumulative energy surrounding a monastery, *sannidhanam* in Tamil; a spiritual shield which protects the monastery and its residents from astral and physical intrusion. Built up through worship, invoking of the Deities, *sādhana, tapas* and disciplined living.

fortitude: The strength to bear misfortune, pain, etc., calmly and patiently; courage.

Gaṇeśa: गणेश "Lord of Categories." (From *gaṇ,* "to count or reckon," and *Īśa,* "lord.") Or: "Lord of attendants *(gaṇa),*" synonymous with Gaṇapati. Gaṇeśa is a Mahādeva, the beloved elephant-faced Deity honored by Hindus of every sect, first son of Śiva and brother of Kārttikeya. He is the Lord of Obstacles (Vighneśvara), revered for His great wisdom and invoked first before any undertaking, for He knows all intricacies of each soul's karma and the perfect path of dharma that makes action successful. He sits on the *mūlādhāra* chakra and is easy of access. See: *Hinduism, Mahādeva.*

Genesis: The first book of the *Bible,* giving the Abrahamic account of creation and a history of the patriarchs.

glacierous: Of or relating to glaciers, huge masses of flowing ice; in the area of glaciers.

Gods: *Mahādevas,* "great beings of light." The plural form of *God* refers to extremely advanced beings existing in their self-effulgent soul bodies in the causal plane. The meaning of *Gods* is best seen in the phrase, "God and the Gods," referring to the Supreme God—Śiva—and the Mahādevas who are His creation. See: *Mahādeva.*

grace: "Benevolence, love, giving," from the Latin *gratus,* "beloved, agreeable." God's power of revealment, *anugraha śakti* ("kindness, showing favor"), by which souls are awakened to their true, Divine nature. Grace in the unripe stages of the spiritual journey is experienced by the devotee as receiving gifts or boons, often unbidden, from God. The mature soul finds himself surrounded by grace. He sees all of God's actions as grace, whether they be seemingly pleasant and helpful or not.

guru: गुरु "Weighty one," indicating a being of great knowledge or skill. A term used to describe a teacher or guide in any subject, such as music, dance, sculpture, but especially religion. For clarity, the term is often preceded by a qualifying prefix. Hence, terms such as *kulaguru* (family teacher), *vīṇāguru (vīṇā* teacher) and *satguru* (spiritual preceptor). According to the *Advayatāraka Upanishad* (14–18), *guru* means "dispeller *(gu)* of darkness *(ru).*" He who Knows and can guide the spiritual aspirant to that Knowing. See: *satguru.*

guru tapas: गुरुतपस् The discipline of working directly under the guidance of the guru in intelligent cooperation, by which inner teachings are conveyed and monastics learn to merge their mind with that of their preceptor.

Hairsplitting: The making of unreasonably or extremely fine distinctions.

Hanumān: हनुमान् In this text, the member of the senior minority group, second in resident seniority, whose main duty is to convey messages to groups. See: *senior minority group.*

harken: To listen attentively.

harrowing: Distressing; tormenting.

hasten: To cause to become faster.

heiau: Hawaiian temple.

herald: To introduce, announce, foretell, etc.

hieroglyphic: A system of writing, such as that of ancient Egypt, using pictorial symbols to represent meaning or sounds or a combination of meaning and sound.

Hinduism (Hindu Dharma): हिन्दुधर्म India's indigenous religious and cultural system, followed today by nearly one billion adherents, mostly in India, but with large populations in many other countries. Also called Sanātana Dharma, "eternal religion" and Vaidika Dharma, "religion of the *Vedas.*" Hinduism is the world's most ancient religion and encompasses a broad spectrum of philosophies ranging from pluralistic theism to absolute monism. It is a family of myriad faiths with four primary denominations: Śaivism, Vaishṇavism, Śāktism and Smārtism. These four hold such divergent beliefs that each is a complete and independent religion. Yet, they share a vast heritage of culture and belief—karma, dharma, reincarnation, all-pervasive Divinity, temple worship, sacraments, manifold Deities, the guru-*śishya* tradition and a reliance on the *Vedas* as scriptural authority. From the rich soil of Hinduism long ago sprang various other traditions. Among these were Jainism, Buddhism and Sikhism, which rejected the *Vedas* and thus emerged as completely distinct religions, disassociated from Hinduism, while still sharing many philosophical insights and cultural values with their parent faith. See: *Sanātana Dharma.*

Homo sapiens: The Latin name of the species which is modern man.

Hyperborean: One of a mythical people known to the ancient Greeks from earliest times, living in a perpetually warm and sunny land near the North Pole.

Imminent: Likely to happen without delay; impending.

impart: To give a share or portion of; give; reveal.

imperceptive: Not able to see or perceive.

impregnate: To saturate or fill; permeate.

incantation: Recitation of verbal charms or spells to produce a magic effect.

incarnate: To take bodily form.

incarnation: From *incarnate,* "to be made flesh." The soul's taking on a human body. **—divine incarnation:** The concept of *avatāra.* The Supreme Being's (or other Mahādeva's) taking of human birth, generally to reestablish dharma. This doctrine is important to several Hindu sects, notably Vaishṇavism, but not held by most Śaivites. See: *reincarnation.*

incognito: Without being recognized; keeping one's identity unrevealed or disguised. Refers in this text to the protocol followed by monks traveling alone from one monastery to another or to rendezvous with other monks on pilgrimage.

indigenous: Native born; originating in a particular country or region.

indwell: To exist as a divine inner spirit or guiding force.

infiniverse: An word coined by Satguru Sivaya Subramuniyaswami as an appropriate alternative to *universe or universes,* because there are realms within realms within realms within known existence, deeper and deepening even now as quantums are found, their energies released from one sphere to another. *Infiniverse,* in fact, describes the Unfathomable that humans have been and are constantly endeavoring to fathom, even unto this very day. While the word *universe* seeks to reduce existence to a one place, *infiniverse* acknowledges the vastly complex possibilities of the Great What Is. See: *microcosm-macrocosm, quantum.*

influx: A mass arrival or collection.

inherent (to inhere): Existing in someone or something as a natural and inseparable quality, characteristic or right.

initiate: A person who has had or is about to have an initiation.

initiation (to initiate): To enter into; to admit as a member. In Hinduism, initiation from a qualified preceptor is considered invaluable for spiritual progress. See: *dīkshā, Hinduism.*

inner ether: Another name for the *ākāśa.*

inner eye: The third eye. See: *ājñā chakra; third eye.*

inner plane: Referring to the inner worlds, usually the Second World, or *Antarloka.*

innovation: Something newly introduced; a change.

instinctive: "Natural or innate." From the Latin *instinctus,* "to impel, instigate." The drives and impulses that order the animal world and the physical and lower astral aspects of humans—for example, self-preservation, procreation, hunger and thirst, as well as the emotions of greed, hatred, anger, fear, lust and jealousy. See: *mind.*

instinctive mind: *Manas chitta.* The lower mind, the controller of basic faculties of perception, movement, ordinary thought and emotion. *Manas chitta* is of the *manomaya kośa.* See: *astral body, mind.*

interrelate: To establish or demonstrate a connection between.

intersperse: Scatter, or randomly distribute among other things.

introvert: To turn within, directing one's interest, mind or attention upon oneself.

intuit: To know or sense without the use of rational processes.

Islam: The religion founded by Prophet Muhammed in Arabia about 625 CE, the youngest of the three Abrahamic faiths. Adherents, known as Muslims, follow the "five pillars" found in their scripture, the *Koran:* faith in Allah (God), praying five times daily facing Mecca, giving of alms, fasting during the month of Ramadan, and pilgrimage. One of the fastest growing religions, Islam has over one billion followers, mostly in the Middle East, Pakistan, Africa, China, Indochina, Russia and neighboring countries.

Jainism: ***(Jaina)*** जैन An ancient non-Vedic religion of India made prominent by the teachings of Mahāvīra ("great hero"), CA 500 BCE. The Jain *Āgamas* teach reverence for all life, vegetarianism and strict renunciation for ascetics. Jains focus great emphasis on the fact that all souls may attain liberation, each by his own effort. Their worship is directed toward their great historic saints, called Tīrthaṅkaras ("ford-crossers"), of whom Mahāvīra was the 24th and last. Jains number about six million today, living mostly in India.

jñāna pāda: ज्ञानपाद् "Stage of wisdom." According to the Śaiva Siddhānta *ṛishis, jñāna* is the last of the four successive *pādas* (stages) of spiritual unfoldment. It is the culmination of the third stage, the yoga *pāda.* Also names the knowledge section of each *Āgama.* See: *Āgama, pāda.*

Judaism: The religion of over 12 million adherents worldwide (over half in the United States), first of the Abrahamic faiths, founded about 3,700 years ago in Egypt-Canaan, now Israel, by Abraham, who started the lineage, and Moses, who emancipated the enslaved Jewish tribes from Egypt. Its major scripture is *The Torah* (the first five books of the *Old Testament* and the *Talmud*).

jyotisha: ज्योतिष From *jyoti,* "light." "The science of the lights (or stars)." Hindu astrology, the knowledge and practice of analyzing events and circumstances, delineating character and determining auspicious moments, according to the positions and movements of heavenly bodies. In calculating horoscopes, *jyotisha* uses the sidereal (fixed-star) system, while Western astrology uses the tropical (fixed-date) method.

Kabbala: Oral tradition of esoteric Jewish mysticism which appeared in the 12th and following centuries. Kabbala claims secret knowledge of the unwritten *Torah,* the "divine revelation" communicated by God to Moses and Adam. While observance of the Law of Moses remains the basic tenet of Judaism, Kabbala provides a means of approaching God directly.

Kali Yuga: कलियुग "Dark Age." *Kali* means "strife, discord, contention: a die marked with one dot, the loosing die." It is the last age of 432,000 years in the repetitive cycle of four phases, a period when only one-fourth of the Central Sun's rays reach Earth. It is comparable to the darkest part of the night, as the forces of ignorance are in full power and many of the subtle faculties of the soul are obscured. See: *yuga, Central Sun.*

kammaba: Shum language term for the feeling, the pressure, the weight of all actions, duties and responsibilities. The karma of another person that is temporarily carried by someone trying to help them, such as when in the midst of solving a problem. See: *karma, Shum.*

karma: कर्म "Action, deed." One of the most important principles in Hindu thought, karma refers to 1) any act or deed; 2) the principle of cause and effect; 3) a consequence or "fruit of action" *(karmaphala)* or "after effect" *(uttaraphala),* which sooner or later returns upon the doer. What we sow, we shall reap in this or future lives. Selfish, hateful acts *(pāpakarma* or *kukarma)* will bring suffering. Benevolent actions *(puṇyakarma* or *sukarma)* will bring loving reactions. Karma is a neutral, self-perpetuating law of the inner cosmos.

Kārttikeya: कार्त्तिकेय Child of the Pleiades, from *Kṛittikā,* "Pleiades." Second son of Śiva, brother of Gaṇeśa. A great Mahādeva worshiped in all parts of India and the world. Also known as Muruga, Kumāra, Skanda, Shaṇmukhanātha, Subramaṇya and more, He is the God who guides that part of evolution which is religion, the transformation of the instinctive into a divine wisdom through the practice of yoga. In the Hindu *Āgamas* and *Purāṇas* appears a story in which Śiva emanates six sparks from His third eye that develop into six beautiful youths that are taken by the six Kṛittikās, or maidens, of the Pleiades and nurtured, hence the name Kārttikeya. These six then merge into one youth with six heads, giving another name: Shaṇmukha. Kārttikeya also appears in much earlier texts of the *Atharva Veda* under the name Skanda, found in the Skanda Yaga section of the *Parisistas,* in which He is referred to as the Son of Śiva, Agni and the Pleiades. Lord Kārttikeya's "birth on Earth" is celebrated near the full-moon day when the Sun is in line with the Pleiades in the month of May/June, the kind of planetary alignment mentioned in *Lemurian Scrolls* for souls to migrate from that star system to Earth. See: *Muruga, Skanda, Subramaṇya, Pleiades, Vedas.*

Kṛita Yuga: कृतयुग "Age of accomplishment." Kṛita also means "good, cultivated, kind action" and names the die of four dots. The first in the repetitive cycle of *yugas,* commonly known as Sat Yuga. See: *yuga.*

kriyā pāda: क्रियापाद "Stage of religious action; worship." The stage of worship and devotion, second of four progressive stages of maturation on the Śaiva Siddhānta path of attainment. See: *pāda, Śaiva Siddhānta,*

Śaivism.

kuṇḍalinī: कुण्डलिनी "She who is coiled; serpent power." The primordial cosmic energy in every individual which, at first, lies coiled like a serpent at the base of the spine and eventually, through the practice of yoga, rises up the *sushumṇā nāḍī*. As it rises, the *kuṇḍalinī* awakens each successive chakra. *Nirvikalpa samādhi,* enlightenment, comes as it pierces through the door of Brahman at the core of the *sahasrāra* and enters! See: *enlightenment, evolution of the soul, nāḍī.*

Laboratory: A room, building or place where scientific experiments are performed. In this text it refers to the places where the first human, flesh bodies were created and perfected.

Lemuria: An ancient continent described in *Lemurian Scrolls* as the first continent on Earth to be inhabited by humans (Lemurians). Lemuria has been revealed by scripture and explained and made popular by numerous clairvoyants and mystics over the past hundred years as a highly advanced civilization with amazing technologies, maintaining the love of nature and appreciating its many gifts. The accounts of various authors closely resemble descriptions found in this text. According to texts read along with *Lemurian Scrolls,* Lemuria once formed a land mass that stretched from the Rocky Mountains in the United States west to South Africa. According to another source, it is an ancient continent thought to have formed a massive connection between India, Madagascar and South Africa. Still another theory places it in the South Pacific between North America and Australasia.

Lemurian and Dravidian Śāstras: The original name for these *Lemurian Scrolls,* revealed from *ākāśic* records in two parts to Sivaya Subramuniyaswami's astral vision in 1973 by Lord Subramaniam's inner-plane librarian. See: *śāstra.*

Lemurian prasādam: Ambrosia made from fruit and cow or goat milk with nuts, seeds and honey that was offered to the Deities and enjoyed as daily nourishment by the Lemurians. At my monasteries, Lemurian Prasādam has become, over the years, a special treat, taken at lunchtime now and then. It is also prepared for days when a *sattvic* diet is needed (such as on *pradosha* days), or as a transition diet when preparing for a fast or ending one. The monks take great joy in making this healthful and simple meal. I have asked them to give a typical recipe for a single, hungry-person serving: One ripe banana and one papaya or the equivalent in other neutral fruits, such as apples, berries, peaches, mangos or pears, cut in bite-size pieces. (Acid fruits, such as oranges, lemons and pineapples, are always taken separately and do not mix well with this meal.) A small handful of raisins, dates and seeds, such as sunflower or sesame, are always added, along with two ounces of nuts, such as almonds, pecans, walnuts or cashews. A special meal can include an ounce of dried figs or currents. Mix all of the above together with one cup of yogurt and add up to one tablespoon of nature's most natural sweetener, honey, as desired. See: *prasādam.*

Lemurians: The term used by the souls in the original bodies that came to this planet in the last Sat Yuga and Tretā Yuga to refer to those souls who were the first to inhabit human bodies that came up from the animal kingdom during the Tretā Yuga.

levitation: The power or ability to float in the air or to cause objects to do so at will.

liberation: *Moksha,* release from the bonds of *pāśa,* after which the soul is liberated from *saṁsāra* (the round of births and deaths), which occurs after karma has been resolved and *nirvikalpa samādhi*—

realization of the Self, Paraśiva—has been attained. In Śaiva Siddhānta, *pāśa* is the three-fold bondage of *āṇava,* karma and *māyā,* which limit and confine the soul to the reincarnational cycle so that it may evolve. *Moksha* is freedom from the fettering power of these bonds, which do not cease to exist, but no longer have the power to fetter or bind the soul. Same as *mukti.* See: *kuṇḍalinī, Paraśiva, Śaiva Siddhānta.*

lo: An exclamation to attract attention or to show surprise.

Lord Subramaniam Śāstras: The three-volume set of inner-plane writings containing the *Lemurian, Dravidian* and *Śaivite Śāstras.*

Magic: Use of charms, spells and rituals in seeking or pretending to cause or control events, or govern certain natural or supernatural forces. Also, wondrous; producing extraordinary results.

mahā: महा A prefix meaning "great."

Mahādeva: महादेव "Great shining one; God." Referring either to God Śiva or any of the highly evolved beings who live in the Śivaloka in their natural, effulgent soul bodies. God Śiva in His perfection as Primal Soul is one of the Mahādevas, yet He is unique and incomparable in that He alone is uncreated, the Father-Mother and Destiny of all other Mahādevas. He is called Parameśvara, "Supreme God." He is the Primal Soul, whereas the other Gods are individual souls. See: *Śivaloka, three worlds.*

mahā tapas: महातपस् State of introspection and intensive striving and purification catalyzed by the grace of the guru and the disciplines of monastic life. A culmination of *sādhana* well-performed; an opportunity to break through inner congestion which has become apparent to the guru's inner vision. During *mahā tapas,* which is given by the guru, often without explanation, a monastic may be relieved of some or all of his regular duties.

mala: मल "Impurity." An important term in Śaivism referring to three bonds, called *pāśa—āṇava,* karma, and *māyā*—which limit the soul, preventing it from knowing its true, divine nature. See: *liberation, pāśa.*

malcontent: Not happy with current conditions or circumstances; not satisfied. A person who is not content.

mantra: मन्त्र "Mystic formula." A sound, syllable, word or phrase endowed with special power, usually drawn from scripture. Mantras are chanted loudly during *pūjā* to invoke the Gods and establish a force field. Certain mantras are used for worshipful incantation, called *japa.* To be truly effective, such mantras must be given by the preceptor through initiation. See: *dīkshā, pūjā.*

Manu Dharma Śāstra: मनुधर्मशास्त्र "Sage Manu's law book." An encyclopedic treatise of 2,685 verses on Hindu law assembled as early as 600 BCE. Despite its caste-based restrictions, which determine one's life unrelentingly from birth to death, it remains the source of much of modern Hindu culture and law.

manvantara: Cycle of 71 *chaturyugas.* See: *cosmic cycle, chaturyuga, yuga.*

maṭha: मठ "Monastery." See: *monastery.*

maṭhavāsi: मठवासि "Monastic; monastery dweller." See: *monk.*

mauna tapas: मौनतपस् The discipline of being silent.

māyā: माया "She who measures;" or "mirific energy." The substance emanated from Śiva through which the world of form is manifested. Hence all creation is also termed *māyā.* It is the cosmic creative force, the principle of manifestation, ever in the process of creation, preservation and dissolution. In Śaivism it is one of the three bonds *(pāśa)* that limit the soul and thereby facilitate its evolution. For Śaivites and most other nondualists, it is understood not as illusion but as relative reality, in contrast to the unchanging Absolute Reality. See: *mala, pāśa.*

Mayans: An advanced civilization that thrived over 3,000 years ago in southern Mexico, Guatemala and northern Belize. The Mayans were adept in astrology, mathematics and agriculture. They built great cities and temples out of stone and believed in many nature Gods.

meditation: The result of successful concentration; uninterrupted thought on a subject, leading to intuitive discovery. *"Dhyāna,"* the seventh of the eight limbs of *ashṭāṅga* yoga. See: *rāja yoga.*

medulla: *Medulla oblongata;* the widening continuation of the spinal cord, forming the lowest part of the brain and containing nerve centers that control breathing, circulation, etc.

mendicant: A beggar; a wandering monk, or *sādhu,* who lives on alms. See: *monk.*

mesmerism: Causing illusions, a form of hypnotism.

microcosm-macrocosm: "Little world" or "miniature universe" as compared with "great world." *Microcosm* refers to the internal source of something larger or more external (macrocosm). In Hindu cosmology, the outer world is a macrocosm of the inner world, which is its microcosm and is mystically larger and more complex than the physical universe and functions at a higher rate of vibration and even a different rate of time. The microcosm precedes the macrocosm. Thus, the guiding principle of the Bhūloka comes from the Antarloka and Śivaloka. Consciousness precedes physical form. In the *tantric* tradition, the body of man is viewed as a microcosm of the entire divine creation. "Microcosm-macrocosm" is embodied in the terms *piṇḍa* and *aṇḍa.* See: *universe, universes*

mind: In the most profound sense, mind is the sum of all things, all energies and manifestations, all forms, subtle and gross, sacred and mundane. It is the inner and outer cosmos. Mind is *māyā.* It is the material matrix. It is everything but That, the Self within, Paraśiva. ℂIn the individual being, mind, or consciousness, is understood in three parts: 1) instinctive mind: the seat of desire and governor of sensory and motor organs; 2) intellectual mind: the faculty of thought and intelligence; 3) superconscious mind: the strata of intuition, benevolence and spiritual sustenance. Its most refined essence is Parāśakti, or Satchidānanda, all-knowing, omnipresent consciousness, the One transcendental, self-luminous, divine mind common to all souls. See: *Parāśakti, Paraśiva, Satchidānanda.*

mingle: To mix together, usually without loss of individual characteristics.

mohan: Often *"mohan* artisan;" a senior swāmī who serves and teaches mainly inside the monastery walls. See: *artisan.*

moksha: मोक्ष See: *liberation.*

monarchy: Rulership by royalty, generally a hereditary head of state, a king or queen.

monastery: "Place of solitariness." *Maṭha.* The age-old tradition, carried forward from Lemurian times into the Hindu culture of India, a sacred place where those of the same gender go through their birth karmas together toward realization of the Self. Living under strict vows, they thrive. Most monasteries are cloisters for men, though monasteries for women, headed by female ascetics, also exist in the Hindu tradition. Male and female monasteries are traditionally situated several miles or more from one another. Monasteries, in the correct sense of the word, are for individuals on the path of enlightenment who have arrived at a certain subsuperconscious state and wish to stay there. Therefore, they release various interactions with the world, physically and emotionally, and seek to remain poised in a contemplative monastic lifestyle. The intention of monastic life is to put oneself in a self-imposed intensity where unfoldment of the spirit can be catalyzed more quickly and more fully than in family life, or in a commune or coed *āśramā* situations where the two genders live together. In monasteries, dedicated to transmutation of the sexual energies, celibacy is strictly upheld and there is no fraternizing with the opposite sex. The karmas of males living together and females living among their own gender are worked though faster than in communes, as they do not distract each other, nor do they offer temptations for additional karmas to be pursued. Such a separation offers safety for sincere seekers, assurance that nothing unseemly will happen as spiritual life is pursued. The purpose of the monastery is to create an environment in which the individual can balance the male and female energies *(piṅgala* and *iḍā)* within himself so that he lives in the spiritual, or *sushumṇā,* energy, which cannot be done when close association with the opposite sex is also occurring. The monastic, whether a monk or a nun, is in a sense neither male nor female, but a pure soul being. By contrast, in communes or *āśramas* in which men and women live together, the men reside mainly in the masculine *(piṅgala)* current, and the women in the feminine *(iḍā)* current. The goal of the monastic, whether male or female, is to live in the depth of his own being, treating all equally, abandoning preferences. He finds points of agreement, forsaking contention and difference. No man is his enemy. No man is his friend. All men are his teachers. Some teach him what to do; others teach him what not to do. He finds security in his own being rather than by attaching himself to outward manifestations of security, warmth and companionship. A Śaiva monastery is a laboratory dedicated to the realization of the Self, an environment in which the *sushumṇā* can come into full power so that the *kuṇḍalinī* can rise to the top of the head and beyond into the fullness of timeless, formless, spaceless Self, Paraśiva. See: *āśrama, cult, monastery, monk, nāḍī.*

monastic: See: *monk.*

monk: A celibate man wholly dedicated to religious life, either cenobitic (residing with others in a monastery) or anchoritic (living alone, as a hermit or mendicant). Literally, "one who lives alone" (from the Greek *monos,* "alone"). Through the practice of yoga, the control and transmutation of the masculine and feminine forces within himself, the monk is a complete being, free to follow the contemplative and mystic life toward realization of the Self within. Benevolent and strong, courageous, fearless, not entangled in the thoughts and feelings of others, monks are affectionately detached from society, defenders of the faith, kind, loving and ever-flowing with timely wisdom. A synonym for *monastic.* See: *sannyāsa.*

moon: In this text, month; one complete cycle of the moon around the Earth.

morass: A place of difficulty or trouble; a swamp, bog or marsh.

mundane: Commonplace, ordinary.

mūrti: मूर्ति "Form; manifestation, embodiment, personification." An image or icon of God or a God used during worship. See: *Deity.*

Muruga: முருகன் "Beautiful one," a favorite name of Kārttikeya among the Tamils of South India, Sri Lanka and elsewhere. See: *Kārttikeya, Skanda, Subramaniam.*

Muslim: "True believer." A follower of Islam. See: *Islam.*

myriad: Countless; an indefinitely large number.

N

nāḍī: नाडी "Conduit." A nerve fiber or energy channel of the subtle (inner) bodies of man. It is said there are 72,000. These interconnect the chakras. The three main *nāḍīs* are named *iḍā, piṅgalā* and *sushumṇā*. ***—iḍā:*** Also known as *chandra* ("moon") *nāḍī*, it is pink in color and flows downward, ending on the left side of the body. This current is feminine in nature and is the channel of physical-emotional energy. ***—piṅgaḷā:*** Also known as *sūrya* ("sun") *nāḍī*, it is blue in color and flows upward, ending on the right side of the body. This current is masculine in nature and is the channel of intellectual-mental energy. ***—sushumṇā:*** The major nerve current which passes through the spinal column from the *mūlādhāra* chakra at the base to the *sahasrāra* at the crown of the head. It is the channel of *kuṇḍalinī*. Through yoga, the *kuṇḍalinī* energy lying dormant in the *mūlādhāra* is awakened and made to rise up this channel through each chakra to the *sahasrāra* chakra. See: *chakra, kuṇḍalinī, rāja yoga.*

naishṭika: नैष्ठिक Virgin from birth. In this text, a monastic or pre-monastic who has maintained the subtle connections with the inner worlds which are closed off or obscured when a connection with a member of the opposite sex is created through sexual intercourse. See: *psychic tubes.*

Nātha: नाथ "Master, lord; adept." Names an ancient Himālayan tradition of Śaiva-yoga mysticism, whose first historically known exponent was Nandikeśvara (CA 250 BCE). *Nātha*—Self-Realized adept—refers to the extraordinary ascetic masters of this school. *Nātha* also refers to any follower of the Nātha tradition. The Nāthas are considered the source of *haṭha* as well as *rāja* yoga. Satguru Sivaya Subramuniyaswami is of the Nandinātha tradition, one of the two major Nātha streams, of which the second is the Gorakshnātha Sampradāya.

nirvikalpa samādhi: निर्विकल्पसमाधि "Enstasy *(samādhi)* without form or seed." The realization of the Self, Paraśiva, a state of oneness beyond all change or diversity; beyond time, form and space. *Vi* means "to change, make different." *Kalpa* means "order, arrangement; a period of time." Thus *vikalpa* means "diversity, thought; difference of perception, distinction." *Nir* means "without." See: *enlightenment, enstasy, Paraśiva, rāja yoga, samādhi.*

north wind: The group within the monastery which provides for and takes care of the monastics, from preparing food to performing the *pūjās* to overseeing the teachings. The north wind is the innermost wind of the monastery. See: *pūjā, winds.*

novitiate: Same as *novice.* A newcomer to a monastic or religious community, on probation, before taking final vows.

nullify: To make invalid or useless.

O

odic: Magnetic—of or pertaining to consciousness within *aśuddha māyā*, the realm of the physical and lower astral planes. Odic force in its rarified state is *prakṛiti*, the primary gross energy of nature, manifesting in the three *guṇas: sattva, rajas* and *tamas.* It is the force of attraction and repulsion between people, people and their things, and manifests as masculine (aggressive) and feminine (passive), arising from the *piṅgalā* and *iḍā* currents. These two currents *(nāḍī)* are found within the spine of the subtle body. Odic force is a magnetic, sticky, binding substance that people seek to develop when they want to bind themselves together, such as in partnerships, marriage, *guru-śishya* relationships and friendships. See: *māyā, nāḍī.*

odic tubes: See: *psychic tubes.*

old soul: One who has reincarnated many times, learned the lessons from life's experiences, matured the soul body through spiritual disciplines and is therefore farther along the path. Old souls may be recognized by their qualities of compassion, self-effacement and wisdom. See: *soul.*

oligarchy: Rulership by a few. Government by a small group, generally empowered by social and financial might.

one-third minority: Same as senior minority group, abbreviated "OTM." See: *senior minority group.*

onrush: A sudden movement forward. Also an attack.

ordain (ordination): To bestow the duties and responsibilities, authority and spiritual power of a religious office, such as priest, minister or *satguru,* through religious ceremony or mystical initiation. See: *dīkshā, initiation.*

original body: Body made from the essences of fruits and flowers. Also referred to as fibrous bodies, they were neither male nor female, nor did they sleep or experience heat, cold or fear. See: *fibrous body.*

overt: Open and observable to anyone; not hidden or secret.

Pāda: पाद "The foot (of men and animals); quarter-part, section; stage; path." Names the major sections of the Āgamic texts and the corresponding stages of practice and unfoldment on the path to *moksha.* According to Śaiva Siddhānta, there are four *pādas,* which are successive and cumulative; i.e. in accomplishing each one the soul prepares itself for the next. ***—charyā pāda:*** "Good conduct stage." The first stage where one learns to live righteously, serve selflessly, performing karma yoga. It is also known as *dāsa mārga,* "path of the slave," a time when the aspirant relates to God as a servant to a master. Traditional acts of *charyā* include cleaning the temple, lighting lamps and collecting flowers for worship. Worship at this stage is mostly external. ***—kriyā pāda:*** "Religious action; worship stage." Stage of *bhakti* yoga, of cultivating devotion through performing *pūjā* and regular daily *sādhana.* It is also known as the *satputra mārga,* "true son's way," as the soul now relates to God as a son to his father. A central practice of the *kriyā pāda* is performing daily *pūjā.* ***—yoga pāda:*** Having matured in the *charyā* and *kriyā pādas,* the soul now turns to internalized worship and *rāja* yoga under the guidance of a *satguru.* It is a time of *sādhana* and serious striving when realization of the Self is the goal. It is the *sakhā mārga,* "way of the friend," for now God is looked upon as an intimate friend. ***—jñāna pāda:*** "Stage of wisdom." Once the soul has attained Realization, it is henceforth a wise one, who lives out the life of the body, shedding blessings on mankind. This stage is also called the San Mārga, "true path," on which God is our dearest beloved. See: *Āgama, Śaiva Siddhānta, Śaivism.*

pagoda: A temple in the form of a pyramidal tower of several stories.

paramount: Ranking higher than any other, as in power or importance.

Parāśakti: पराशक्ति "Supreme power; primal energy." God Śiva's second perfection, which is impersonal, immanent, and with form—the all-pervasive, Pure Consciousness and Primal Substance of all that exists. There are many other descriptive names for Parāśakti—Satchidānanda ("existence-consciousness-bliss"), light, silence, divine mind, superconsciousness and more. See: *rāja yoga, Satchidānanda.*

Paraśiva: परशिव "Transcendent Śiva." The Self God, Śiva in His first perfection, Absolute Reality. God Śiva as That which is beyond the grasp of consciousness, transcends time, form and space and defies description. To merge with Him in mystic union is the goal of all incarnated souls, the reason for their living on this planet, and the deepest meaning of their experiences. Attainment of this is called Self Realization or *nirvikalpa samādhi.* See: *nirvikalpa samādhi, samādhi, Śiva.*

pāśa: पाश "Tether; noose." The whole of existence, manifest and unmanifest. That which binds or limits the soul and keeps it (for a time) from manifesting its full potential. Pāśa refers to the soul's three-fold bondage of *āṇava,* karma and *māyā.* See: *āṇava, karma, māyā, mala, liberation.*

perceptive: Having the ability to perceive and understand.

permeate: To spread or flow throughout.

pervasive: Diffused throughout; existing in.

petition: A solemn, earnest request to a superior, Deity, person or group in authority.

phenomenal: Extraordinary; outstanding.

philosophical quiz: A verbal test given by the senior minority group to a monastic seeking entrance to the monastery.

Pleiades: *Kṛittikā* कृत्तिका A star cluster, also known as M45, located in the zodiacal constellation Taurus, approximately 400 light-years (2,400 trillion miles) from our solar system, of which six or seven stars can be seen by the unaided eye. The Pleiades are referred to in stories from religions and cultures the world over. In the Hindu scriptures appears a story in which Lord Kārttikeya is nurtured by the six maidens of the Pleiades, known as the Kṛittikās. This story is paralleled in Greek mythology where the "Seven Sisters" are believed to have been turned into stars by Zeus. Referred to in the poet-astronomer Omar Khayyam's *Rubaiyat* as "beginning all things," the Pleiades were simultaneously known in ancient Peruvian legend as "the arbiters of human destiny." The *Koran,* the holy book of Islam, tells of Najm, the Pleiades, from which a spirit (the angel Gabriel) came to tell the Prophet Muhammed the laws of the Muslims. The Pleiades are also well known to the Chinese, the Freemasons, and are one of the few star clusters mentioned in the *Bible.* See: Kārttikeya.

pliable: Easily bent or shaped; moldable.

poignant: Sharp; penetrating; pointed. Also emotionally intense or distressing.

polarize: In common usage, to separate into diametrically opposed parts. In this text, to draw upon the cosmic forces and channel them for a particular purpose, or to attract and sustain the presence of divine beings.

populace: The public or masses.

portend: To serve as an omen or a warning.

pragmatic: Concerned with actual practice, everyday matters, etc.; practical.

prasādam: प्रसाद् "Clarity, brightness; grace." 1) The virtue of serenity and graciousness. 2) Food offered to the Deity or a guru, or the blessed remnants of such food. 3) A propitiatory offering. See: *Lemurian Prasādam.*

prebiotic: Before life.

precipitate: To bring on; cause; hasten. Also to condense moisture from vapor to water.

premeditate: To plan or arrange in advance.

preordain: To appoint or order in advance.

prism: To collect, channel or redirect the spiritual energies, or darshan.

proficient: Having or marked by an advanced degree of ability, as in an art, craft, profession or knowledge.

progenitor: A direct ancestor.

progeny: Something born of or derived from another; an offspring or descendant.

promulgator: Someone who makes something known publicly.

proportionate: Being in relationship between things or parts of things.

prudence: Careful management; discretion.

psychic: "Of the psyche or soul." Sensitive to spiritual processes and energies. Inwardly or intuitively aware of nonphysical realities; able to use powers such as clairvoyance, clairaudience and precognition. Nonphysical, subtle; pertaining to the deeper aspects of man. See: *clairaudience, clairvoyance.*

psychic entanglements: See: *psychic tubes.*

psychic tubes: Channels of astral matter which connect a man and woman who have had sexual intercourse. Such connections persist for a 12 year period, though are greatly diminished after 6 years. Psychic tubes also persist between child and mother up until age 24. Through the process of *brahmacharya* all such connections are gradually dissolved and a new connection established with the guru. See: *brahmacharya.*

puberty: Time in youth when sexual capacity and characteristics develop.

pūjā: पूजा "Worship, adoration." An Āgamic rite of worship performed in the home, temple or shrine, to the *mūrti* or other consecrated object, or to a person, such as the *satguru.* Its inner purpose is to purify the atmosphere around the object worshiped, establish a connection with the inner worlds and invoke the presence of God, Gods or one's guru. During *pūjā,* the officiant *(pujārī)* recites various chants praising the Divine and beseeching divine blessings, while making offerings in accordance with established traditions.

pulsate: To beat or throb in rhythm.

pungent: Producing a sharp sensation of taste or smell; stimulating.

Purāṇa: पुराण "Ancient." Hindu folk narratives containing ethical and cosmological teachings relative to Gods, man and the world. They revolve around five subjects: primary creation, secondary creation, genealogy, cycles of time and history. There are 18 major *Purāṇas* which are designated as either Śaivite, Vaishṇavite or Śākta. See: *Hinduism.*

purusha: पुरुष "The spirit that dwells in the body/in the universe." Person; spirit; man. Metaphysically, the soul, neither male nor female. Purusha can also refer to the Supreme Being or Soul, as it sometimes does in the *Upanishads.* In the *Ṛig Veda* hymn "*Purusha Sūkta,*" Purusha is the cosmic man, having a thousand heads, a thousand eyes, a thousand feet and encompassing the Earth, spreading in all directions into animate and inanimate things.

Quiescent: Being quiet, still, or calm; inactive.

quantum: Quantity or amount. In science's quantum theory: a fixed basic unit, usually of energy. **—quantum particles of light:** Light understood not as a continuum, but as traveling bundles each of a same intensity. Deeper still, these particles originate and resolve themselves in a one divine energy. **—at the quantum level (of the mind):** Deep within the mind, at a subtle energy level.

quell: Put an end to, subdue, make quiet.

Rāja yoga: राजयोग "King of yogas." Also known as *ashṭāṅga* yoga, "eight-limbed yoga." The classical yoga system of eight progressive stages to Illumination as described in various yoga *Upanishads*, the *Tirumantiram* and, most notably, the *Yoga Sūtras* of Patañjali. The eight stages are: *yama* (restraints), *niyama* (observances), *āsana* (posture), *prāṇāyāma* (breath control) *pratyāhara* (withdrawal), *dhāraṇa* (concentration), *dhyāna* (meditation) and *samādhi* (enstasy, mystic oneness). See: *nirvikalpa samādhi, samādhi.*

ramification: Effect, consequence, result.

reincarnation: "Re-entering the flesh." *Punarjanma;* metempsychosis. The process wherein souls take on a physical body through the birth process. The cycle of reincarnation ends when karma has been resolved and the Self God (Paraśiva) has been realized. This condition of release is called *moksha.* Then the soul continues to evolve and mature, but without the need to return to physical existence. See: *evolution of the soul, karma, Paraśiva, soul.*

remorse: Mental state of feeling sorry or regretful for one's past actions.

requisite: Required; essential.

resplendence: Radiance; brilliance.

retrospect: A looking back on; thinking about the past.

revelation: The act of revealing or disclosing something; a vision or understanding.

Ṛig Veda: ऋग्वेद् *"Veda* of verse *(ṛik)."* The first and oldest of the four *Veda* compendia of revealed scriptures *(śruti),* including a hymn collection *(Saṁhitā),* priestly explanatory manuals *(Brāhmaṇas),* forest treatises *(Āraṇyakas)* elaborating on the *Vedic* rites, and philosophical dialogs *(Upanishads).* The *Ṛig Veda Saṁhitā,* which in length equals *Homer's Iliad* and *Odyssey* combined, is the most important hymn collection, for it lends a large number of its hymns to the other three *Veda Saṁhitās* (the *Sāma, Yajur and Atharva).* Chronologically, after the *Saṁhitās* came the *Brāhmaṇas,* followed by the *Āraṇyakas,* and finally the *Upanishads,* also called the *Vedānta,* meaning *"Veda's* end." See: *Vedas.*

ṛishi: ऋषि "Seer." A term for an enlightened being, emphasizing psychic perception and visionary wisdom. In the Vedic age, *ṛishis* lived in forest or mountain retreats, either alone or with disciples. These *ṛishis* were great souls who were the inspired conveyers of the *Vedas.* Seven particular *ṛishis* (the *sapta-ṛishis*) mentioned in the *Ṛig Veda* are said to still guide mankind from the inner worlds. See: *Hinduism.*

Sacrifice: *Yajña.* 1) Giving offerings to a Deity as an expression of homage and devotion. 2) Giving up something, often one's own possession, advantage or preference, to serve a higher purpose. The literal meaning of *sacrifice* is "to make sacred," implying an act of worship. It is the most common translation of the term *yajña,* from the verb *yuj,* "to worship." In Hinduism, all of life is a sacrifice—called *jīvayajña,* a giving of oneself—through which comes true spiritual fulfillment.

sādhaka: साधक "Accomplished one; a devotee who performs *sādhana."* A serious aspirant who has undertaken spiritual disciplines, is usually celibate and under the guidance of a guru. He wears white and may be under vows, but is not a *sannyāsin.*

***sādhaka* monastery:** A monastery in which most of the senior members are *sādhakas* dressed in white.

sādhana: साधन "Effective means of attainment." Religious or spiritual disciplines, such as *pūjā,* yoga, meditation, *japa,* fasting and austerity. The effect of *sādhana* is the building of willpower, faith and confidence in oneself and in God, Gods and guru. *Sādhana* harnesses and transmutes the instinctive-intellectual nature, allowing progressive spiritual unfoldment into the superconscious realizations and innate abilities of the soul. See: *pūjā, spiritual unfoldment.*

***Śaivite Śāstras*:** The inner-plane prophecy that has guided Śaiva Siddhānta Church since Sivaya Subramuniyaswami read it from the *ākāśa* in 1973. *The Śaivite Śāstras* were written for the Śaiva Siddhānta Yoga Order by a group of *devas* in the Second World, in English. Their purpose is to bring forward the applicable patterns of the Lemurian and Dravidian monasteries, molding the monastics into the culture and ideals expressed therein, including relationships with the *guru,* attitudes and guidelines for monastic life.

Śaiva Siddhānta: शैवसिद्धान्त "Final conclusions of Śaivism." The most widespread and influential Śaivite school today, predominant especially among the Tamil people in Sri Lanka and South India. It is the formalized theology of the divine revelations contained in the twenty-eight *Śaiva*

Āgamas. For Śaiva Siddhāntins, Śiva is the totality of all, understood in three perfections: Parameśvara (the Personal Creator Lord), Parāśakti (the substratum of form) and Paraśiva (Absolute Reality which transcends all). Souls and world are identical in essence with Śiva, yet also differ in that they are evolving. See: *Hinduism, Śaivism*.

Śaivism (Śaiva): शैव The religion followed by those who worship Śiva as supreme God. Oldest of the four sects of Hinduism. The earliest historical evidence of Śaivism is from the 8,000-year-old Indus Valley civilization in the form of the famous seal of Śiva as Lord Paśupati, seated in a yogic pose. See: *Hinduism*.

samādhi: समाधि "Enstasy," which means "standing within one's Self." From verb-root *dhā* with prepositional prefixes *sam* and *ā*, "to hold together completely." Sameness; contemplation; union, wholeness; completion, accomplishment. *Samādhi* is the state of true yoga, in which the meditator and the object of meditation are one. *Samādhi* is of two levels. The first is *savikalpa samādhi* ("enstasy with form or seed"), identification or oneness with the essence of an object. Its highest form is the realization of the primal substratum or pure consciousness, Satchidānanda. The second is *nirvikalpa samādhi* ("enstasy without form or seed"), identification with the Self, in which all modes of consciousness are transcended and Absolute Reality, Paraśiva, beyond time, form and space, is experienced. This brings in its aftermath a complete transformation of consciousness. See: *enstasy, nirvikalpa samādhi, Paraśiva, Satchidānanda*.

Sanātana Dharma: सनातनधर्म "Eternal religion" or "everlasting path," based on two supremely divine bodies of revealed scripture, *śruti* (that which is heard from God), the *Vedas (Ṛig, Sāma, Yajur and Atharva)* and the *Āgamas*. Sanātana Dharma is a traditional name for the Hindu religion and one still used in India. See: *Hinduism*.

sanction: Authoritative permission or approval.

sandhyā: संध्या Twilight, end of an era (*yuga, chaturyuga, manvantara*, etc.) the transitional period as one era ends and a new one begins. See: *cosmic cycle*.

sannidhānam: சன்னிதானம் "Nearness; proximity; taking charge of." A South Indian title for heads of monasteries: *guru mahāsannidhānam*. See: *sānnidhya*.

sānnidhya: सान्निध्य "(Divine) presence; nearness, proximity." The radiance and blessed presence of *śakti* within and around a temple or a holy person.

sannyāsa: संन्यास "Renunciation." "Throwing down or abandoning." Sannyāsa is the repudiation of the dharma, including the obligations and duties, of the householder and the acceptance of the even more demanding dharma of the renunciate. See: *monastic, monk*.

Sarasvatī: सरस्वती "The flowing one." Śakti, the Universal Mother; Goddess of the arts and learning, mythological consort of the God Brahmā. Sarasvatī, the river Goddess, is usually depicted wearing a white *sārī* and holding a *vīṇā*, sitting upon a swan or lotus flower. Prayers are offered to her for refinements of art, culture and learning.

śāstra: शास्त्र "Sacred text; teaching." Any religious or philosophical treatise, or body of writings. Also a department of knowledge, a science; e.g., the *Artha Śāstras* on politics.

Satchidānanda: सच्चिदानन्द "Existence-consciousness-bliss." A synonym for Parāśakti. Lord Śiva's Divine Mind and simultaneously the pure superconscious mind of each individual soul. It is perfect love and omniscient, omnipotent consciousness, the fountainhead of all existence, yet containing and permeating all existence. It is also called pure consciousness, pure form, substratum of existence. See: *Parāśakti*.

satguru (sadguru): सद्गुरु "True weighty one." A spiritual preceptor of the highest attainment—one who has realized the ultimate Truth, Paraśiva, through *nirvikalpa samādhi*—a *jīvanmukta* able to lead others securely along the spiritual path. He is always a *sannyāsin*, an unmarried renunciate. All Hindu denominations teach that the grace and guidance of a living *satguru* is a necessity for Self Realization. He is recognized and revered as the embodiment of God, Sadāśiva, the source of grace and of liberation. See: *guru, Hinduism, Paraśiva.*

Sat Śiva Yuga: सत्शिवयुग् Another name for the next Sat Yuga. See: *Sat Yuga.*

Sat Yuga: सत्युग् (Also Satya) "age of Truth," also called Kṛita, "accomplished, good, cultivated, kind action; the winning die of four dots." The first in the repetitive cycle of *yugas*, lasting 1,728,000 years, representing the brightest time, when the full light of the Central Sun permeates Earth. See: *yuga, Central Sun, cosmic cycle.*

scripture (scriptural): "A writing." A sacred text or holy book having authority for a given sect or religion. See: *śāstra.*

Second World: The astral or subtle plane. Here the soul continues its activities in the astral body during sleep and after the physical body dies. The Second World exists "within" the First World or physical plane. See: *Antarloka, astral plane, Devaloka.*

Self: See: *Paraśiva, Self Realization.*

Self Realization: Direct knowing of the Self God, Paraśiva. Self Realization is known in Sanskṛit as *nirvikalpa samādhi;* "enstasy without form or seed;" the ultimate spiritual attainment (also called *asamprajñata samādhi).* Esoterically, this state is attained when the mystic *kuṇḍalinī* force pierces through the *sahasrāra* chakra at the crown of the head. See: *enlightenment, kuṇḍalinī, nirvikalpa samādhi, Paraśiva, rāja yoga.*

semblance: The likeness or similarity of something else.

senior minority group: The one-third most senior members of the monastery. They meet regularly, in private, to oversee cleanliness, general procedures and the flow of guests and act as a channel to the guru and convey his instructions to the monastery in a formal way. See: *one-third minority.*

sentience: The state of being conscious.

serf: A slave.

Shinto: The indigenous religion of Japan, based on the sacred power or God, *kami,* within a variety of forms, mainly of nature.

Shum: A Nātha mystical language of meditation revealed in Switzerland in 1968 by Sivaya Subramuniyaswami. Its primary alphabet looks like this:

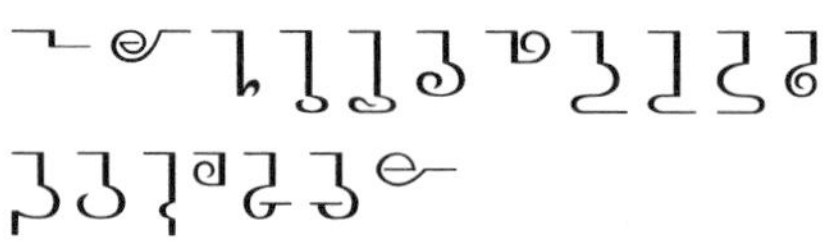

siddha: सिद्ध A "perfected one" or accomplished *yogī,* a person of great spiritual attainment or powers. See: *siddhi, yogī.*

siddhānta: सिद्धान्त "Final attainments or conclusions." The ultimate understanding arrived at in any field of knowledge. See: *Hinduism, Śaiva Siddhānta.*

siddhi: सिद्धि "Power, accomplishment; perfection." Extraordinary powers of the soul, developed through consistent meditation and deliberate, grueling, often uncomfortable *tapas,* or awakened naturally through spiritual maturity and yogic *sādhana.* Through the repeated experience of Self Realization, *siddhis* naturally unfold according to the needs of the individual. Before Self Realization, the use or development of *siddhis* is among the greatest obstacles on the path because it cultivates *ahaṁkāra,* I-ness, and militates against the attainment of *prapatti,* complete submission to the will of God, Gods and guru.

Sikhism: "Disciple." Religion of nine million members founded in India about 500 years ago by the saint Guru Nānak. A reformist faith which rejects idolatry and the caste system, its holy book is the *Ādi Granth,* and main holy center is the Golden Temple of Amritsar. See: *Hinduism.*

Śiva: शिव "The auspicious, gracious or kindly one." Supreme Being of the Śaivite religion. God Śiva is All and in all, simultaneously the creator and the creation, both immanent and transcendent. As personal Deity, He is creator, preserver and destroyer. He is a one being, perhaps best understood in three perfections: Parameśvara (Primal Soul), Parāśakti (pure consciousness) and Paraśiva (Absolute Reality). See: *Hinduism.*

Śivaloka: शिवलोक "Realm of Śiva." See: *three worlds.*

Śiva Purāṇa: शिवपुराण "Ancient [lore] of Śiva." A collection of six major scriptures sacred to Śaivites. Also the name of the oldest of these six texts, though some consider it a version of the *Vāyu Purāṇa.* See: *Hinduism, Purāṇas.*

Skanda: स्कन्द Name for Muruga as the ultimate Divine Warrior. See: *Kārttikeya, Muruga, Subramaniam.*

sober: Marked by seriousness, or solemnity of conduct or character.

socialism: A system of government in which private ownership and production is superceded by community or state control.

soul: The real being of man, as distinguished from body, mind and emotions. The soul—known as *ātman* or *purusha*—is the sum of its two aspects, the form or body of the soul and the essence of the soul. —**essence or nucleus of the soul:** Man's innermost and unchanging being—Pure Consciousness *(Parāśakti* or *Satchidānanda)* and Absolute Reality *(Paraśiva).* This essence was never created, does not change or evolve and is eternally identical with God Śiva's perfections of Parāśakti and Paraśiva. —**soul body:** *ānandamaya kośa* ("sheath of bliss"), also referred to as the "causal body" *(kāraṇa śarīra),* "innermost sheath" and "body of light." *Body of the soul,* or *soul body,* names the soul's manifest nature as an individual being—an effulgent, human-like form composed of light (quantums). See: *evolution of the soul, reincarnation, Parāśakti, Paraśiva.*

south wind: The group within the monastery who are the craftsmen, the builders, maintenance men, printers and publishers. See: *artisan, winds.*

spiritual unfoldment: The unfoldment of the spirit, the inherent, divine soul of man. The gradual expansion of consciousness as *kuṇḍalinī śakti* slowly rises through the *sushumṇā nāḍī.* The term *spiritual unfoldment* indicates this slow, imperceptible process of uncovering soul qualities that are already there, likened to a lotus flower's emerging from bud to effulgent beauty. See: *kuṇḍalinī, nāḍī, sushumṇā nāḍī.*

Śrīmad Bhāgavatam: श्रीमद् भागवतम् Also known as *Bhāgavata Purāṇa,* a work of 18,000 stanzas. A major *Purāṇa* and primary Vaishṇava scripture, from oral tradition, written down CA 800. It provides the stories of all incarnations of Vishṇu, filled with the *bhakti,* inner current of devotion. It falls in the category of secondary scripture, *smṛiti,* "that which is remembered," along with the *Mahābhārata, Rāmāyaṇa,* the *Bhāgavad Gītā,* the *Tirukural* and countless other works by man, as opposed to *sṛuti,* "that which is heard," wisdom revealed by God—a category reserved for the four sacred *Vedas,* the *Āgamas* and few rare texts throughout history that rise to this level of superconscious receptivity between our First World and the realm of the Gods. See: *Purāṇa.*

stabilizing the force field: Consciously working to quiet the instinctive forces and thus permit the influx of superconsciousness into the monastery. Done through various means of regulated cultured living and obedience to the *śāstras* and the guru. See: *force field.*

static: Unchanging; unmoving.

status quo: The existing state of affairs.

stratum: A section or layer of something. Plural: strata.

subconscious mind: *Saṁskāra chitta.* The storehouse of past impressions, reactions and desires and the seat of involuntary physiological processes. See: *aura, mind.*

subdue: To quiet or bring under control.

sublime: Noble, grand. Inspiring awe or reverence.

Subramaniam: சுப்பிரமணியம் (Sanskṛit—Subramaṇya: सुब्रमण्य) "Very pious; dear to holy men." A name of Lord Kārttikeya. See: *Kārttikeya, Muruga, Skanda.*

Subramuniya: சுப்பிரமுனியி Tamil spelling of the Sanskṛit *Śubhramunya* (not to be confused with *Subramaṇya).* It is formed from *śubhra* meaning "light; intuition," and *muni,* "silent sage." *Ya* means "restraint; religious meditation." Thus, *Subramuniya* means a self-restrained soul who remains silent or, when he speaks, speaks out from intuition. Name of the author of *Lemurian Scrolls,* current and 162nd satguru (1927–) of the Nandinātha Sampradāya's Kailāsa Paramparā.

subsuperconscious mind: *Anukāraṇa chitta.* The superconscious mind working through the conscious and subconscious states, which brings forth intuition, clarity and insight.

subtle body: *Sūkshma śarīra,* the nonphysical, astral body or vehicle in which the soul encases itself to function in the Antarloka, or subtle world. The subtle body includes the *vijñānamaya kośa* (mental, cognitive-intuitive sheath), *manomaya kośa* (instinctive-intellectual sheath) and the *prāṇamaya kośa* (life-energy sheath) if the soul is physically embodied. It consists of only *manomaya and vijñānamaya* after death, when *prāṇamaya kośa* disintegrates. And it consists of only *vijñānamaya kośa* when *manomaya kośa* is dropped off just before rebirth or when higher evolutionary planes are entered. Also part of the subtle body are the *antaḥkaraṇa* (mental faculty: intellect, instinct and ego—*buddhi, manas* and *ahaṁkāra*), the five *jñānendriyas* (agents of perception: hearing, touch, sight, taste and smell); and the five *karmendriyas* (agents of action: speech, grasping, movement, excretion and generation). Its composition spans the 6th to the 36th *tattva.*

succeed: To follow after. To accomplish something intended.

suffuse: To spread through, as with liquid, color or light.

Sufism: A mystical Islamic belief and practice in which Muslims seek to find the truth of divine love and knowledge through direct personal experience. See: *Islam.*

superconscious mind: *Kāraṇa chitta.* Mind of light. Śiva's Divine Mind. Satchidānanda. The intuitive or knowing state of mind; "the mind of light." One of the three phases of the mind: instinctive, intellectual and superconscious. See: *mind, Satchidānanda.*

supplement: Something added to complete a thing or strengthen the whole.

sushumṇā nāḍī: सुषुम्णानाडी "Most gracious channel." Central psychic nerve current within the spinal column. See: *nāḍī.*

synchronicity: The state or fact of being simultaneous.

syphon: To draw off of, take away or channel from.

Tapas: तपस् Literally, "to burn;" state of accelerated unfoldment and working with the forces through spiritual practices. A state of humble submission to the divine forces and surrender to the processes of inner purification which occur almost automatically at certain stages. In the monastery *tapas* is administered and guided by the guru. Denotes religious austerity, severe meditation, penance, bodily mortification, special observances; connotes spiritual purification and transformation as a "fiery process" which "burns up" impurities, ego, illusions and past karmas that obstruct God-Realization. See: *mahā tapas, mauna tapas.*

***tapas* monastery:** A monastery where most senior members are in yellow, on *tapas.*

tattva: तत्त्व "That-ness" or "essential nature." *Tattvas* are the primary principles, elements, states or categories of existence, the building blocks of the universe. Lord Śiva constantly creates, sustains the form of and absorbs back into Himself His creations. Ṛishis describe this emanational process as the unfoldment of *tattvas,* stages or evolutes of manifestation, descending from subtle to gross. At *mahāpralaya,* cosmic dissolution, they enfold into their respective sources, with only the first two *tattvas* surviving the great dissolution. The first and subtlest form—the pure consciousness and source of all other evolutes of manifestation—is called Śiva *tattva,* or Parāśaktināda. But beyond Śiva *tattva* lies Paraśiva—the utterly transcendent, Absolute Reality, called *attava.* That is Śiva's first perfection. The Sāṅkhya system discusses 25 *tattvas.* Śaivism recognizes these same 25 plus 11 beyond them, making 36 *tattvas* in all. (See chart on page 292.)

telepathy: Communication that transcends the five senses, such as thought transmission.

tenure: The length of time under which something is held.

terrocracy: Rulership through fear and intimidation. Government that gives permission for guerilla force, propelled by ruthless, unconscionable outlashes.

theocracy: Divine rulership. Government by religious leaders supported ideally by the inner worlds, such as the Dalai Lama's spiritual and political leadership of the Tibetan people.

Theosophy: Greek for "God" and "wisdom." The beliefs of a religious sect, the Theosophical Society, founded in New York City in 1875, incorporating aspects of Buddhism and Hinduism. Its goals include intense studies of ancient world religions and civilizations, especially Lemuria, for the purpose of deriving a universal ethic. See: *Lemuria.*

third eye: The *ājñā* chakra. The inner organ of psychic vision, located above and between the two physical eyes. See: *ājñā chakra, chakra.*

Third World: Śivaloka,"Realm of Śiva." The spiritual realm or causal plane of existence wherein Māhadevas and highly evolved souls live in their own self-effulgent forms. See: *Śivaloka, three worlds.*

three worlds: The three worlds of existence, *triloka,* are the primary hierarchical divisions of the cosmos. 1) Bhūloka: "Earth world," the physical plane. 2) Antarloka: "Inner or in-between world," the subtle or astral plane. 3) Śivaloka: "World of Śiva," and of the Gods and highly evolved souls; the causal plane, also called Kāraṇaloka. These are also known as the First World, Second World and Third World.

tone and tenor: The subtle tendencies and qualities of something.

transcendental: Supernatural; beyond known reality.

transition: Passing from one condition or place to another. A synonym of *death* which implies, more correctly, continuity of the individual rather than annihilation.

translucent: Partially transparent; allowing some light to shine through.

transmigration: Passage of a soul into another body after death.

transmutation: Changing of a gross force into a finer one, referring specifically to changing or transforming the sexual/instinctive energies into intellectual and

The 36 Tattvas: Categories of Existence

Atattva: Paraśiva (Śivaliṅga, Absolute Reality), beyond all categories

The Five Śuddha Tattvas
Actinic or Pure Spiritual Energy

1) *Śiva tattva:* Parāśakti-Nāda (Satchidānanda, pure consciousness)
2) *Śakti tattva:* Parameśvara-Bindu (Naṭarāja, Personal God), energy, light and love
3) *Sadāśiva tattva:* the power of revealment (Sadāśiva)
4) *Īśvāra tattva:* the power of concealment (Maheśvara)
5) *Śuddhavidyā tattva:* dharma, pure knowing, the powers of dissolution (Rudra), preservation (Vishṇu) and creation (Brahmā)

The Seven Śuddhāśuddha Tattvas
Actinodic or Spiritual-Magnetic Energy

6) *māyā tattva:* mirific energy
7) *kāla tattva:* time
8) *niyati tattva:* karma
9) *kalā tattva:* creativity, aptitude
10) *vidyā tattva:* knowledge
11) *rāga tattva:* attachment, desire
12) *purusha tattva:* the soul shrouded by the above five *tattvas*

24 Āśuddha Tattvas
Odic or Gross-Magnetic Energy

13) *prakṛiti tattva:* primal nature
14) *buddhi tattva:* intellect
15) *ahaṁkāra tattva:* external ego
16) *manas tattva:* instinctive mind
17) *śrotra tattva:* hearing (ears)
18) *tvak tattva:* touching (skin)
19) *chakshu tattva:* seeing (eyes)
20) *rasanā tattva:* tasting (tongue)
21) *ghrāṇa tattva:* smelling (nose)
22) *vāk tattva:* speech (voice)
23) *pāṇi tattva:* grasping (hands)
24) *pāda tattva:* walking (feet)
25) *pāyu tattva:* excretion (anus)
26) *upastha tattva:* procreation (genitals)
27) *śabdha tattva:* sound
28) *sparśa tattva:* feel
29) *rūpa tattva:* form
30) *rasa tattva:* taste
31) *gandha tattva:* odor
32) *ākāśa tattva:* ether
33) *vāyu tattva:* air
34) *tejas tattva:* fire
35) *āpas tattva:* water
36) *pṛithivī tattva:* earth

spiritual ones. The primary aim of life in the monastery.

transmute: To change from one nature, form, substance or state into another; to transform.

transparent: Not drawing attention to oneself, unobtrusive. Cultured living. A term used to describe the state of mind and being in which one is centered within oneself and, though behaving in a natural and relaxed manner, does not ruffle one's surroundings.

Tretā Yuga: त्रेतायुग "The age of triads," second of the four *yugas,* lasting 1,296,000 years, in which three-forths of the spiritual light of the Central Sun still permeates Earth. Much of the refinement of the Sat Yuga still exists in the Tretā Yuga. The end of Tretā Yuga is described in this text as a time when the dusk of externalization of consciousness approaches. See: *yuga, cosmic cycle, Central Sun.*

tribulation: Great misery or distress.

turmoil: Commotion; uproar; confusion.

Umādeva: उमादेव In this text, the messenger of the senior minority group, or "one-third minority" (OTM). The member of the OTM with the least resident seniority. See: *senior minority group.*

Umāgaṇeśa: उमागणेश In this text, the member of the senior minority group with the most resident seniority in the monastery. He is the guru's secretary and chairman of the senior minority group, with the duty of keeping the guru informed of all activities. See: *senior minority group.*

unanimous: Having the same opinions or views; being in complete harmony or agreement.

unbeknownst: Without the knowledge of a specified party.

unfoldment: Progression into the soul nature through awakening of *kuṇḍalinī* force within the chakras, subtle spiritual/psychic forces centers within the being of man. See: *kuṇḍalinī, spiritual unfoldment.*

unhindered: Free of obstacles or resistence. Not restrained.

universal language: The process of thought projection and immediate translation into one's own language by the astral brain, a process employed in some *ākāśic* writings in which readers see words of another language and understand them fully by catching the meaning through mental pictures, like the mental language of dreams.

universe, outer: A term from *unus,* "one," and *versus* (pp. of *vertere,* "to turn"), meaning the totality of all existence; the creation or the cosmos. It can also refer to a specific field or sphere, as of thought or activity.

universe, inner: Referencing the inner, nonphysical worlds—the astral plane or Antarloka, and the causal plane or Śivaloka.

universes: A term used in this book to refer to the outer universe and the inner universe, and also to imply that the fullness of God's creation is not a simple one thing, but a profoundly complex, divine, and even incomprehensible and interwoven Whole. It exists on many planes, in many dimensions, some known now, others yet to be known. Metaphysically it names the beyond of the beyond of the beyond, both inner and out and much, much more. Even now, contemporary science proposes matter and anti matter, which are two complete and completely different "universes." Expanding the mind, we know that this simple physical universe is not all there is, but exists as one of many "universes," subtle and gross, in God's infinitely creative expression. See: *infiniverse, microcosm-macrocosm.*

unobtrusive: Not noticeable; inconspicuous.

upheaval: A sudden disruption or upset.

Vadivel: வடிவேல் The youngest in physical years in a monastery, honored as such and whose duty it is to calculate the membership of the senior minority group each time the population of the monastery changes. See: *senior minority group.*

valor: Courage or bravery.

Veda: वेद "Wisdom." Sagely revelations which comprise Hinduism's most authoritative scripture. They, along with the *Āgamas,* are *śruti,* "that which is heard." The *Vedas* are a body of dozens of holy texts known collectively as the *Veda,* or as the four *Vedas: Ṛig, Yajur, Sāma and Atharva.* In all they include over 100,000 verses, as well as additional prose. The knowledge imparted by the *Vedas* is highly mystical or superconscious rather than intellectual. Each *Veda* has four sections: *Saṁhitās* (hymn collections), *Brāhmaṇas* (priestly manuals), *Āraṇyakas* (forest treatises) and *Upanishads* (enlightened discourses). The *Saṁhitās* and *Brāhmaṇas* (together known as the *karmakāṇḍa,* "ritual section") detail a transcendent-immanent Supreme-Being cosmology and a system of worship through fire ceremony and chanting to establish communication with the Gods. The *Āraṇyakas* and *Upanishads* (the *jñānakāṇḍa,* "knowledge section") outline the soul's evolutionary journey, providing yogic-philosophic training and propounding a lofty, nondual realization as the destiny of all souls. The oldest portions of the *Vedas* are thought to date back as far as 6,000 BCE, written down in Sanskṛit in the last few millennia, making them the world's most ancient scriptures. See: *Hinduism.*

veiling grace: *Tirobhāva śakti.* The divine power that limits the soul's perception by binding or attaching the soul to the bonds of *āṇava,* karma and *māyā*—enabling it to grow and evolve as an individual being.

vel: வேல் "Spear, lance" *(śūla* in Sanskṛit.) The symbol of Lord Kārttikeya's divine authority as Lord of yoga and commander of the *devas.* The *vel* is Lord Kārttikeya's *jñāna śakti,* which is His power to vanquish darkness, or ignorance. The flame-shaped *vel* is also the symbol of Kṛittikā, the Pleiades. See: *Kārttikeya.*

venerable: Deserving respect by virtue of age, dignity, character or position.

verge: The extreme edge or border.

verification: A statement of agreement; a confirmation.

vision: Sight. Also an inner experience where something is seen by other than normal sight; something perceived in a dream, trance or state of higher awareness; may foretell the future.

viśvagrāsa: विश्वग्रास "Total absorption." The final merger of the soul in Śiva at the fulfillment of its evolution. It is ultimate union of the individual soul body with the body of Śiva—Parameśvara—within the Śivaloka, from whence the soul was first emanated. See: *evolution of the soul.*

Wall: The monastery wall. The boundary of the monastery, both physical and psychic. Here newcomers sit and beg entrance and adjust their vibration to that of the monastery.

wane: To decrease. "On the wane:" in the process of decreasing or disappearing.

west wind: The group within the monastery which oversees income and expenditures.

winds: Flows of force within the monastery according to the laws of transmutation, each of the four winds—north, east, west and south—moving further into creative manifestation. The winds correspond to the basic functions of a monastery: the north wind taking care of nourishment, physically (through the kitchen) and spiritually (through the temple); the east wind giving forth the teachings; the west overseeing income and expenditures; and the south building and maintaining the property and producing the printed word. The fifth wind, the *ākāśic* wind is of the guru, which harmonizes all the other winds.

winds of the body: Five *prāṇas* or forces of the physical body. When they are in perfect balance, vibrant health is experienced. In Lemurian times, balance was achieved through nutrition, exercise and by ingesting or applying oils to the body.

wither: To cause to shrivel or fade.

worldly: Materialistic, unspiritual. Devoted to or concerned with the affairs or pleasures of the world, especially excessive concern to the exclusion of religious thought and life. Connoting ways born of the lower chakras: jealousy, greed, selfishness, anger, guile, etc.

Yoga: योग "Union." From *yuj,* "to yoke, harness, unite." The philosophy, process, disciplines and practices whose purpose is the yoking of individual consciousness with transcendent or divine consciousness. See: *bhakti yoga, haṭha yoga, rāja yoga.*

yoga pāda: योगपाद् The third of the successive stages in spiritual unfoldment in Śaiva Siddhānta, wherein the goal is Self Realization. See: *pāda, yoga, Śaiva Siddhānta.*

Yogaswami: யோகசுவாமி "Master of yoga." Sri Lanka's most renowned contemporary spiritual master (1872–1964), a Śivajñāni and Nātha *siddha* revered by both Hindus and Buddhists. He was trained in and practiced *kuṇḍalinī* yoga under the guidance of Satguru Chellappaswami, from whom he received guru *dīkshā.* Sage Yogaswami was in turn the *satguru* of Sivaya Subramuniyaswami, current preceptor of the Nātha Sampradāya's Kailāsa Paramparā. Yogaswami conveyed his teachings in hundreds of songs called *Natchintanai,* "good thoughts," urging seekers to follow dharma and realize God within. Four great sayings capsulize his message: *Thanai ari,* "Know thy Self by thyself;" *Sarvam Sivam Ceyal,* "Śiva is doing it all;" *Sarvam Sivamaya,* "All is Śiva;" and *Summa Iru,* "Be still." See: *Nātha.*

yogī: योगी One who practices yoga, especially *kuṇḍalinī* or *rāja* yoga.

yoginī: योगिनी Feminine counterpart of *yogī.*

yoking: To be joined together or united.

yore: Time long past; long ago.

young soul: One who has gone through only a few births, and is thus inexperienced or immature, has not matured the soul body through spiritual discipline and learning the lessons from life's experiences. See: *old soul, soul.*

yuga: युग "Period, age." One of four ages in which our solar system experiences graded levels of consciousness: Sat (or Kṛita), Tretā, Dvāpara and Kali. In the first period dharma and virtue reigns supreme, but as the ages revolve, the rays of the Cental Sun diminish by one-fourth in each (from which their name is derived) and ignorance and injustice increase. (Kṛita=**4**/4; Tretā=**3**/4; Dvāpara=**2**/4 and Kali=**1**/4) At the end of the Kali Yuga, the cycle begins again with the Sat Yuga. See: *cosmic cycle, chaturyuga, manvantara, Central Sun, Sat Yuga, Tretā Yuga, Dvāpara Yuga, Kali Yuga.*

Zenith: Highest point; apex; summit.

Zoroastrian: Of or related to Zoroastrianism, a religion founded in Persia by Spenta Zarathustra (CA 600 BCE). It has roughly 150,000 adherents today, mostly near Bombay, where they are called Parsis. The faith stresses monotheism while recognizing a universal struggle between the force of good (led by Ahura Mazda) and evil (led by Ahriman). The sacred fire, always kept burning in the home, is considered the only worshipful symbol. The primary Zoroastrian scripture is the *Zend Avesta.*

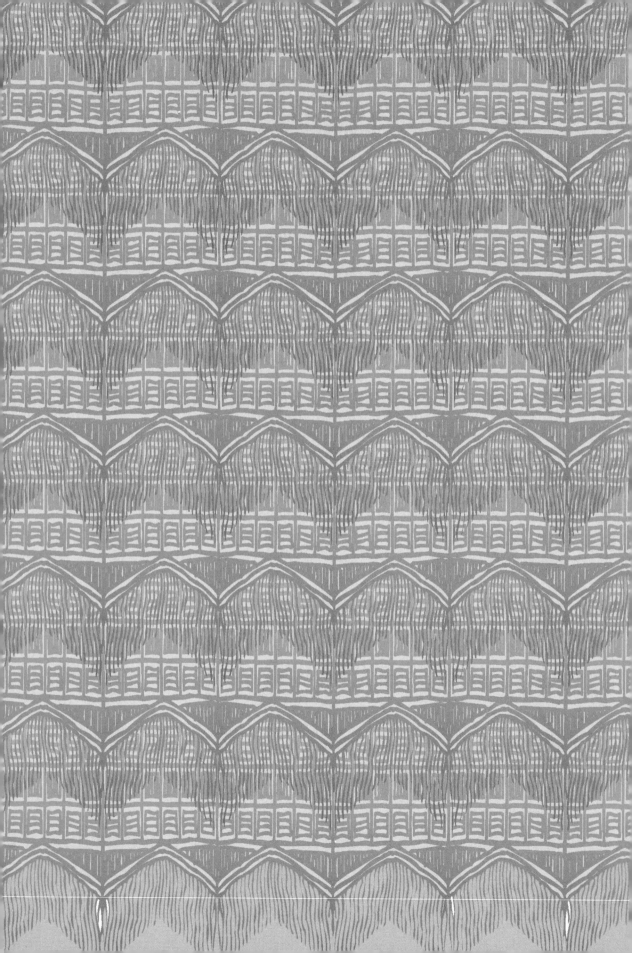

Index

अनुक्रमणिक

A

B

C

E

F

I

J

K

L

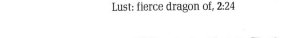

M

N

O

Q

R

S

T

U

p.216–217; giving and, **9**:122; instinctive nature, **27**:360; *kuṇḍalinī* and, p.217, **26**:341; OTM membership, **23**:295; service and, **14**:179, 181; yoga, p.143
Universe: knowledge of from Deities, **25**:330; habitable planets, **1**:9, **3**:37; Śiva and, **12**:160–162, **16**:195, **26**:344; knowledge of, infinite, **25**:334; Lord of the, **7**:91; travel, **3**:42; see also *Central Sun, Galaxy*
Universes (inner and outer): Self beyond, **26**:350; guiding, **23**:299; Gurudeva's vision of, p.259
Upliftment: *chakram* for, **21**:275

V

Vadivel: becoming, **19**:241; ego and, **20**:251; OTM calculation, **20**:250, **19**:238; OTM and, p.32–33; reports, **19**:240; see also *One third minority, Senior minority group*
Vedas: on origins of man, xiv, p.256
Vel: of Lord Muruga, p.257; vision of Muruga holding, xxvii
Vegetables: picking and eating, **17**:213; power through, **24**:315; protective qualities, **24**:310; see also *Milk, Nourishment, Seeds*
Vigil: inside the walls, **4**:50; special Umāgaṇeśa, **19**:236
Violence: at awakening, **25**:338
Vision: galaxies converging, p.259; loss of, **12**:156; on San Mārga, xxxviii–xxxix
Visitors: gifts from, **9**:121; neighboring planets, **25**:332; not seeking admittance, **22**:291; seeking admittance, **5**:67, having no, **8**:104; teaching, **24**:319; wearing white, **9**:124
Viśvagrāsa: final merger, p.261
Voices: guru's and Mahādeva's, **10**:140

W

Waiting: *tapas* of, **20**:254
Wakonda: mind of, xvi; p.256
Walking distance: monasteries, **3**:46
Wall(s): activities at, **22**:283, p.142–143; carriers of darshan **23**:293; darshan through, **4**:49; dismantling, **18**:224, **19**:243; First and Second Worlds, **17**:215; gold, **9**:121; gurus' coming to, **4**:47, **18**:228; Hanumān oversees, **19**:234, **20**:257, **22**:292; helping *sādhaka* monasteries, **21**:266; leaving through at night, **26**:350; living by after break in residency, **23**:294; *mahā tapas,* **19**:238; name changes, **20**:260; nature of, **4**:49, **22**:284, p.20–21, p.32–33; newcomers at, **5**:67–68, **7**:94, **7**:98, **17**:216–217, **19**:241, **20**:249, **20**:256, **21**:272, **21**:278, **22**:286, **27**:354–355; newcomers not admitted, **22**:289–290; no one's sitting by, **19**:237; protection, **3**:44, **6**:86, **17**:215, **17**:218–219, **17**:222; protocol at, **22**:280–292; sleeping in, **11**:150; speaking through, **5**:63, **11**:149, **16**:196, **17**:220, **20**:263, **22**:285, **22**:287, **27**:358; vigils at, **4**:50; visitors, **22**:291; see also *Guards, Holes in walls*
Wands: of power, **26**:351
Wars: between *devas* and demons, **2**:18; Second and First worlds, **17**:221
Water: great bodies of, **12**:164, **15**:189; large mammals, **2**:27; negotiating for, **20**:263; old monastery sites, **6**:85–86; see also *Condensation, Lake, Swimming*
Watery abyss: jubilation in, xix
Wealth: renunciation of, **23**:305
Weather: variations and food, **6**:76; see also *Diet, Food, Nourishment*
Weaving: clothing, gold, **3**:35; fine fabrics that wouldn't be worn, **11**:153
Wheel: use as a tool, **3**:35
White: brother wearing, **23**:304; milk, drink, **24**:314; monasteries, colors of, **22**:290, **23**:302; pilgrimage, worn on, **3**:45; *sādhakas* in, **19**:238, **21**:265; skills, **23**:306; worn by whom, **9**:124; see also *Sādhaka*
Winds: east wind, **20**:259; five and healing, **13**:174–176, **14**:181; five great, p.108–109; four in monastery, **14**:178, **19**:231–234, **19**:243, **24**:316; Lemurian Prasādam, **6**:76, **6**:79; meetings of, **20**:255; negativity and, **19**:244; protection from, **11**:142; *see also Ākāśic wind*

Colophon

अन्त्यवचनम्

LEMURIAN SCROLLS, ANGELIC PROPHECIES REVEALING HUMAN ORIGINS WAS DESIGNED AND PRODUCED BY THE ĀCHĀRYAS AND SWĀMĪS OF THE ŚAIVA SIDDHĀNTA YOGA ORDER AT KAUAI'S HINDU MONASTERY ON THE GARDEN ISLAND OF KAUAI. This first book in the Siddha Collection was edited and assembled using QuarkXpress on a network of Powermacs with Gurudeva's original input for final editing on Macintosh Powerbooks. The text is 10-point Dominante on 14-point linespacing. Sanskṛit and Tamil fonts include those by Ecological Linguistics, Brahmi Type and Srikrishna Patil of Cupertino, California. Pages were output to film by BookCrafters in Chelsea, Michigan, and printed by offset press on 70# Enviro-text paper. The oil portraits of Satguru Yogaswami on page iv and of Gurudeva on the back cover were gifted by India's renowned artist Sri Indra Sharma. The intricate line drawings for each chapter were produced in 1974-75 by Bruce Andre of the Big Island of Hawaii. The cover art is a watercolor by Tiru S. Rajam of Chennai, India, commissioned in 1999 for the second printing, based on Bruce's drawing for chapter one. The Deity paintings on the title page and after the introduction are also the work of S. Rajam. The painting of Iraivan Temple and Mount Waialeale on page xxxviii is by Kauai's visionary artist D.J. Khamis, his gift to the temple in 1996. The paintings on pages xxxvii and xxix depicting Gurudeva's visions of Muruga and Śiva and all the numerous computer graphic patterns were done by a gifted soul among our *sannyāsi* order. Gurudeva enjoyed drawing numerous Aums for the patterns you see at the end of certain chapters. The painting of Gurudeva's monastic order on page xliv was by I. Wayan Marya of Ubud, Bali. Sanskṛit proofreading was provided by Sri Swami Satyam, a *sannyāsin* of the Arya Samaj of Bangalore, and Dr. P. Jayaraman, Executive Director of Bharatiya Vidya Bhavan, Woodside, New York. Assistance in graphics, indexing and glossary was provided by Brahmacharis Jothi Param, Japendra Mahesvaran and Jyothi Palani. Indexing was done by Jordan and Vita Richman of Writer's Anonymous, Phoenix, Arizona. Finally, we give great thanks to all devotees worldwide who have supported this first edition of *Lemurian Scrolls* with *pūjās* and prayers.

About Gurudeva

ONCE IN A WHILE ON THIS EARTH THERE ARISES A SOUL WHO, BY LIVING HIS TRADITION RIGHTLY AND WHOLLY, PERFECTS HIS PATH AND BECOMES A LIGHT TO THE WORLD. SATGURU SIVAYA Subramuniyaswami is such a being, a living example of awakening and wisdom, a leader recognized worldwide as one of Hinduism's foremost ministers. In 1947, as a young man of 20, he journeyed to India and Sri Lanka and was initiated into *sannyāsa* two years later by the renowned *siddha yogī* and worshiper of Śiva, Sage Yogaswami of Sri Lanka, regarded as one of the 21st century's most remarkable mystics. For over four decades Subramuniyaswami, affectionately known as Gurudeva, has taught Hinduism to Hindus and seekers from all faiths. He is the 162nd successor of the Nandinātha Kailāsa lineage and *satguru* of Kauai Aadheenam, a fifty-one-acre temple-monastery complex on Hawaii's Garden Island of Kauai. From this verdant Polynesian *āśramā* on a river bank near the foot of an extinct volcano, he and his monastics live their cherished vision, following a contemplative and joyous existence, building a jewel-like white granite Śiva temple, meditating together in the hours before dawn, then working, when rainbows fill the sky, to promote the dharma together through Śaiva Siddhānta Church, Himalayan Academy and Hindu Heritage Endowment. Gurudeva is known as one of the strictest gurus in the world. His Church nurtures its membership and local missions on five continents and serves, personally and through books and courses, the community of Hindus of all sects. Its mission is to protect, preserve and promote the Śaivite Hindu religion as expressed through three pillars: temples, *satgurus* and scripture. Its congregation is a disciplined, global fellowship of family initiates, novitiates and students who are taught to follow the *sādhana mārga*, the path of inner effort, yogic striving and personal change. Gurudeva is the recognized hereditary guru of 2.5 million Sri Lankan Hindus. His is a Jaffna-Tamil-based organization which has branched out from the Śrī Subramuniya Ashram in Alaveddy to meet the needs of the growing Hindu diaspora of this century. He has established a branch monastery on the island of Mauritius and gently oversees more than 40 temples worldwide. Missionaries and teachers within the family membership provide counseling and classes in Śaivism for children, youth and adults. HINDUISM TODAY is the influential, award-winning, international monthly magazine that Gurudeva founded in 1979. It is a public service of his monastic order, created to strengthen all Hindu traditions by uplifting and informing followers of

The photograph at left of Satguru Sivaya Subramuniyaswami, taken in July of 1997, is the image from which Indra Sharma modeled his color portrait that you see on the back cover of *Lemurian Scrolls*.

You can visit Gurudeva at his home page on the World Wide Web: www.gurudeva.org/gurudeva/

dharma everywhere. Gurudeva is author of more than 30 books unfolding unique, practical insights on Hindu metaphysics, mysticism and *yoga.* His *Master Course* lessons on Śaivism, taught in many schools, are preserving the teachings among thousands of youths. Hindu Heritage Endowment is the public service trust founded by Gurudeva in 1995 to establish and maintain permanent sources of income for Hindu institutions worldwide. In 1986, New Delhi's World Religious Parliament named Gurudeva one of five modern-day Jagadāchāryas, world teachers, for his international efforts in promoting a Hindu renaissance, then in 1995 bestowed the title of Dharmachakra for his remarkable publications. The Global Forum of Spiritual and Parliamentary Leaders for Human Survival chose Subramuniyaswami as a Hindu representative at its unique conferences. Thus, at Oxford in 1988, Moscow in 1990 and Rio de Janiero in 1992, he joined religious, political and scientific leaders from all countries to discuss privately, for the first time in history, the future of human life on this planet. At Chicago's historic centenary Parliament of the World's Religions in September, 1993, Gurudeva was elected one of three presidents to represent Hinduism at the prestigious Presidents' Assembly, a core group of 25 men and women voicing the needs of world faiths. In 1996, he transformed HINDUISM TODAY to a magazine, a quantum leap that placed it on newsstands everywhere. In 1997 he responded to US President Bill Clinton's call for religious opinions on the ethics of cloning and spearheaded the 125th anniversary and diaspora pilgrimage of Sri Lanka's Sage Yogaswami. Today Gurudeva continues—with unique effectiveness and practicality—a daily dialog with religious leaders and institutions of all sects that promote Sanātana Dharma, setting a new example of cooperation and harmony among Hinduism's diverse one billion followers. In recent months he has, as part of his "think globally and act locally" emphasis, been a key member of Vision Kauai, a small group of inspirers (including the mayor and former mayor, business and education leaders and local Hawaiians) that meets to fashion the island's future based on spiritual values. If you ask people who know Gurudeva what it is about him that is so remarkable, they may point to his uncanny power to inspire others toward God realization in its truest sense, to change their lives in ways that are otherwise impossible without disciplined penance and *sādhanas* leading to release from karmic burdens—also his ability to take care of little things so that bigger happenings are kept at bay. He is the light on the spiritual path toward liberation from rebirth to all of his hundreds of thousands of devotees. He is a mother and father to all who draw near.

Come to Lemuria!

Satguru Sivaya Subramuniyaswami is depicted here by Indra Sharma, one of India's greatest living artists, at his Hawaiian Temple Monastery complex. Gurudeva is standing before our extinct volcano with the San Mārga Iraivan Temple in the background. He holds the sacred trident, a traditional Śaivite Hindu symbol with three prongs, representing the divine powers of love, wisdom and action.

WELCOME, SERIOUS SEEKER, TO OUR TROPICAL HAWAIIAN PARADISE ON THE GARDEN Island of Kauai, the Lemurian mountaintop monastery and home of Satguru Sivaya Subramuniyaswami, the extraordinary being who brought forth *Lemurian Scrolls*. Every day spiritual visitors and devout pilgrims come from all over the world to enjoy his darshan, to be in his presence at the sacred place where the life you have just read about is being lived. Kauai Aadheenam is one of the Hindu religion's most dynamic monasteries. This is by no means a public place or a tourist attraction. It is a destination for profoundly sacred pilgrimage, open to serious seekers who prepare well in advance. Expectations at this traditional and secluded Sanātana Dharma sanctuary are strict. For information on how to prepare and what to anticipate, including a schedule of tour days:

See our Web Site at www.hindu.org/ka/
Phone 1-808-822-3012 ext. 237
Or e-mail: thondu@hindu.org

Aum Namaḥ Śivāya!

There are a few unusual young men who have had enough of the materialstic world and choose to serve as Hindu monks as these scrolls describe.

THESE RARE SOULS FOLLOW THE PATH OF THE TRADITIONAL HINDU MONASTIC, VOWED TO POVERTY, HUMILITY, OBEDIENCE AND PURITY. THEY PURSUE THE DISCIPLINES OF *CHARYĀ*, *KRIYĀ*, yoga and *jñāna* that lead to realization of the Self. It is this ancient faith that most fully carries forward the traditions spoken of in *Lemurian Scrolls.* There are one billion Hindus on the planet today, and by conservative estimate, three million swāmīs, *sādhus* and *satgurus* in India alone. The Swami Narayana order has well over 800; Ramakrishna Mission over 700 worldwide. Other organized Hindu orders range into the thousands. Temples to the Gods of Sanātana Dharma are estimated at 500,000—with 1,000 in the USA. The priests serving in these temples outnumber those in several of the great religions. We invite you, if you feel a calling and are under the age of 25, to consider joining our order, the Śaiva Siddhānta Yoga Order. Knowing God Śiva and serving others is our only goal in life. We live in monasteries apart from the world to worship, meditate, serve and realize the truth of the *Vedas* and *Āgamas,* uplifting the world by our example. Guided by our *satguru,* Sivaya Subramuniyaswami, and headquartered at Kauai Aadheenam in Hawaii, our order ranks among Hinduism's foremost traditional monastic orders, accepting candidates from every nation on Earth. Young men considering life's renunciate path who believe they have found their spiritual master in Gurudeva are encouraged to write to him—he is available—sharing their personal history, spiritual aspirations, thoughts and experiences, and to visit his monastery and meet others who are following this highest path on Earth. Entrance is slow. The first step is to come on a noncommital taskforce program for six months, then return home and think over the experience. After that, vows for six months at a time are given for the first year or two. Renewable two-year vows are given until final lifetime vows, Holy Orders of *Sannyāsa,* may be given after ten to twelve years of training. More about our order can be found at: www.hindu.org/monks/

Satguru Sivaya Subramuniyaswami
Guru Mahāsannidhānam, Kauai Aadheenam
107 Kaholalele Road, Kapaa, Hawaii 96746-9304 USA
E-mail: gurudeva@hindu.org

The Hindu Heritage Endowment

HINDU THOUGHT AND CULTURE THREAD THROUGH ALMOST EVERY CIVILIZATION ON THE PLANET, WEAVING A SUBTLE TAPESTRY OF LOFTY PHILOSOPHY AND EARTHY, PRAGMATIC WISDOM. Whose life has not been touched? Some have been raised in India and enjoy memories of warm extended families and cool temples resounding with ancient mantras. Others find peace of mind in Hindu yoga practices. Many find solace in the concepts of karma, dharma and reincarnation, which express their own inner findings and beliefs. If you are one who has been touched by Hindu thought and culture, you may wish to further enrich your life by giving back to India and helping to preserve her rich heritage for future generations. Hindu Heritage Endowment (HHE) provides such an opportunity. A public charitable trust founded by Satguru Sivaya Subramuniyaswami and recognized by the United States government, HHE was created to maintain permanent endowments for Hindu projects and institutions worldwide. Its endowments benefit orphanages, children's schools, *āśramas* and temples. They support priests and publish books, and they are designed to continue giving that financial support year after year, decade after decade, century after century. Whether you are inspired to give a few dollars to support orphanages, or bequest millions in your will, the staff at HHE is one-pointed in their dedication to seeing that qualified donations will be used effectively for the purposes intended. Write, give us a call, or visit us on the Internet. Find out how to enrich your life by helping to preserve the treasures of a profound heritage for generations as yet unborn. Ask about pooled income funds to provide yourself and a loved one an income for life and then remit to an HHE fund of your choosing.

HINDU HERITAGE ENDOWMENT
Kauai's Hindu Monastery
107 Kaholalele Road
Kapaa, Hawaii, 96746-9304 USA
Phone: (800) 890-1008, Ext. 222
Outside US: (808) 822-3152, Ext. 222
Fax: (808) 822-4351
www.hindu.org/hhe/
E-mail: hhe@hindu.org

The Mini-Mela Giftshop

For all our books, visit *store.himalayanacademy.com.*

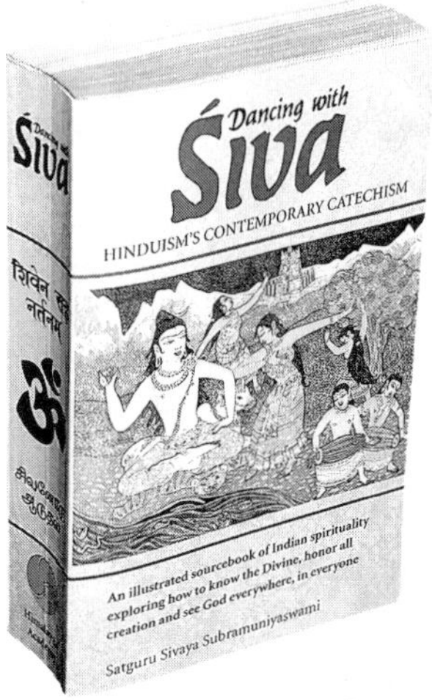

Dancing with Śiva

Hinduism's Contemporary Catechism

Question the meaning of life and find the right answers! Gurudeva's splendid sourcebook on Hinduism answers all your queries in a way that will make you wise. Clearly written and lavishly illustrated, expertly woven with 600 verses from the Vedas, Āgamas and other holy texts, 165 South Indian paintings, 40 original graphics, a 40-page timeline of India's history and a 190-page lexicon of English, Sanskṛit and Tamil. A spiritual gem and great value at twice the price. "The most comprehensive and sensitive introduction to the living spiritual tradition of Hinduism ...a feast for the heart and the mind" (Georg Feuerstein). Fifth edition, 1997, 8.5" x 5.5", softcover (isbn 0-945497-48-2), $29.85.

Weaver's Wisdom

Ancient Precepts for a Perfect Life

The jewel of South India's classical literature, the Tirukural, by the weaver saint, Tiruvalluvar. Translated from Tamil by two of Gurudeva's sannyasins, this is the finest English edition of this 2,200-year-old masterpiece. Yet it's all about today's world, short aphorisms of earthy advice: keys for running a business, strengthening relationships, dealing with money, coping with enemies and personal fears; about gambling, politics, diet and health. You will want to keep it with you as a daily guide to wise conduct. Illustrated with 108 original South Indian paintings. "In this unique book, the life, spirit and meaning of the original are well preserved. It will enlighten millions of people to lead a meaningful life" (Sri Swami Buaji Maharaj). First edition, 408 pages, 5.5" x 8.5", paper, (ISBN 0-945497-76-8) $19.95.

Merging with Śiva

Hinduism's Contemporary Metaphysics

The ultimate book of self transformation, undoubtedly the richest volume on meditation, realization and the inside of you ever written. Yet, it's user-friendly, easy to follow, sensible and nonacademic! *Merging with Śiva* is about God, about the mystical realm of the fourteen chakras, the human aura, karma, force fields, thought and the states of mind, the two paths, *samādhi* and so much more. A treasury of Satguru Sivaya Subramuniyaswami's fifty years of yogic realizations and personal teachings composed in 365 daily lessons, one for each day of the year. Reading it is like sitting at the feet of a living master. "An imperative lesson book for all in quest of a conscious life and inner freedom" (Maya Tiwari). Beautifully illustrated with more than fifty original South Indian paintings. First edition, 1999, 8.5" x 5.5," 1,408 pages, softcover (ISBN 0-945497-74-1), $39.75.

Inspiration by E-mail

Send an e-mail to *sadhu@aloha.net* to receive via e-mail daily inspiration at no charge. Options include verses from *Vedas, Tirukural, Tirumantiram, Hymns of Saint Thayumanavar, sūtras* from *Living with Śiva,* excerpts from *Dancing with Śiva* and lessons from *Merging with Śiva.*

Loving Gaṇeśa

Hinduism's Endearing Elephant-Faced God

NEW, SECOND EDITION. No book about this beloved elephant-faced God is more soul-touching. Here Gurudeva makes approaching this benevolent Lord easy and inspiring. Through such magical contact *Loving Gaṇeśa* has improved the lives of thousands and can bring new clarity and peace to yours, too. Learn about Gaṇesa's powers, pastimes, nature, science, forms, the astounding "Milk Miracle of 1995," sacred symbols, and specific mantras to use. "Lord Gaṇeśa comes to life through the pages of this inspired masterpiece. *Loving Gaṇeśa* makes approaching Gaṇeśa easy and inspiring" (The Mystic Trader). Second Edition, ©2000, 8.5" x 5.5", 592 pages, with classical Rajput paintings and newly commissioned pen-and-ink drawings. Softcover (ISBN 0-945497-77-6), $29.85.

Śaivite Hindu Religion

What every Hindu parent needs: intelligent, nonviolent, traditional texts for their kids. This is Gurudeva's authentic, illustrated, seven-book course teaching philosophy, culture and family life. Based on the *Vedas,* the world's oldest scripture, an excellent resource for educators and parents, it explains the "why" of each belief and practice in simple terms in three languages. Prominent leaders of all sects have given enthusiastic endorsements. "A commendable, systematically conceived course useful to one and all with special significance to fortunate children who shall be led on the right path (Sri Sri Sri Tiruchi Mahaswamigal, Bangalore, India)." Book One (5- to 7-year-old level) is available in a Hindi-Tamil-English edition. Softcover, 8.5" x 11," 170 pages, $15.95. Book Two (6- to 8-year-old level), English-Tamil-Malay, 196 pages, $15.95.

The Vedic Experience

We could hardly believe our eyes when we came upon this brilliant anthology from the Vedic *Saṁhitas, Brāhmaṇas, Āraṇyakas* and *Upanishads* and other scriptures. This Vedic epiphany tells the story of the universal rhythms of nature, history and humanity. The translation and abundant commentary are the work of renaissance thinker Raimon Panikkar—the fruit of twelve years of daily *sādhana* in Varanasi between 1964 and 1976 while he lived above a Śiva temple on the Ganges. He considers it perhaps his most significant literary contribution. This classic makes the *Vedas* available to all. Motilal Banarsidass, Delhi, 1977, smythe-sewn and case bound, cloth cover, 5.5" x 8.5," 1,000 pages, $41.

Hinduism Today

International Magazine

Enjoy a bimonthly spiritual experience with the foremost international journal on Sanatana Dharma, published by Gurudeva and his swamis. Breaking news, ancient wisdom, modern trends, world-class photos, family resources, humor—you'll treasure every issue! Hot issues, trimphs, challenges, health, yoga, fascinating people and places. Reporting from the spectrum of Hindu lineages, leaders and personalities, it is clear, articulate and stunning, in full-color photos and art. "Hinduism Today is a beautiful example of the positive possibility of the media being fulfilled, a bright ray of light in a darkened world" (Anne Shannon, Portland). Introductory offer (US only): one-year subscription for $29.95! ISSN 0896-0801; UPC: 0-74470-12134-3. See order form for subscription rates.

Monks' Cookbook

Vegetarian Recipes from Kauai's Hindu Monastery

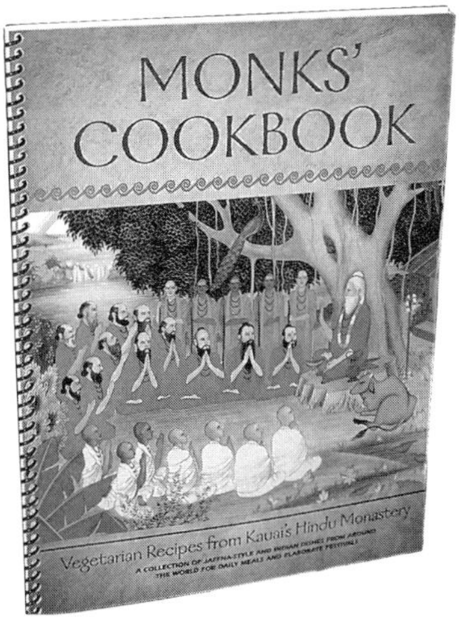

Gurudeva calls it the "Yum-Yum Cookbook!" Here are the secret recepies that have made our Hindu monastery on Kauai famous for its fabulous food. They believe good food is the best medicine, and there is an energy in these culinary contemplations, called *prāṇa,* that nourishes body and soul alike. Enhance all your meals at home and with special friends with this cornucopia of Jaffna-style and Indian dishes from around the world for daily menus and elaborate festivals. Every chef will appreciate the 30-page ready reference on the unique *āyurvedic* qualities of a vast array of spices, grains, fruits and vegetables. First Edition, 1997, 8.5" x 11", 104 pages, lightly illustrated, durable paper, maroon spiral binding. Softcover, ISBN 0-945497-71-7, $16.95.

Namaḥ Śivāya Bracelet

With this handsome piece of Indian jewelry for men or women, you can wear the most sacred Śaiva mantra, "Aum Namaḥ Śivāya," all day as a reminder of God's grace at work in your life. Best quality, made in India from silver, copper and brass, with the mantra in Sanskṛit Devanāgarī script. Band is five-eighths inches wide. Excellent for gifts. $30.

Hand-Picked, Hawaiian-Grown Rudrāksha Beads

Here is a 36-bead strand, packed with Hawaii's sublime life energy. The beads, gathered fresh each year from the Rudrāksha forest floor at Kauai's Hindu Monastery, lovingly cleaned an strung, are five-faced and roughly 3/4-inch in diameter. $39.

Indian Rudrāksha Prayer Bead Necklaces

It's very hard to find *rudrāksha* prayer strands of this quality, and the price is unbeatable. These *japa* beads are sacred to Śiva and endowed with healing properties. The beads are of uniform size, 3/8 inches in diameter, in two styles: 108 beads on flexible thread, or 54 silver capped beads. Can be worn as a necklace or around the wrist. Grown in the Himālayas, $25.

Order Form

☐ Please send me free literature.

☐ I consider myself a devotee of Satguru Sivaya Subramuniyaswami. I kindly request to receive my first 52 *sādhanas* (spiritual discipline).

☐ I wish to subscribe to Hinduism Today. (Please inquire for international rates.)
☐ 1 year, $29.95 ☐ 2 years, $59.95 ☐ 3 years, $89.95 ☐ Lifetime, $800

I would like to order:

☐ *Loving Gaṇeśa*, $29.85 ☐ *Dancing with Śiva*, $29.85 ☐ *Monks' Cookbook*, $16.95
☐ *Śaivite Hindu Religion:* Book 1 (ages 5-7), $15.95; ☐ Book 2 (ages 6-8), $15.95
☐ 108 *rudrāksha bead* strand, $25 ☐ 54 *rudrāksha* strand, silver-capped, $25
☐ 36 *rudrāksha* bead strand from Hawaii, $39 ☐ Namaḥ Śivāya bracelet, $30
☐ *Living with Śiva*, $29.85 (available Spring 2001) ☐ *Vedic Experience*, $41
☐ *Merging with Śiva*, $39.75

Prices are in U.S. currency. Add 20% for postage and handling in USA and foreign, $1.50 minimum. Foreign orders are shipped sea mail unless otherwise specified and postage is prepaid. For foreign airmail, add 50% of the merchandise total for postage.

☐ My payment is enclosed. Charge to: ☐ Master Card ☐ Visa ☐ Amex

Card no.: ☐☐☐☐ ☐☐☐☐ ☐☐☐☐ ☐☐☐☐

Expiration: ☐☐ / ☐☐ Total of purchase: $ ____________________

Name on card: [Please Print] ____________________________________
Signature: ____________________________________
Address: [Please Print] ____________________________________
____
____
Phone: ______________ Fax: ______________E-mail: ______________

Mail, phone, fax or e-mail orders to:

Himalayan Academy Publications, Kauai's Hindu Monastery, 107 Kaholalele Road, Kapaa, Hawaii 96746-9304, USA. Phone (US only): 1-800-890-1008; outside US: 1-808-822-7032 ext. 238; Fax: 1-808-822-3152; E-mail: books@hindu.org; World Wide Web: store.himalayanacademy.com

Also available through the following. (Write or call for prices.)

Sanāthana Dharma Publications, Bukit Panjang Post Office, P. O. Box 246, Singapore 916809. Ph: 65-362-0010; Fax: 65-442-3452. E-mail: sanatana@mbox4singnet.com.sg

Śaiva Siddhānta Church of Mauritius, La Pointe, Rivière du Rempart, Mauritius, Indian Ocean. Phone: 230-412-7682, Fax: 230-412-7177.

Iraivan Temple Carving Site, PO Box No 4083, Vijayanagar Main, 560040 Bangalore, India. Phone: 91-80-839-7118; Fax: 91-80-839-7119; E-mail: jiva@vsnl.com

Om Vishwa Guru Deep Hindu Mandir, Europe: Phone/Fax: 36 11143504; E-mail: ervin@mail.matav.hu

Page 334 (Ram Swarup's comments continued from inside front cover) on Earth has an unknown astral source. Some form of seed life floated to Earth and, finding an hospitable habitat, evolved into its present variegated forms. Others hold that there are beings on other planets very much like us here, and they may even be trying to establish electronic contact with us. ¶What is intriguing is that *Lemurian Scrolls* claims to tell us of an event that actually took place. Its philosophic rationale is that nothing that happens is altogether lost but is taken up and recorded in the subtle medium of space *(akasha);* that if we can read these *akashic* records, we can recapture the past. The account in *Lemurian Scrolls* is based on the author's capacity to read these records. In the yogas, such a capacity and much more is admitted. In this system of thought nothing is so distant, nothing so hidden, that it cannot be known. The book is ultimately about Gods, the Self, the sages, entelechy, about seeking and *sadhana,* which are of interest to all on a spiritual quest. ¶I also find the book in keeping with the spirit of old sages who gave primacy to the subtle over the gross, who derived the visible from the invisible, the lower from the higher seed-form. They believed that man is an epitome of all reality, that he is the whole world and all times in miniature, a veritable microcosm *(pinda).* To study him is to study the whole macrocosm *(brahmanda).* The approach makes a deep philosophic sense. ¶As the sages looked within, they saw that the truths of the spirit are also the basis of man's more physical and social welfare, *yoga-kshema;* that when men follow spiritual and moral excellence, they are also rich in things of life and nature's gifts. Their basket is full, and the earth yields more abundantly and freely, their herbs are more nourishing. But as men shrink in spiritual and moral qualities, they also shrink outwardly in welfare and well-being. They are short-lived and they live in want and poverty. They live by the sweat of their brow. ¶When projected on the time screen, the concept gives us the theory of ages *(yugas),* which are beautifully described in the *Mahabharata,* the *Puranas,* the *Ramayana* and in the Buddhist literature. There is a beautiful account of these *yugas* in the *Pathika-vagga* of *Digha Nikaya.* ¶Now, a little more about *akasha* and *akashic* records and the capacity to read them. In the system of yogas, this kind of knowledge and other knowledges come under the discipline of *samyama.* Though these are seldom pursued for their own sake. They come more often than not, when necessary, as by-products to those who pursue *brahma-jnana.* ¶The *Chandogya Upanishad* speaks not only of the *akasha* outside man, but also of the inner *akasha (antah-akasha),* and even of *akasha* within the heart. Not many can read the *akashic* records, but many are alive to what is recorded in the inner *akasha.* But even that needs the development of an inner seeing and inner hearing. All this requires *yama* and *niyama, ekagrata* (one-pointedness), *sattva samshuddhi* (purification of the inner being). ¶*Lemurian Scrolls* discusses this subject in great earnest; it discusses the problems connected with receiving and transmitting this knowledge. It discusses the continuity of spiritual knowledge *(jnana-pravaha),* its channels, its masters and disciples, the temples, *ashramas, viharas* and monasteries, the need for and the problem of training, establishing and stabilizing spiritual communities that are able to protect and transmit this knowledge.

Chakrapani Ullal,
renowned Jyotisha Shastri, named by the Indian Council of Astrological Sciences as Jyotisha Kovid and Jyotisha Vachaspati; Los Angeles, California

The *Lemurian Scrolls* by Satguru Sivaya Subramuniyaswami is an inspired account of human evolution, documenting the journey from Satya Yuga to the present Kali Yuga, comprising millions of years. It bears an interesting relationship to ancient mythology and epics including the *Ramayana* and the *Mahabharata*. In these and other ancient literatures references are made to human life in subtle light bodies of vastly refined abilities. This indicates that exalted states of human consciousness existed in the distant past. It makes fascinating reading, and I recommend it to anyone who has thoughtfully pondered our origins.

Dee See Mana,
Founder, Touch the Earth Foundation, representative of the Hopi Native American tribe of Arizona; Solana Beach, California

Throughout the Hopi creation stories, our art, rituals, the solar and lunar cycles, there is always a reminder of those who have come before and left the knowledge for those to follow, weaving a rich tapestry of origin and humanity together as one spiritual family. Instructions, warnings and prophecy acted out and demonstrated daily in stories, art, songs and rituals serve as a living record of a Divine Ancestry. It is common knowledge, even if unspoken, among all our Indigenous Ancestors of a greater heritage left to us from Lemuria and Mu, the "Mother Land." Our elders have long taught from these ancients who left us messages etched in stone on tablets and carved in special places—the places of the unseen "akashic" records—of how mankind has a deeper heritage in the Sky Nations and how for thousands upon thousands of years there was order and bounty here on Mother Earth, our true physical home. We are taught, as revealed in *Lemurian Scrolls,* that we came to the Earth to be of service, to learn deep spiritual lessons and help others do the same. The Ancient Hopis, when viewing the world, look at a universe in balance and bring this balance in concert with other worlds which support our experience here on the Mother Earth, the inner knowing of the Sun as father, and that together we are here to look after the well being of the land and life. Although using different names, Satguru Sivaya Subramuniyaswami has bridged and woven the enlightening truth. Ever patiently a spiritual guide and teacher of Sanatana Dharma, Gurudeva again reveals that "Truth is One, paths are many." This truth from our Ancient Ones reminds us of where our very souls originate, a place where all creation stories are the same, the place where we are all one, where the Holy Ancestors have been with us through our whole development and always came to interface with us in these special times in history, as described so well in *Lemurian Scrolls*. It was a time when "the ones who walk the Earth were Knowers of the Unknowable and held the Truth in the palms of their hands" throughout all the worlds and stages of development on these Many Beads. This has happened and is most likely still happening today.

Dr. David Frawley, O.M.D.,
Vedacharya; Director of the American Institute of Vedic Studies; author: *Ayurvedic Healing, Astrology of the Seers;* co-author, *The Yoga of Herbs,* Santa Fe, New Mexico

According to Hindu Dharma, consciousness pervades the entire universe. Our own planet Earth is closely connected with other worlds, both physical and astral, and their inhabitants. *Lemurian Scrolls* weaves a fascinating account of how human life derives from these realms beyond and remains linked to a higher evolutionary purpose. The book discloses deep secrets of how the various worlds and dimensions interrelate, including how to contact the forces and beings of the higher planes. Satguru Sivaya Subramuniyaswami, reflecting the vision of a *rishi,* shows the spiritual basis of human evolution and guides us to a new transformation in planetary consciousness. He reveals the occult history of humanity

Page 336 that science has so far failed to discover, offering a radical change in the estimation of our species and its potentials. *Lemurian Scrolls* will greatly expand the awareness of the reader, putting human history in a cosmic perspective and aiding in the reconciliation of scientific, occult and spiritual knowledge. The book can be used to harmonize New Age insights with ancient wisdom, bringing Hindu Dharma to the forefront of the emerging global age. It certainly provides one of the most innovative views of Hinduism to come out in modern times.

John Grimes, Ph. D, Professor in the Dept. of Religious Studies, Michigan State University; education from University of Madras; author: *Ganapati: Song of the Self,* and *A Concise Dictionary of Indian Philosophy;* East Lansing, Michigan

There are more things in heaven and earth, past and future, than one could ever dream of. In this new groundbreaking book, internationally renowned Satguru Sivaya Subramuniyaswami reveals a subject which at first sight appears obscure and arcane, and explores, elucidates, digests and distills it. If the subject matter was originally ancient and mystical, here is a treatment which is fresh and insightful and most relevant to today's world.

Sri Sri Swami Chidanand Saraswati (Muniji), President, Parmath Niketan; Editor of the forthcoming *Encyclopedia of Hinduism;* Founder, India Heritage Research Foundation; Rishikesh, India

This divine book, *Lemurian Scrolls,* records the mystic readings of H.H. Sivaya Subramuniyaswami. As you delve into this sacred text, you will learn invaluable truths regarding the divine origin of life and how souls journeyed to the Earth four million years ago. Further, Gurudeva's beautiful work insightfully reveals the early struggles of man, shining light on both our human and our divine heritage. As one reads, it becomes clearer and clearer how deep our need is for spiritual guidance and inspiration in this age of Kali Yuga. The message of this book is beautiful and uplifting, yet it has been restricted to monks for a quarter of a century. By the grace of H.H. Satguru Sivaya Subramuniyaswami, this wisdom is now available to seekers around the world. H.H. Satguru Sivaya Subramuniyaswami is a wonderful example of service and devotion. His life has been one filled with piety, dedication and commitment. God has bestowed wonderful blessings upon him and his work. Those who are graced to know him or to read his words receive boundless gifts of wisdom, inspiration and spiritual upliftment. I pray to the Lord Almighty that this book will get the widespread attention and praise of which it is worthy.

P. R. Krishna Kumar, M.D., Managing Director, Arya Vaidya Pharmacy; Managing Editor of the reputed journal *Ancient Science of Life;* Trustee, Vishwa Hindu Parishad; Managing Trustee, Ayurvedic Trust; Coimbatore, India

Lemurian Scrolls is indeed a work from an enlightened person. Only Gurudeva could have written a book so divine and deep. To all those who are inclined towards spirituality and seeking the Truth, this book is a must. Most revered Satguru Sivaya Subramuniyaswami, in his fervent efforts as a panthentheist to delve deep into the fathoms of the unbelievable changes if Sat Yuga (Krita Yuga) cuts across the Pancha Dweep and Sapta Sagaras, was beckoned by the Lord to Jambu Dweep, also known as Lemuria, to receive the bliss of enlightenment of Sat Yuga. The revelation is unique and singular and the narration so captivating and absorbing, giving an insight into the supernatural powers with the wondrous spectacular shows of how the race of Sat Yuga could freely change their bodies from one form to another and move from place to place, lifting themselves in the air, living without food, sleep and all other necessities of life as we see now in this Kali Yuga, solely powered by the spine's powerhouse of *muladhara* chakra located at the lowest three and one-half rings and transmitted through *sahasraradala padma.* Indeed, this marvelous book, *Lemurian Scrolls,* is a gift to mankind to be treasured by people of all ages as coming from the divine spirit of Gurudeva, the greatest explorer to unravel the mysteries of *yugas* dating back many millions of years, and is a priceless presentation to mankind to reach the Ultimate. The human race should be eternally indebted to Gurudeva for his tireless efforts for the emancipation of mankind and attainment of Ultimate Bliss.

Arthur Pacheco, well-known counselor, healer, astrologer, theosophist, occultist, medium and parapsychologist, lecturer on psychic development, cosmic laws, mediumship and astrology; Honolulu, Hawaii

Not since the days of the Theosophical seers Madame Blavatsky and Charles Leadbeater has there been in print such in-depth and detailed reading of the *akashic* records as is found in the *Lemurian Scrolls.* Having been fascinated by their work in this area for many years, it was with great delight that I enjoyed reading this great manuscript. And just as their works collectively pointed always to a higher version of mankind's true origins and history than was commonly accepted at the time, so also do the *Lemurian Scrolls* clearly define man's divine history and destiny. This is the "big picture" that science is looking for. One reads of how Helena Blavatsky would sit open-eyed for hours at a time reading from some invisible volumes held before her gaze, and from these drew all the information that was compiled and later presented as *Isis Unveiled* and *The Secret Doctrine*. And then to read of Satguru Sivaya Subramuniyaswami's account of how he received this information is to hear the same story told again of how these things are revealed at intervals when Higher Forces choose certain people through whom to pour this enlightening information. May it be well received by a humanity seeking its spiritual "roots."

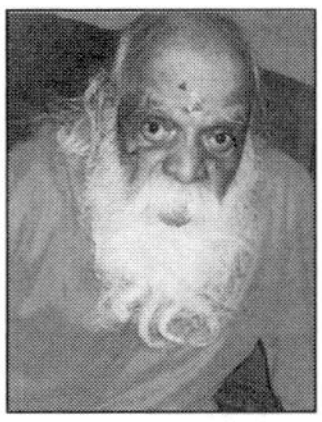

Sri Sri Swami Bua Maharaj, Centenarian, Founder and Head, Indo-American Yoga-Vedanta Society, New York; Teacher of Sanatana Dharma in South America and elsewhere; New York

Mystics have pondered over the mystery of this universe from beginningless time and have arrived at different conclusions according to their understanding. The conclusions are divergent because they are arrived at from different angles. It is to be noted that all these are about that great mystery which cannot be known in its totality. Divine wisdom reveals itself to the chosen and deserving souls who become channels of dissemination of that secret knowledge to posterity. *Lemurian Scrolls* are not ordinary spiralled bunches of some unestablished, unintelligible or unproven hallucinations or imaginative dreams of an individual. They are angelic prophecies retrieved from Lord Subramaniam's Library and revealed to the inner eyes of one of the greatest saints of modern times who read these *akashic* scripts through his clairvoyance. Such revelations are quite probable and possible according to the wonderful powers of yoga. We are extremely fortunate now to be exposed to these revelations due to the magnanimity of Satguru Sivaya Subramuniyaswami, who has decided to put these in print after keeping them within the reach of only his cloistered monks for 25 years. The question whether the planet Earth came into being first or life was existing before bas been answered in this revelation to Gurudeva. During Satya Yuga man migrated from other planets to Earth. Life

Page 338

was not produced out of nothing. Life always existed in one form or other. This is the message of reassurance to the human beings who are now and then threatened with Pralaya, Black Day, End of the World, *et al.* There are 27 chapters here that narrate the upward evolution of the soul from the time of the advent of man on this planet. *Yugas* after *yugas* roll as time marches on and the human spirit, undaunted by new challenges of time, proceeds towards its goal, ably directed by the Gods, the gurus and the doctrine. The importance of developing the yogic power of *kundalini* is outlined. The divine qualities of foods are emphasized. The need for dispassion and a genuine turn in life is equally stressed. Devotion to guru is highlighted. The supremacy of monastic life is upheld. Spiritual discipline and cultivation of the cardinal virtues of life are exhorted. The ordinary beings are given the chance to know the secrets and mysteries of monasteries by opening the iron doors and creating cleavages in the stone walls. This is the greatness of Gurudeva. The births of temples, formation of monasteries, identification of *devas* and Mahadevas and the guru-shishya relationship are all explained in detail. The messages are that life is to live, live purposefully and there is no end to life.

M.C. Bhandari, President, Bharat Nirman NRI Foundation; Chairman, Occult Foundation of India; Editor-in-Chief, *Mystic India* monthly magazine; named Jyotish Ratna by the World Astrological Institute; Calcutta, India

"Cosmos exists, life comes and goes. How does it happen, none of us knows. Who made the stars and who made all these suns? How they affect us, how we take breath? What is that consciousness, where we go after death? What a miraculous creation, what a miraculous mind? Is not all that mystic, should we not them find?" These words appearing in the beginning of each issue of our monthly magazine *Mystic India* are the perennial questions being asked by humanity from time immemorial. Satguru Sivaya Subramuniyaswami of Saiva Siddhanta Church has now made it easy to find answers to them in his new book, *Lemurian Scrolls,* which he has transcribed from the messages that he has received from the cosmos by his clairvoyant powers. In the mystic world, it is possible to connect one's inner self with the cosmic forces attunable to him and receive as well as perceive happenings of the past, present and future. Sri Subramuniyaswami, attuning himself to his link in the outer world, has found answers to many mysteries of the world. In this book, he gives vivid description of how this world, particularly our planet Earth, came into being and how all the systems of health, healing, diet, waters, gases, flowers, fruits, animals and human beings came into existence and got evolved. He also describes gold and jewels and all other matter. He also tells about *devas, satgurus,* religion, monasteries, priests and everything on Earth on the basis of his cosmic messages. This book indeed is very enlightening, educative and exciting.

Sri Sri Swami Pragyanand, Founder/Patron, Sai Pragya Dham, Pragya Mission International, Pragya Mitra Pariwar and Pragya Yoga Foundation, New Delhi, India; Vishwa Mata Gayatri Trust, Delhi, India

Satguru Sivaya Subramuniyaswami is recognized as a legend, one of the foremost personalities of Hinduism. This book reveals to the readers his inner vision in a lucid and candid transparency presented through clairvoyant *siddhis* gifted to him by his satguru, Siva Yogaswami. The origin of life in the universe has been forever the greatest mystery and challenge for exploration. Nevertheless, many theories, such as the Darwinian theory of evolution, Yin-Yang, Big Bang, Purusha and Manu, have been advanced and widely accepted. Yet, all remain imperfect, as most suffer from the basic lack of the most important factor—the element of Godliness. It is now established that physical existence is not the ultimate Truth, and a transcendental intelligence, rather wisdom, is inherent in the evolution of the Universe. The present book is a divine effort to clarify the advent of life on Earth and the experience of man on Earth through various *yugas.* Vivid description of monastic life—admission, training, dietary regimen and Divinity vis-à-vis seasonal changes and illness, discipline and avenues of selfless service to suffering humanity—can easily coax and cajole interest in and envy of a highly advanced Siva-Sakti *sadhaka.* In this time of transition, this nectar-like book renders a simple and fluent reading of, keeping interest alive until the last word and beyond. ¶It may not be out of context to refer to the scientifically developed theory of Stephen Hawking on how time began and his conclusion that it will never end. Hawking's new theory of "Open Inflation" is widely accepted by scientists but still held in skepticism by the astronomers in his latest investigation of the fraction of a second before the Big Bang, discovering the fuse that detonated the primordial explosion that created the universe 12 billion years ago, hence forming time, space and matter. The theory anticipates important support when an American satellite will be launched in two years time to map the microwave radiation left over by the Big Bang. The universe has a creator and is certainly infinite. ¶Referring back to *Lemurian Scrolls,* such a book wouldn't be forthcoming if its author did not have communion with the Lord, the almighty Siva. Such a gem of creativity shall be a prized and much-coveted possession of all mankind interested in Self Realization, the ultimate Truth and goal of every mystic. Thus I offer divine endorsement to *Lemurian Scrolls* and wish a global reading making life more meaningful, effective and enlightening by luminary exposure to the Divine.

Sri Sri Paramhans Swami Maheshwarananda,
named Saravbhom Sanatan Jagadguru by the World Religious Parliament; Spiritual Head, International Sri Deep Madhavananda Ashram Fellowship; Vienna, Austria

With *Lemurian Scrolls,* Satguru Sivaya Subramuniyaswami introduces us to an exciting thesis which challenges Western science and the popular belief held in many religions about the origin of man. Contradicting the Darwinistic postulate that human beings have evolved from lesser earthly species, it represents a new view of the evolutionary process: the evolution of souls originated from other planets towards Self Realization. We learn that millions of years ago our progenitors, highly-developed divine souls from several planets of the galaxy, undertook the risk of migrating to Earth where they could complete their unfoldment to the final realization of the Self, willing to undergo the experience of duality which comprehends love and joy as well as stress and pain. In a thrilling journey through time and space the divine visions of Satguru Sivaya Subramuniyaswami lead us through the cycles of the four *yugas,* describing in a very lively manner the development of consciousness, its descendence into matter as well as its ascendence to enlightenment and liberation. His disclosures about the origins of temples, monastery culture and the master-disciple relationship are in accordance with the tradition of Sanatana Dharma and spiritual scriptures of other religions of the world. Holy adepts preserve the knowledge of our divine origin, abilities and meaning. Though not bound to this planet, they remain here to rescue the souls who have lost their subtle nature and have sunk into the darkness of ignorance. The revelations of *Lemurian Scrolls* expand our view and understanding of the essential questions mankind has always asked: from where do we come, where will we go, what is the origin and mission of our lives? They ensure us that there

Page 340 exists a divine course of evolution, that we are guided by illustrious and enlightened souls who have helped and guarded us since the beginning of our physical existence and who will lead us eventually to our goal, the complete realization of our Divine Self. The writer rightly hopes that reading of this book would invest the reader with a new vision or outlook on life. He wants the reader to take these scrolls in their totality and make them a living, vital reality of life. I am sure that if the readers adopt this attitude, they will find the scrolls meaningful and delightful.

Dr. Shripad Dattatraya Kulkarni, renowned historian, author of *Bhishma, Study of Indian History and Culture* (18 volumes), translator of the *Vedas;* Mumbai, India

The current Sat Yuga has begun. Thus reveals Sivaya Subramuniyaswami, Gurudeva, as he is affectionately called by his millions of followers in over 40 countries of the globe. He is the seer of the *Veda,* the book of knowledge walking in flesh and blood, mixing amongst us. He has brought to us, stubborn as we are, this message of love and hope for our more secure future. Gurudeva, the *siddha,* the spiritualist *par excellence*, declares in no uncertain terms that "Sat Yuga began around 1879 CE when the inhabitants of the Earth were able to light the night with their own devices." What a world-shaking angelic prophecy! ¶Lemuria is a mythical heaven on Earth, Hawaii's Garden Island of Kauai where he has his *ashrama* on a river bank near the foot of an extinct volcano. There Gurudeva's inner eye has opened on an array of great manuscripts in the inner library of Lord Subramaniam. He read these volumes, and in the sequel these *Lemurian Scrolls* have seen the light of the day. They record accurately what was revealed to Gurudeva about human origins. In unmistakable terms Gurudeva records the most pregnant revelation, "Human life did not evolve from lesser Earthly species." The early societies had developed an integral vision of life, the harmony between the spiritual and the temporal aspects of life resulting in a wealthy, highly productive, harmonious society. For this to happen, spiritual men and women, spiritual sharing of power had to guide the individual and societal effort. The example of such a society is the Dalai Lama's Tibet where something like one third of the social order was a monastic group which served the spiritual and political needs of the two-thirds family group. Their society remained stable for hundreds and hundreds of years. ¶The Dravidian (Hindu) *shastras* tell us more or less the same story. This type of society can be ushered in by subordinating the political power to the spiritual one. The fourfold division of society based on aptitude and profession achieved this miracle. It is prophesied that stable and peaceful societies will once again emerge when mankind adopts these wise protocols of the earlier times. Gurudeva is confident that this will happen, for according to him Sat Yuga has begun. ¶Gurudeva, by his revelations, confirms the Puranic account of human origin. The fourfold cycle of *yugas,* Sat, Treta, Dvapara and Kali, is also what he saw through his inner eye. According to the *Puranas,* the Kali Yuga covers a span of 432,000 human years. The four *yugas* together cover 4,320,000 years and this is one cycle. Seventy-one such cycles form one *manvantara,* and age of man. This works out to 306,720,000 years. Six such *manvantaras* have so far elapsed from the beginning of this epoch *(kalpa)* and the seventh *manvantara,* that of the Vaivasvata, has begun, and seven more such *manvantaras* have yet to come. ¶These fourteen *manvantaras* constitute one day of Brahman—the Creator Brahma's life is 100 years. Fifty such years have elapsed. We are now in the first day of the fifty-first year. In figures, that means 306,720,000 (one *manvantara*) x 14 *manvantaras* (this is the day of Brahman) x 14 (his night) x 365 (days of the year) x 100 (years). This is the life of the Brahman. This is a mind-boggling figure, projected by Surya Siddhanta. In brief, this is the Puranic conception of the beginninglessness and endlessness of the cosmos. Surprisingly, Gurudeva, who has clairvoyantly read the volumes placed at his disposal by Lord Skanda's private librarian, confirms this universal time line. ¶The *Scrolls* give the signs of the advent of the Kali Yuga as, "man kills man,... war and turmoil prevails,... drastic climactic changes occur," and so on. In this way the *Scrolls* have given in detail the signs of the advent of the other *yuga* cycles. We are, however, more interested in knowing the signs of the advent of Sat Yuga as from 1879 CE than those of the others. ¶Gurudeva's personality of Godhead is Skanda, the six-faced Deity who looks in all directions, and will thus inspire us all to lead the life of enlightenment, befitting the Sat Yuga in which we live and have our being. For giving us this vision we are all under deep obligation to Gurudeva. I offer my salutations hundred and thousand fold at his lotus feet.

Dr. Vidya Sagar Anand,
Hindu statesman in the UK, Chairman of the European Council of Hindu Organisations; London, England

A *rishi* with tremendous inner spiritual powers attained through life-long meditation and austerities shares with us and posterity divine insights into the origin of human kind on this planet. For the past two centuries, mainly in the West, this subject has been treated superficially, giving, or attempting to give, scholastic and scientific backing to the alleged superiority of Nordic Man. The theories of Darwin and some Western charlatans have helped to create the unsustainable myth that "God has made some of us, and not all of us, in His own image." The scientific mind and the spiritual mind interpret nature and its origins differently. While one, because of its serious limitations and prejudices, sees and perceives the veneer only, the other's vision is more profound, embracing the external and the internal dimensions. Rarely have the twain met. In *Lemurian Scrolls*, the illustrious Sivaya Subramuniyaswami illuminates with his graceful and penetrating pen the origins, progress and decline of the human race from time immemorial. Rarely in living memory has this eternally intriguing subject been delineated so painstakingly, authoritatively and lucidly. This is an impressive and enlightening document, a modern and revealing *purana*, deserving of close study in the East and the West.

Pundit Ramesh Tiwari,
President General, Edinburgh Dharmic Sabha; Chaguanas, Trinidad & Tobago

This is a masterpiece of dharmic tapestry interwoven with cosmic philosophy which can only come out from such a highly realized soul as Satguru Sivaya Subramuniyaswami. May Lord Siva guide Swamiji to lead us into the Golden Age—Sat Yuga.

Pundit K.N. Navaratnam,
M.A.F.A., F.A.A.; Jyotisha Marthand and National Astrologer of Australia; close devotee of Satguru Siva Yogaswami; Sivathondan Center; Hallam, Australia

Satguru Sivaya Subramuniyaswamigal is a living legend forever—a great visionary like his great *satguru,* Siva Yogaswamigal, as evidenced by many. On the full-moon day in May 1949, when he received the divine strong slap from his master, Satguru Siva Yogaswamigal, he received the graceful enlightenment and thus the visions. If not, how could he have discovered the long-lost ancient Siva Temple at Hawaii related to the ancient Saint Manikkavasagar Swami, narrated in

Page 342 his Hindu scripture known as *Holy Thiruvasagam* more than 10,000 years or before? ¶Not to mention that I am a visionary, a strong disciple of Satguru Siva Yogaswamigal, born and bred in his Land of Jaffna, associated with him for more than fifteen years. I had a beautiful vision in the year 1991 in that I saw loving Ganesha carrying Satguru Sivaya Subramuniyaswamigal on his right shoulder and Gurudeva blessing all of us by his right hand. What more testimony is needed?

Thiru Satkunendran,
Assistant Secretary,
Sivathondan Nilayam;
Toronto, Ontario, Canada

An excellent presentation, interesting to read, easy to understand by any lay person, revealing the long past, present and future of humankind, and the *yugas.* This rare production of Gurudeva's with his third eye is a must for every Hindu and all those seeking the truth!

Thiru L. Nellaiappan,
devotee of Satguru Sivaya Subramuniyaswami of 25 years;
Former Joint Director of Industries, Government of Tamil Nadu, India;
Chennai, Tamil Nadu, India

Lemurian Scrolls, the spiritual treasure of *akashic* reading revealed through clairvoyance of my beloved guru, Sivaya Subramuniyaswami, the spiritual head of Kauai Aadheenam, released after two decades of mystic research and input, is one of the holiest of holy unfoldments for the benefit of mankind during this century. Certainly the future will generate valuable debate, discussion, seminars and intense research among scholars and spiritual seekers about the coming into being of the human race in this world, contrary to other evolutionary scientific theories in belief. It is a rare publication, comparing the concept of other beliefs in an invaluable timeline. This may be called a testament to the values of mankind and a guide book to all monasteries.

Dr. Canagasabay M. Pillay,
Former Chairman, Mauritius Medical Association; Former President, Hindu Maha Jana Sangham; Former Editor, *La Lumière;* Former Mayor, Vacoas-Phoenix, Mauritius

The body of scientific knowledge about man's origin is increasing rapidly. Evolution, followed by the Big Bang theory and recent genetic studies situate the arrival of *Homo sapiens* at 150,000 years ago in East Africa. Far from being doubly wise through a science outlook, man suffers from a spiritual vacuum. Drug addiction and AIDS are threatening to assume pandemic proportions. There is a crying need for a spiritual worldview of our planet's history. *Lemurian Scrolls* brings this spiritual dimension to the arrival of man on Earth, with Earth being part of the wider universe, rather than an Earth-centered genesis. We are privileged that this book, which was unfolded to Satguru Sivaya Subramuniyaswami in a unique spiritual experience, has been made available to the public. Satguru Sivaya Subramuniyaswami is, of course, the ideal person to receive and transmit this spiritual treasure.

Dr. Kadress Pillay,
Minister of Education and Human Resource Development;
Mauritius

The mode of life depicted is exactly what one would expect to live when one has attained *moksha* or *satchidananda.* Only the blessed could have envisioned such a highly divine form of social organization.